UNIVERSITY ADULT EDUCATION

UNIVERSITY

ADULT EDUCATION

A GUIDE TO POLICY

by RENEE PETERSEN
and WILLIAM PETERSEN

A Project Planned and Directed by WARREN ROVETCH
Director, Education Research Associates

HARPER & BROTHERS, PUBLISHERS, NEW YORK

UNIVERSITY ADULT EDUCATION

CONTENTS

Appendices

FOREWORD

by ROLAND R. RENNE, President
Montana State College

University Adult Education: A Guide to Policy is an important
and a disturbing book. It is important because it combines a
broad factual survey of university adult education with a principled, perceptive, and sharp critical analysis. It is disturbing if the
authors are correct in their view that, while the education of adults
is a significant function of universities, much of what passes for
adult education in many institutions is substandard, commercial-
ized, or not education at all.

This poses a dilemma. For if the failings prevalent in university
adult education occur seemingly without regard for the administrative or organizational pattern, then a neat administrative revision
will not solve the problem. It may not be out of order to re-
emphasize one point the authors make so well. The origin of the
problem lies deep within the institution and what it perceives to
be its purposes. A workable solution can be found only when the
institution as a whole attaches purpose, priority, and standards to
the education of adults and indeed the whole of the institution's
extension activities.

For this reason the book offers no blueprint appropriate for
large and small universities, public and private, rural and urban;
and the fact that the authors do not suggest one indicates they
are well aware of the complexity of the question. But under the
heterogeneity, as is pointed out, are universal principles, which
in the hectic effort to balance budgets and meet schedules both
administrators and faculty may forget. Most who have discussed
the contentious subject of university adult education have either
defended it *in toto*, or proposed throwing out the baby with the

bath. Whether or not one agrees with the specific proposals offered in this book, the fact that a serious effort is made to distinguish legitimate from illegitimate, necessary from dispensable, makes this a thought-provoking stimulus to any university administrator and all persons concerned with adult education in America.

In one respect I share responsibility for this work. Three years ago, as part of a major review of extension activity at Montana State College, I asked Mr. Rovetch to initiate a national survey and evaluation of experiences in other institutions. This task was carried out by Renee and William Petersen and, after much elaboration and expansion, has resulted in this book. The Deans' Council, Mr. Rovetch, and I met in a number of day-long deliberations, using the preliminary draft of this book as a base for our discussions. We found it relatively easy to agree on what we do *not* want for extension (low standards, low pay, educational cafeteria, etc.) and even to outline structural features that would guarantee these negative requirements. We saw that those outside the resident faculty who regularly participate in adult education have to be given some kind of status within the appropriate department or division; that equal pay for equal work is a prerequisite to any demand for equal quality of teaching; that if the several departments and divisions are given some budgetary responsibility, this can help tie extension work to the standards and purpose of the whole institution; that some system for cutting through divisional and departmental lines is required to call on institutionwide resources, particularly with public policy education for adults; that noncredit work offers an opportunity for creative initiative without the sacrifice of educational quality. In all these matters we found the book most helpful in finding our own answer. As such it is a most valuable aid to policy definition.

Montana State College's positive goals in adult education, not surprisingly, have been a more difficult question. A permanent committee, consisting of the deans of Agriculture, Education, Letters and Science, and the Graduate Division, has been charged with the task of proposing a broad definition of institutional policy, which, with careful experimentation to see what really works as a guide, the Deans' Council and I will eventually implement. Here, too, we have found our prior agreement on principles a useful guide to first steps and temporary arrangements.

Because Montana State College is a land-grant institution, we faced a special question—that of the relationship of the Cooperative Extension Service to adult education and vice-versa. We are finding the answer less in examining the traditional function of Cooperative Extension than in the new opportunities and responsibilities which the transformation of rural America, and indeed our whole society, offers to the land-grant institution. Once again, we have found the discussion of this matter in *University Adult Education* a most valuable aid.

Each institution must, of course, seek its own answer to adult education responsibility. The form this takes will reflect the unique diversity among institutions of higher education in America. This is as it should be. However, many of the faults of university adult education, as is clear in the Petersens' detailed discussion, are related to the fact that it "just growed" here and there in odd corners of the institution, with no one able even to state what is being done, much less to assess or control it. *University Adult Education: A Guide to Policy* introduces the concept of the "total extension function," or everything supplementary to regular daytime instruction of adolescents and faculty research. This is not, as it may seem to those closely bound to existing patterns, an elusive will-o'-the-wisp; we have found the concept to be a most useful framework, both theoretical and practical, within which to approach extension policy.

We must take this book seriously if we are seriously concerned about the major issues our nation faces and the consequent demand for every individual's highest possible level of performance. University adult education is too important a job to be done casually or badly. Many institutions of higher education have done much to advance the cause of adult education, and we at Montana State College are grateful to those who have taken the lead. However, most of these universities, even those with a great tradition of extension work, are now faced with many of the problems this work analyzes.

The Petersens have done an excellent job of careful analysis, intelligent appraisal, and effective writing. Mr. Rovetch has not only done an outstanding job of effective planning and directing the project, but has pointed up the tremendous possibilities of improved services of Cooperative Extension and land-grant institutions generally. In addition, the study emphasizes the basic principles, policies, and procedures which are most likely to bring about maximum realization of these service possibilities. For myself and my colleagues who are reevaluating extension activities and trying to establish a new over-all policy, this is a timely and significant book.

INTRODUCTION

by CYRIL O. HOULE, Professor of Education
The University of Chicago

Not long ago the president of a very large university, while speaking to a group of extension administrators, made a point which was at least refreshingly frank. Universities are outstanding, he pointed out, chiefly because of the excellence of their various parts. As a college of law, a department of English, or a research center in physics achieves distinction, so does the whole institution which contains them. But—and here he administered the lethal needle—no university has yet been helped to become outstanding, or even famous, because of the excellence of its work in adult education.

Strictly speaking, he was wrong. Such a comment challenges listeners (or, at least, one of them) to find examples which refute it, and it proved to be easy to think of exceptions to the rule which he laid down so authoritatively. How about the Extension Division of the University of Wisconsin, a program now so safely hallowed by reverent mention as to be beyond controversy? At that institution, a group of outstanding men and women have carried on their work for more than fifty years at a level of excellence so high as to attract the admiration of their colleagues, the people of their state, and the administrators and faculties of other universities. And anyone who wished to be daring would not need to stop with this one example. Yet the president's comment was essentially valid, for while it is possible to think of outstanding extension units which are jewels in the crowns of their universities, one comes to the end of the list fairly quickly.

Mr. and Mrs. Peterson and Mr. Rovetch have some clear ideas about why university adult education is so often carried out without great distinction. They suggest among other things that the president is usually at fault himself because adult education is a function which should properly be exercised by the whole institution and therefore only he can oversee it properly. In this regard it is like the student personnel program, like library service, and like publishing. To be sure there is often a specialized central unit for adult education—a general extension division, a cooperative extension service, or an evening college—just as there is a dean of students' office, a central library, or a university press. But the performance of all such functions is and, by its very nature, never can be completely centralized.

Since presidents are busy men, they must expect the administrators of specialized extension units to exert leadership in directing the program of the whole university. But if we are to believe the high authority cited at the beginning of this Introduction, it is precisely these units which do not achieve very much eminence. Here, too, the authors of this book believe they know the reasons why: the relatively low level of aspiration of extension and evening college deans and directors; their failure to rise to their responsibilities; and their delusion or confusion by false doctrines.

Having explored the basic situation, the book goes on to its major task, the suggesting of remedies. Here some very interesting, useful, and provocative things are said. The three authors have not themselves grown up within the ranks of those who devote their lives to university adult education but they have studied that field with care and they bring to their examination of it their competence in the social sciences, their experience with university life, and their belief in the importance of a strong program of extension for the community and for the institution itself.

The book, though essentially unitary, is divided into three different explorations of its central theme. The first deals with broad questions of university responsibility and policy, the second examines the implications of this approach in the subject matter field of world affairs, and the third is a contribution to the slim body of literature dealing with the important organizational question of how general and cooperative extension may be brought within a single administrative framework. Underlying all three essays, however, is the belief that university adult education has reached a fairly advanced level of maturity and should be taken seriously.

There was a time—only yesterday, it seems—when there was a doubt about whether the education of adults is an appropriate university function. Every setback—a budget cut; an inquiry by the University Senate; a sudden unexplained drop in enrollment; the replacement of a strong, dedicated leader by a weak, uncommitted one; or a re-organization which reduced some of the functions of the Division—seemed an ominous warning of an approaching end. But every year now, some division celebrates its fiftieth anniversary, and the growth of university adult education far over-shadows any momentary set-backs. A year or so ago, several deans and directors of extension who thought themselves threatened by a wave of reaction held an emergency session at which they discussed how to combat "the national attack on extension." Seeking to discover the seriousness of that attack and to gather ammunition and support, they sent out a circular letter to their fellow deans. As the answers came back, it turned out that, at most universities, adult educational units were stronger and healthier than they had ever been before. And even some of the deans who had cried havoc found their own programs emerging into a more solid status than they had previously known.

What is gradually becoming clear is that, as with every other part of the university, the extension unit often passes through cycles of development, of growth and decay and growth again. Since 1925, there have been a number of studies of the eminence of universities which show with what dramatic suddenness the reputation of a department of instruction may fall or rise. If extension units had been included in such studies, they would have shown a similar variability. Compared with instructional units their orbits may be more rapid and their peaks may not be as high. But whether or not their depths are lower is a fair matter for speculation and there is a good deal to be said on either side of the matter.

There is also a second cycle through which university adult education seems to pass, one extreme of which is marked by the dispersion of the function, the other by its integration. In every university, there are these centrifugal and centripetal movements; sometimes one prevails, sometimes another. But at no university is there complete centralization or complete dispersion of the function.

Space does not permit a further detailing of these two kinds of cycles or their relationship to each other. But there is at least one fairly clear connection between them. If the staff of an extension unit strives for quality and accepts no lower aim than that of giving lustre to the university itself, the tendency toward centralization of responsibility for adult education will be enhanced because the university's board, administrators, and faculty will have greater confidence in the capacity of the extension unit.

It is not always easy to know what is meant by "quality," particularly in university adult education which has so many different approaches and programs. The authors of "University Adult Education" have faced this matter directly, however. They have no patience with anything less than the effort to be first-rate; they have strong ideas about what excellence would mean; and they have decided views about how it should be achieved. What they have to say is often provoking and that is precisely what they intend it to be. Some practitioners in the field will be led to change their minds, others to change their arguments, and still others to dig deeper than they have ever gone before to find out why they believe as they do.

The reason that I know these results will occur is because all three have happened to me. From time to time this book points out how very wrong I am to hold certain views. It would be spiritless not to respond in kind, so let it be recorded that, persuasive though the authors are, I hold the same opinion still on most of the matters about which they think me incorrect. I disagree with them at a number of other points as well, nor is such disagreement always a matter of nuance or shade of opinion. But the reading of their views has caused me to reconsider my own position, occasionally to change it, but more often to find some excellent new arguments to support it. These matters are minor, however; I am happy to discover that on most matters of policy or strategy I seem to have come to the same conclusions as have the authors of *University Adult Education.*

It is an honor to be asked to write this introduction and to have a first opportunity to wish the book Godspeed. If it is widely and thoughtfully read, there will be more universities whose claim to eminence is based in part on the distinction of their programs of adult education.

ACKNOWLEDGMENTS

This book was issued in a preliminary multilithed form and circulated among a number of persons with an expert knowledge of university adult education, or of one of the topics discussed in the various chapters and appendices. Almost all who were sent the manuscript, or a portion of it, were kind enough—in spite of their own full work schedules—to read it carefully and offer us their thoughtful comments and criticisms. And a few went far beyond the usual bounds of scholarly cooperation. In particular, we want to acknowledge a large debt of sincere gratitude to Cyril O. Houle, professor of education at the University of Chicago, who went over the whole manuscript twice and discussed it in detail with Renee Petersen; to Paul A. McGhee, dean of the Division of General Education, New York University, who commented section by section, almost page by page, on the first version; and to Russell I. Thackrey, executive secretary of the American Association of Land-Grant Colleges and State Universities, who discussed the book in person with Mr. Rovetch and was especially helpful with respect to Cooperative Extension and over-all university policy.

Other readers helped us in various ways. Some gave us their general impressions, some corrected errors in fact, some offered welcome encouragement to what they deemed a useful venture. Without here specifying in each case the kind of assistance we received, we want to acknowledge it most gratefully from all of the following, listed here in non-invidious alphabetical order: Henry C. Alter, American Foundation for Continuing Education; John A. Baker, legislative director, National Farmers Union; Reinhard Bendix, professor of sociology, University of California, Berkeley; M. E. Campbell, General Extension, Pennsylvania State University; Robert H. Cory, Jr., assistant professor of political science, Denison University; Edward D. Eddy, Jr., provost, University of New Hampshire; C. R. Elder, director, Information Service, Iowa State University; Harold L. Enarson, executive director, Western Interstate Commission on Higher Education; C. M. Ferguson, administrator, Federal Cooperative Extension Service, Washington; C. Hartley Grattan, author, then consultant to the Fund for Adult Education; Jessie W. Harris, dean, College of Home Economics, University of Tennessee; Cannon C. Hearne, director, Foreign Training Division, U. S. Department of Agriculture; E. N. Holmgreen, director, Office of Food and Agriculture, International Cooperation Administration; Bernard J. James, director, Program in Government Administration, Downtown Center, University of Chicago; E. L. Keller, director of General Extension, Pennsylvania State University; Grant McConnell, professor of political science, University of Chicago; Carl Malone, Extension economist, Iowa State University; Paul A. Miller, provost, Michigan State University; Hans J. Morgenthau, professor of political science and director, Center for the Study of American Foreign Policy, University of Chicago; James R. Morton, dean, Extension Division, University of Alabama; Julius M. Nolte, dean, General Extension Division, University of Minnesota; Charles O'Brien, chief assistant to the attorney general, State of California—at the time West Coast director, Foreign Policy Association; Hilton Power, associate regional director, Foreign Policy Association; Hugh G. Pyle, Informal Instruction Division, Pennsylvania State University; Dwight C. Rhyne, associate director, University Extension Division, University of North Carolina; Paul H. Sheats, dean, University Extension, University of California; Russell F. W. Smith, associate dean, Division of General Education and Extension Services, New York University; Ernest Van den Haag, adjunct professor of social philosophy, Division of General Education, New York University; Philip Van Slyck, editor, Program Materials, Foreign Policy Association, and Editorial Associate, Education Research Associates; James B. Whipple, assistant director for operations, Center for the Study of Liberal Education for Adults; A. L. Winsor, dean, School of Education, Cornell University; Jane Zahn, head, Department of Conferences and Special Activities, Northern Area, University Extension, University of California.

As part of our research, we wrote to a great many persons and organizations throughout the country. The personnel of the Center for the Study of Liberal Education for Adults—in particular Mr. Roger De Crow, clearinghouse director—were especially helpful. We also want to thank the following, who answered the questions we put to them, or sent us relevant materials, or both: Frank Anderson, director, Bureau of Community Development, University of Washington; Wilmer V. Bell, director of adult education, Baltimore Public Schools; Roger P. Bristol, deputy TV grant director, Alderman Library, University of Virginia; James E. Crimi, dean, Aurora College; Joan Dorfman, secretary to Edwin H. Spengler of Brooklyn College, the executive secretary of the Association of University Evening Colleges; Arthur H. Dugan, president, State Normal and Industrial College, Ellendale, N. D.—at the time supervisor of off-campus instruction, University of Wyoming; Joseph P. Flannery, director, Division of Management Operations, Federal Cooperative Extension Service, Washington; The Fund for Adult Education; G. H. Griffiths, vice-president, Fund for Adult Education; George L. Hall, director of development, Educational Television and Radio Center; James Harrison, dean, Utica College, Syracuse University; Richard Hill, assistant professor of sociology, University of California at Los Angeles; Joint Council on Educational Television; E. L. Keller, director of General Extension, Pennsylvania State University; Clark Kerr, president, University of California; Paul A. McGhee, dean, Division of General Education, New York University; Lawrence E. McKune, television coordinator, Continuing Education Service, Michigan State University; M. H. McMichael, assistant director, Division of Extension, Summer Session and Community Services, University of New Mexico; J. R. Morton, dean, Extension Division, University of Alabama; Frank R. Neuffer, dean, Evening College, University of Cincinnati; Julius M. Nolte, dean, Extension Division, University of Minnesota, and secretary-treasurer, National University Extension Association; Fayette W. Parvin, assistant to the president, University of Florida; John R. Richards, chancellor, Oregon State System of Higher Education; Robert H. Schacht, director, Bureau of Information and Program Services, University of Wisconsin; Beatrice Schenk, educational materials director, American Heart Association; T. W. Schultz, professor of economics, University of Chicago; Raymond C. Scott, director, Division of Agricultural Economics Programs, Federal Cooperative Extension Service, Washington; Theodore J. Shannon, director of field services, University Extension Division, University of Wisconsin; Edwin H. Spengler, executive secretary, Association of University Evening Colleges; Glenn Starlin, director, Inter-Institutional TV Teaching Project, University of Oregon; Richard N. Swift, Department of Government, New York University; Russell I. Thackrey, executive secretary, American Association of Land-Grant Colleges and State Universities; Robert S. Warner, Wyeth Laboratories.

We appreciate especially the significant assistance of President Renne and the Council of Deans of Montana State College. Early in 1957, when they were trying to work out an adult-education policy for that institution, they commissioned Warren Rovetch to prepare a study based on the experiences of other general-extension divisions. A preliminary multilithed draft of *University Adult Education* was one basis of protracted deliberations on how Montana State College ought to establish and control its total extension function. This fact, that the first version of the study was actually used as a guide to policy, gave us constructive and practical help in preparing the present, much revised and enlarged book.

RENEE PETERSEN
WILLIAM PETERSEN
WARREN ROVETCH

UNIVERSITY ADULT EDUCATION

1

THE SIGNIFICANCE
OF ADULT EDUCATION TODAY

Adult Americans have lived, though few of them realize it, through a period of change momentous enough to be termed—adopting what has become a cliché—a social revolution. Many in this country, however, still lack the training necessary either for living the full life that our economic abundance makes possible, or for performing in sufficient number some of the most essential tasks in a complex industrial society. If the world were moving at a slower rate, we might be tempted to write off the under-educated portion of the adult population and wait until the longer schooling now being received by the country's youth significantly increases the average learning. But the United States cannot post-pone a generation or two facing up to the tasks—technical and economic, cultural and political—that urgently demand more skills. We must try to develop the human resources available in that portion of the adult population capable of contributing more fully to their own welfare and that of their society. And in particular we must try to realize more of the potential at the level of university training.

The Twentieth-Century Revolution[1]

Over the past fifty years the population of the United States has doubled. Average expectation of life at birth increased from about fifty years in 1900 to about seventy years in 1950.

In 1900, though industrialization was well under way, 38 per cent of the gainful workers were still occupied in agriculture;

[1] Unless otherwise indicated, the data in this section are from the U.S. Bureau of the Census, as compiled in its *Historical Statistics* with the *Continuation to 1952* of this series; and in Taeuber and Taeuber, *The Changing Population*. For complete bibliographical details about these and other foot-note references, see Bibliography, pp. 237 ff.

fifty years later this figure was only 12.5 per cent and continuing to decline. At the turn of the century, six Americans out of ten lived in rural areas; in 1950, 64 per cent lived in towns and almost 60 per cent in the country's 168 metropolitan areas. This shift is no longer a simple country-to-town movement; the differences between "urban" and "rural" are diminishing. The intermediate suburbs are growing much faster than either city centers or small towns and villages, and what were once urban amenities are becoming available to a larger and larger proportion of the remaining rural population.

Mechanical and electrical energy has been substituted for human. The production of electric energy increased over the half century from 6 billion to 389 billion kilowatt hours, while the average workweek of production workers in manufacturing fell from 51 hours (in 1909) to 40.5. The decline over the whole past century is even more spectacular: the average workweek in all occupations fell from seven 10-hour days in 1850 to five 8-hour days in 1950.

In spite of the rapidly growing population and the steady reduction of the average workweek, productivity increased fast enough to provide a steady, substantial rise in living standards. The average annual gross national product, expressed in billions of 1929 dollars, rose from 29.4 in 1891-1900 to 149.3 in 1941-1950.[2] The tremendously increased national income, moreover, came to be distributed more equitably among the whole population.[3]

Rapid as the change was between 1900 and 1950, in most respects it has accelerated since mid-century. During 1959 *Fortune* published a series of articles projecting to 1970 the progress to date in technology, production, and living standards.[4] The prognoses are extravagant, but to be at all realistic they must be. During the 1950's, some $60 billion was spent on scientific research and development; the sum for the following decade will be twice that, and we can expect a corresponding increase in both basic discoveries and practical applications. Productivity

[2] U.S. Bureau of Labor Statistics, *Economic Forces*, p. 46.
[3] Dewhurst et al., *America's Needs and Resources*, pp. 91-93; Tucker, "The Distribution of Income"; Kuznets, *Shares of Upper Income Groups*.
[4] Harper later published these as a book, *America in the Sixties*.

per man-hour, which increased by 1 per cent per year between 1850 and 1889, by 2 per cent between 1889 and 1919, by 2.5 per cent between the wars, and by about 3 per cent since 1945, will continue to increase at at least this last rate during the 1960's. With a rapid increase in the labor force and a no more than moderate decrease in the workweek, the gross national product may well shoot up to a fantastic $750 billion by 1970.

According to *Fortune*'s estimate, by 1970 some 25 million families, or nearly two-fifths of the total, will have an annual income after taxes of more than $7,500. About half of this will be spent on necessities like food, clothing, and shelter; the other half will be discretionary, available for a widely increased range of consumers goods, personal investment, cultural activities. Certainly there will be more of everything; whether also more and better is a question, already much debated, that will depend on whether taste improves as rapidly as purchasing power rises.

Even today, before these projected developments, man's basic needs are better satisfied in the United States than at any time in all history. Social problems are now often the effects of the country's economic and cultural abundance, paradoxical as this still sounds. Overeating is a far greater threat to health than malnutrition. Infant mortality has all but disappeared, but the number of aged grows steadily. The new mass audience sometimes threatens to engulf high culture in *Kitsch*. With the rapid population growth, some of what economists term "free goods" have become, or are likely to become, commodities: water in the semi-arid West, air in smog-ridden Los Angeles, space in any city to park a car.

Apart from such anomalies, *the* problem of economic theory—how to allocate scarce goods among alternative uses—seems to be in the process of becoming obsolete. With productivity as efficient as it has become, it is often not necessary to choose one or the other commodity, but rather possible to have both. For instance, the classic example of the economic problem, the distribution of productive factors between military and civilian needs, had a brand new solution in the United States during World War II— guns *and* butter. To some degree, this unique affluence is disguised by a reversal in the traditional relation between supply and demand. In any nonindustrial society, demand comes first—the

need for food, clothing, housing, or something almost as fundamental; and production tends to rise in an effort to meet this
demand. In the United States today, on the contrary, supply often
comes first, and the demand for the goods produced is then
stimulated by advertising and other, more subtle means of exciting
social emulation. Galbraith terms this relation the Dependence
Effect: "The production of goods creates the wants that the
goods are presumed to satisfy."[5] So long as this kind of squirrel
cage remains in operation, the economic system can never achieve
psychological satiation in consumers goods, for with greater and
greater production more and more economic "wants"—in this
new sense—remain unsatisfied.

The Dependence Effect operates, however, only with respect
to commodities sold on the market, not with respect to social
services. It is now far less important to increase industrial production than to find means of redressing the balance between
opulence in consumers goods and public poverty. Any American
city shows a marked contrast between rising retail sales and, on
the other hand, crowded schools, understaffed police forces, dirty
streets, and overworked transportation systems. Any discussion of
education, and particularly of adult education, must take cogni-
zance of this contrast. In the wealthiest country in history, even
so obvious a demand on the public purse as schooling is not adequately satisfied.

The Educational System: Achievements and Lacks[6]

The economic and social metamorphosis of American society
was accompanied, both as cause and as effect, by a no less complete change in its educational system. In the nineteenth century,
the main problem was getting free public education established,
especially at the primary level. A hundred years ago, less than half
of those aged five to nineteen years attended school; and almost a
tenth of the native-born white, plus virtually all of the slave
population and a considerable portion of the foreign-born, were
totally illiterate. The full establishment of a free universal school

[5] Galbraith, *The Affluent Society*, p. 155.
[6] Unless otherwise specified, the data in this section are from Taeuber and
Taeuber, *The Changing Population*, Chap. 10; Dewhurst et al., *America's
Needs and Resources*, Chap. 12.

system during the second half of the nineteenth century made possible, among other things, the assimilation of millions of immigrants and their children into a unified culture.

At the end of the century, however, education beyond grammar school was still limited to a very small minority. Of those aged fourteen through seventeen years, the proportion enrolled in high school has increased from 7 per cent in 1890 to 88 per cent in 1959. Thus, in sixty years, the American high school has changed from a preparatory school for a small elite to an institution almost as universally accessible as elementary school; and this trend is continuing. Over the same period, college enrollment has grown even faster; only about 4 per cent of persons of college age entered college in 1900, and about 30 per cent in 1959. In absolute terms, college enrollment increased by more than ten times, or from about 237,000 in 1900 to about 2.7 million in 1955.

While the United States can be justly proud of this expansion in educational opportunities, its very rapidity left a gap among the substantial number of adults who had lacked these advantages. When today's very old people were children, about a quarter of the population were given no more than four years of schooling, an amount now considered so inadequate that it is used to define the upper limit of the "functionally illiterate." In 1950, the proportion functionally illiterate among whites ranged from 18 per cent of those aged sixty-five through sixty-nine down to only 3 per cent of those aged twenty-five through twenty-nine. Put another way, the median number of school years completed in 1950, 9.3 for the total adult population, ranged from 8.2 for those sixty-five and over up to 12.1 for the twenty-five to twenty-nine age group. The gradual improvement in the country's educational system during the past generation or two was not, of course, at an equal rate among all social classes, and differences persist by region, urban–rural residence, and race, as well as by age. Thus, rural Negroes in the South, by reason of all three of these characteristics, have both the least schooling and the poorest present educational facilities.

In short, millions of adult Americans have less education than would be most beneficial both to themselves and to their society. In 1950, three-tenths of the adult population had not graduated from grammar school, two-thirds had not graduated from high school, 94 percent had not graduated from college. A portion, but only a portion, of these deficiencies was based on innate limitations, but accidents of birth played a greater role.

The rapid expansion of America's school system has not been without travail. As even the most casual reader of newspapers knows, the whole educational system has been undergoing a thorough, and often a hostile, review. Three topics in this important debate are worth summarizing here—the finances of education, the effect of the rapid population increase, and the question of standards.

1. "Education costs money. Though expense does not guarantee success, more and better education always costs more."[7] Obvious as this truism may appear to be, the question of how to pay for public education is a complex one. The increase in expenditures per pupil in elementary and secondary schools was spectacular—from $20 in 1900 (or $62 in 1949-1950 dollars) to $259 in 1950. But the rise in costs was even faster. Today the United States spends less proportionately on its public schools than it did in the depth of the interwar depression.[8]

Public schools are locally financed, and their funds thus derive principally from the relatively inflexible general property tax. New sources of tax income are hard for local governments to find: personal and corporate income is already taxed by the federal government and many of the states. Municipalities have tried to keep up with their growing financial responsibilities by

[7] Brown, "Have Our Schools Failed?" p. 471. For three excellent book-length discussions, see Committee for Economic Development, *Paying for Better Public Schools*; Harris, *How Shall We Pay*; Van den Haag, *Education as an Industry*.

[8] The percentage of gross national product spent on public schools was highest in 1932—namely, 3.7. In 1944, with a small school population and extraordinary outlays for the war, it had fallen to 1.2 per cent. Since 1946, it has gradually risen again, reaching 3.0 in 1958; but this increase has not kept pace with either the greater ability of a prosperous country to pay or the mounting costs of adequate education. The same curve (from the high point in the 1930's, to the low during the war, to a moderate upward trend in the postwar years) is described also by other indices of outlay for education—for example, expenditures for public schools as a per cent of total tax collections. See National Education Association, *Status and Trends*, Table 26, p. 21.

levying sales taxes[9] or by broadening the property tax base; but these can be nothing more than stopgap measures. The solution for public education, in the opinion of some, is federal financing; but this attacks, or seems to attack, local control of the schools—one of the most revered of America's large herd of sacred cows. Thus, the many bills introduced in Congress to establish federal aid to public education have all, for one reason or another, failed to pass.[10] Only about 4 per cent of the cost of public education is now paid by the national government, which collects three out of every four tax dollars.

American higher education also rests on an inadequate and *ad hoc* financial base. College revenue is derived from student fees, which have risen alarmingly during the past decade; from municipal and state legislatures, which are under constant pressure to allocate monies elsewhere; from alumni and other donors, who are sometimes more interested in football than in education; from personal and foundation endowments, always inadequate in amount and sometimes arbitrarily restricted to certain uses; and from greatly underpaid faculties.[11] This haphazard patchwork is not a satisfactory way of financing so important an institution as the country's higher education.

2. The difficulties in financing schools and colleges, moreover, have been considerably aggravated by the baby boom. During the first postwar decade, more than 36 million infants were born to American parents, and as these children move up into adult life,

[9] This expedient has been strongly resisted, however, particularly by liberals. In Galbraith's view, opposition to sales taxes in an economy abundantly provided with consumers goods is not warranted, but this argument—like many that he offers—expresses the point of view of a maverick (*The Affluent Society*, pp. 316-317).

[10] The principal issue in recent years has been desegregation, and the principal opponents were the representatives of the South, which has by far the worst schools and the greatest need for federal aid. Dependence on local taxation means, of course, that differences in wealth among regions tend to increase over time, since poor states are likely to have poor schools and thus inadequately prepared citizens in the next generation.

[11] "The plain fact is that the college teachers of the United States, through their inadequate salaries, are subsidizing the education of students, and in some cases the luxuries of their families, by an amount which is more than double the grand total of alumni gifts, corporate gifts, and endowment income of all colleges and universities combined" (President's Committee on Education Beyond the High School, *Second Report*, p. 6).

they are disrupting one institution after another built to accommodate more modest numbers. Greatly swollen student bodies have burst the grammar schools, and the flood is just beginning to engulf the high schools.[12] Administrators of universities are well aware that their turn is coming. In their case, a double increase must be anticipated, one in the number of persons of college age and another in the proportion of this age group that attends college.

Today we have 3 million students in colleges and universities. By 1975 the college population will be at least 7.5 and perhaps as many as 12 million—a little less than 50 per cent of the eligible age groups. . . . Today the total annual expenditure of higher education, including capital investment, is probably around $5 billion. Twenty years hence it may exceed $25 billion.[13]

The rapid increase in the school population has effected an unprecedented strain on educational facilities and personnel. The so-called "normal capacity" of elementary and secondary schools is presently exceeded by some 2.3 million pupils, and their enrollment will increase by another 30 per cent over the next decade. Even if every person who gets a Ph.D. were to become a college teacher, the shortage in faculties would grow. "Unless the supply of competent college teachers is increased, the next 20 years may do damage to higher education in the United States which the following 100 years will find it impossible to repair."[14]

3. Partly as a consequence of the shortage of funds and the overabundance of pupils, but partly also for other reasons, the

[12] According to Census Bureau estimates, the number of persons aged 5 to 17 will increase from 30.6 million in 1950 to 48.8 million in 1963. Between 1950 and 1959, the school-age group increased at about double the rate of the whole population. See U.S. Bureau of the Census, *Current Population Reports*, Series P-25, No. 201, June 1, 1959.

[13] Drucker, *America's Next Twenty Years*, pp. 53, 65-66. According to a Roper poll, if the aspirations of their parents are realized, 69 per cent (rather than under half) of the children under 18 in 1959 will go to college (*Time*, September 28, 1959).

[14] Hamilton, "The Recruitment," p. 210. See also, for example, Coombs, "How Will Institutions of Higher Education Secure and Maintain an Adequate Supply of Qualified Teachers?" For discussions of possible extenuating factors, see various publications of the Fund for the Advancement of Education—for example, Eurich, "Better Instruction," and, for a recent review of the Fund's experimental programs, Paschal, "What New Developments."

quality of American education has suffered. There has been, depending on which books in this heated dispute one reads, either a shocking deterioration in educational standards or—at best, by the most optimistic appraisal—a failure to improve quality nearly fast enough to satisfy the educational prerequisites of an industrial democratic society.[15] Differences are sharp over where to put the blame—whether at the door of teachers colleges, or in the lap of a public unwilling to pay for a good educational system, or wherever. That the products of the American public schools are less knowledgeable and competent than they ought to be, however, hardly anyone would deny. Under the stresses outlined in the previous paragraphs, moreover, it will be particularly difficult for elementary and high schools to improve, or even to maintain, the quality of their instruction over the next decade or so. And if colleges will not be able to take it for granted, as seems reasonable enough in the abstract, that applicants for admission will be well prepared in basic subjects, then their talk of raising standards may well also remain—talk.

This short and incomplete review of the economics of American education has perhaps been sufficient to indicate how complex the question is. Automatically, on principle, all Americans are "for" more and better schools; *whether* there should be good educational facilities is never a political issue, with candidates and parties aligned for and against. Nevertheless, the proportion of the national income allotted to education is grossly inadequate. The subsistence financing of the schools is the product in large part of a rather inflexible institutional structure. A fundamental reform in the manner by which school revenue is allocated is called for, but this will not be accepted overnight. In the interim, some of the educational gaps that the school system leaves can be repaired by devoting more attention to the education of adults.

The Functions of Adult Education

Education as a lifelong process, at least for a portion of the population, is an ideal as old as Western civilization. For the

[15] For responsibly critical views, see Woodring, *Let's Talk Sense, A Fourth of a Nation*; Bestor, *Educational Wastelands*.

Greek citizen, the medieval scholar, the Renaissance man, learning was an attribute of life, continuing until death. The central purpose of American adult education today is to preserve this ideal in the more formal structure of an organized program, and to apply it to as large a portion of the total population as is capable, by both innate intelligence and interest, of continuing to learn.[16] This purpose is sought at all levels, from remedying the lack of primary skills to keeping persons with graduate degrees up to date in their profession:

1. In 1950, there were nearly 10 million adults who were functionally illiterate, that is, who had had four years or less of schooling. While many of these, both Negro and white, were reared in the rural South, there are illiterates in virtually every state of the union.[17] Many of those who can read and write, moreover, were never taught much more. One out of four of the healthy young men drafted into the Army are unable to learn any task more complicated than digging ditches or washing pots and pans[18]; and while some of these soldiers are undoubtedly of low native intelligence, the staggering size of the inept proportion suggests that the principal cause of their deficiency is inadequate schooling.

2. Even the simplest function of an educational system, vocational training, is relatively complex in an economy changing as fast as ours. Among manual jobs, those that require no skill are becoming proportionately fewer; and in the labor force as a whole, the percentage of white-collar and professional positions is increasing even faster. The significance of these trends to each individual American is obvious: they mean that the traditional opportunity to raise himself up the social ladder still exists to a marked degree. The main prerequisite to a significant rise, however, has become the formal education appropriate to the position he is seeking. A degree pays for itself many times over: a four-year college education that costs a total of about $9,000 (including the amount that could be earned by a teenager at relatively un-

[16] For an interesting history of adult education, see Grattan, *In Quest of Knowledge.*
[17] Caliver, "For a More Literate Nation."
[18] *New York Times,* May 4, 1958.

skilled work) increases one's lifetime income by about $100,000.[19]

That the efforts of an individual to get ahead are commendable in terms of American values need hardly be said, and it is also a commonplace that the society as a whole is in great need of more highly educated specialists. The number of persons engaged in professions associated with industrialization has grown tremendously—from 30,000 engineers in 1890 to more than 530,000 in 1950,[20] for example, and by similar ratios among chemists, physicists, biologists, accountants, and, most recently, administrators. Even this growth has not been fast enough, however, and there are serious and in some cases increasing shortages in several essential professions. Which these are depends to some degree, of course, on one's definition both of "essential" and of "shortages."

The most obvious, though not necessarily the best, criterion of a shortage of professional personnel is a large number of unfilled openings and a consequent disproportionate rise in salaries or earnings. But this definition, in spite of the fact that it has the sanction of economic theory, applies only to professionals subject to market conditions, such as engineers working for corporations or physicians in private practice. Persons who work for a government and are thus paid out of a tax fund often have lower salaries even if their services are more important to society. The shortages of physicians in salaried positions in health departments, for example, or of nurses in hospitals, or of teachers, must be defined by comparing the number and quality of the supply with some standard of what the society needs. Sometimes such a need—for example, for a greater number of highly qualified theoretical physicists—can be appreciated only by one himself trained in the profession.[21]

The principal reason for such shortages is that, in spite of the rapid expansion of America's educational system, too few young people are learning nearly as much as they can absorb. Furthermore:

[19] The figures, obviously rough approximations, are the estimates of two statisticians of the Census Bureau, Glick and Miller, "Educational Level," pp. 310-311. The recent rise in the cost of a college education, though sharp, has not been great enough to affect this contrast appreciably.

[20] National Manpower Council, *A Policy*, p. 162.

[21] *Ibid.*, Chap. 7.

Today, less than half of those capable of acquiring a college degree enter college. About two-fifths of those who start college—many with superior ability—do not graduate. For every high school graduate who eventually earns a doctoral degree, there are twenty-five others who have the intellectual ability to achieve that degree but do not.[22]

A long-term policy demands that greater incentives be devised to keep some of these "underdeveloped human resources" in school for a longer period. For the immediate future, the only remedy is more and better adult education.

3.   The differentiation between vocational skills and general cultural knowledge that we have made is to some degree artificial. Indeed, it may be potentially dangerous.

Vocational education conceived as job-training represents the greatest threat to democratic education in our time. It is a threat to democracy because it tends to make the job-trained individual conscious only of his technological responsibilities, but not of his social and moral responsibilities. He becomes a specialist in "means" but indifferent to "ends" which are considered the province of another specialist.[23]

In any case, if even a liberal arts degree generally results in a higher salary, and if a larger income is valued in part for the greater access to culture it makes possible, then economic roles are not really as rigidly separated from the rest of life as in the usual analysis. The function of a liberal education is to prepare a student both to earn his own living and to live fully with what he earns.

Perhaps the greatest boon that their technology has brought Americans, at least potentially, is more free time. Leisure has been increased in three ways: people generally work less hard and thus have reserves of energy at the end of the working day; as has been noted, over the past century the average workweek has been cut from 70 to 40 hours, and is still going down; and during the last fifty years the average life has been extended by twenty years, and is still going up. However, this free time is often less a boon than a burden, particularly for the aged.

So long as work was the main waking activity of the vast ma-

[22] *Ibid.*, p. 19.
[23] Hook, *Education*, pp. 156-157.

jority of the population, "leisure" was regarded simply as respite from work. This merely negative view of free time has been maintained in our value system after its relevance disappeared. Americans are a hard-working people. Veblen to the contrary notwithstanding, the United States has never had a leisure class. The so-called "idle rich" have seldom been idle, for no matter how great their wealth they have been typically as much imbued as the rest of the population with the stern Protestant ethic epitomized in Benjamin Franklin's maxims. This moral imperative to work made possible the overnight conversion of a wilderness into a great civilization, and it still continues to be a conspicuous element of the American national character.

In twentieth-century America, leisure is misconceived as idleness, vacationing (which involves "vacancy"), play, recreation, relaxation, diversion, amusement and so on. . . . Leisure, properly conceived, . . . consists in activities which are neither toil nor play, but are rather the expressions of moral and intellectual virtue—the things a good man does because they are intrinsically good for him and for his society.[24]

In theory, the whole rich storehouse of Western culture is now available for all to draw from, but many have not learned how to open the door.

By far the favorite reading matter of the wartime Army, that cross-section of young America, was comic books. Half of the students in a major state university do not know who Karl Marx is.[25] A much larger proportion do not recognize the Bill of Rights of the United States Constitution when they see it.[26] The failure of the educational system to teach students the elements of their own culture is greater even than the failure to provide the

[24] Kelso and Adler, *The Capitalist Manifesto*, pp. 16-17.

[25] Several hundred freshmen and sophomores were asked to identify twenty famous persons, and fewer than a quarter of them recognized as many as half the names in the list. "In fact only four of the twenty names were clearly identified by as many as half the students. These were [Adlai] Stevenson (86 per cent), John Dillinger (78 per cent), Peter Townsend (66 per cent), and . . . Karl Marx (50 per cent). At the bottom of the list was Norman Thomas; only seven students (2 per cent) knew who he is" (Norman and Sawin, "What Johnny Don't Know").

[26] When the Bill of Rights was converted into an opinion questionnaire, and administered to a random sample both of the regular student bodies of the University of Wisconsin and Northwestern University and that portion of the summer student body that had taught in primary or secondary schools,

American economy with a sufficient number of trained persons.
4. "Popular government without popular education," in the
words of James Madison, "is a prologue to a farce or a tragedy."

It is a truism that democracy requires a higher general level of education, and a much higher level of political understanding and experience, than other forms of government; yet it is difficult to be
convinced that it is a truism which we have taken very seriously, and
equally difficult to see how we can claim to be taking it seriously
without a considerable development of adult education and of university participation in it.[27]

In the American democracy the level of ignorance of the
populace is an important determinant not only of public policy
but, with the growing power of the United States, of world affairs
as well. Over the past half century the relation between the United
States and the rest of the world has changed at least as dra-
matically as its domestic social economy. In 1900, this country
was still in many respects a cultural appendage of Europe,
having just made in the Spanish-American War its first, brash
entry on the world scene. Today the United States is the core of
Western democracy. The rest of the nontotalitarian world looks
to it, not always hopefully, for both material aid and political
guidance. In a fundamental sense, this leadership is legitimate:
the many demands of the peoples of the world can be summed up
in two—political and social democracy, and mass-produced consumers goods—and these are significant features of American
society today. In political terms, however, world leadership was
thrust on the United States before the necessary experience and
tradition had fully developed. America's national interest must
be more effectively defined in the nation's schools and—again,
to make up for past and present deficiencies—in adult-education
programs.

If, as we have tried to show, the many important changes that
have taken place in American society over the past fifty years
necessitate special educational facilities to help adults adapt to

as many as three-quarters of the respondents disagreed with some of the
points. And, what is even more disturbing, apparently most of these college
students and public school teachers did not recognize the Bill of Rights
through its thin disguise. See McGinnis and Mack, "A Study of Belief."
[27] Raybould, *The English Universities,* p. 15.

them, this does not mean that the role of adult education is only adaptive. Education, including adult education, ought to help people adjust to changing conditions—but also to see that they do not adjust too far. The *main* function of education is to furnish cultural continuity from one generation to the next, and the more rapid the change in society, the more essential it is to stress the enduring verities that, without help, students tend to overlook. The appropriate response to what in articles on education is invariably termed our "dynamic" world is not simply flexibility, but flexibility combined with fundamental stability. "The greatest task of adult education and the greatest obligation laid upon state universities in this disordered present is to restate the cultural and political ideals of America."[28]

To what degree are the tasks of adult education fulfilled? That it has failed to realize the potential that exists among the large number of possible participants, that it has not made good the gaps between existent and needed knowledge, even its own practitioners would hardly deny. The reasons for this partial failure are many and complex. One of the most important, according to the thesis of this book, is that, in spite of the vast literature on the subject, few people in adult education know precisely either what they are trying to do or what means are appropriate.

If adult education is important, as we have tried to demonstrate in this chapter, a guide to policy concerning it is necessary; and in the following chapters we attempt to furnish this with respect to the university's role.

Summary

Over the past fifty years, the economy, social structure, and educational system of the United States have all undergone a fundamental transformation. For many Americans, this rapid change has made possible a richer life, achieved by the vocational training and cultural orientation their education gave them. For many others, however, the potential has not been realized; and both they as individuals and society as a whole suffer as a consequence. The under-educated sector of our population can be brought up to par only by offering it the opportunity to learn

[28] Nolte, "The Role of the State University," p. 66; see also Browne, "Winds of Doctrine"; Gideonse, "On Re-Thinking Liberal Education."

more. Of the many conclusions that might be drawn from this review of the past half century, thus, we wish to suggest only one —that significant adult education may well be as worthy an object of public support as the primary school itself.

In general terms, the functions of adult education can be defined as follows:

1.   *Remedial*[29]: To eliminate illiteracy, teach adult immigrants English, and in other respects bring the entire normal population up to the level of grammar school graduates.

2.   *Vocational:* To provide the means by which adults can improve themselves in the way they earn a living, either within their vocation or by changing to another one; to alleviate specific shortages of professional personnel by teaching suitable adults; and to teach women how to perform better their roles as housewives and mothers.

3.   *Cultural:* To give adults some understanding of the natural world, their cultural heritage, the society in which they live, and themselves, so that they can live more fully and make richer use of the increasing years of leisure available to them.

4.   *Political:* To train adults as citizens and give them a better basis for taking sides on public issues; particularly, to correct the very serious deficiency in Americans' understanding of foreign affairs.

Stated baldly, these purposes of adult education may seem to be too axiomatic to be worth writing down. But neither these ends nor especially the means by which they might be achieved are agreed on among adult educators. On the contrary, whether we speak of aims, or content, or method, or whatever, there is hardly a thesis in adult education without its counter thesis. In Chapter 2, we will examine the most important of these disputes and attempt to resolve them.

[29] This is now often called, following the euphemism of UNESCO terminology, "fundamental" education. See, for example, Spence and Cass, *Guide for Program Service,* p. 39.

ADULT EDUCATION:
PRINCIPLES AND PROBLEMS

American education is in a turmoil. Vigorous disputes over the philosophy of education, curricula, teaching methods, standards, the training of teachers, and so on and on, have engaged the attention of the entire teaching profession and a sizable portion of the general public. In some respects, the controversy in adult education is parallel to the more familiar one between progressive and traditionalist educators, between those who "teach children" and those who "teach subject matter." There are, however, several important differences.

Standard education (that is, all but adult education) has established a number of relatively inviolable functions: pupils in primary grades are to learn the three R's; college teaching is governed by the several disciplines. The complaint is that Johnny can't read, and the dispute is over the efficacy of various methods of teaching him. No one so much as raises the question whether he should learn to read at all. Similarly, the range of the divergence concerning higher education is generally not so great that the opponents get out of sight of each other. Advocates of polar positions—say, Sidney Hook at one extreme and Mortimer J. Adler at the other—agree that the college's function is to transmit a "liberal education."[1] The differences are over how to define the key term and especially over how to attain this goal. When all more or less agree on ends and differ mainly over means, it may be possible to resolve the dispute. Whether knowledge of

[1] In Adler and Mayer, *The Revolution in Education*, the authors discuss the "modernist" Sidney Hook as the antithesis to their own "traditionalist" position. While this chapter, entitled "The Appearance of Agreement," argues that the differences are unbridgeable in spite of similar formulations of educational goals, the book ends with proposed "Roads to Resolution" of this and other similar oppositions in standard education.

17

Latin improves the student's English, for instance, or whether learning algebra teaches him to reason better, can be tested. However difficult it may be to devise such tests, the point is that in standard education evaluation is generally possible to some degree, and advocates of various philosophies usually find it expedient to argue in terms of the educational effects of the curricula and methods they propose.

Adult education is a different world. It is, most practitioners agree, unorganized, confused, chaotic; and some of them believe that this is as it should be. One of the things about an adult-education conference that, amazingly, "most cheered" a visiting colleague from Canada was that "a certain amount of confusion, apparent contradictions and unresolved difficulties not only were present but were tolerated."[2] We would agree that a democratic movement must have a place for differing positions, and that a dynamic movement is likely to reflect past rapid change in present variety, but what is the value to education of confusion, even "a certain amount"? And any movement, even the most democratic and the most dynamic, is meaningful only if there is a minimum core of invariable consensus. Whether this exists in adult education is a moot question.

A potpourri of heterogeneous organizations interested in "reaching" adults, each in its own fashion and for its own purposes, defines each in its own way the institution, its functions, the means of achieving the goals set. Among adult educators the very word *education*, for instance, is markedly imprecise: for some, it means the process by which new knowledge or attitudes or skills are transmitted, and for others that by which persons participate together in an activity and come to feel a sense of identification with a group. Distinctions between such opposed positions are not ordinarily sharply drawn. While adult educators feel, of course, that the orientation they prefer is the best, they almost always concede that every other "approach" also has its value. Tolerance of others' views, flexibility, exciting experimentation, imagination, and creativity—these are seen by most practitioners as prime virtues, overriding such mundane characteristics as consistency, practicality, and logic.

---

[2] Kidd, "The Observer's Report." For other expressions of similar sentiments, see, for example, Knowles, "Philosophical Issues," pp. 238-239.

In order to analyze the basic trends in adult education, where should one begin in this welter of contradictory, sometimes self-contradictory, tenets and practices, most of which are neither validated nor even capable of being evaluated? One frequent device is to take the extreme positions and compare them. According to Birnbaum, for example, the "two major schools of adult education today" are as follows:

1. The "traditionalist"—"those who see mental functions or cognition as the central phenomenon in learning, who stress content as against method, who see their task as the liberal education of the individual, who stress the development of a mature value system, and who would, moreover, make substantial use of the content of past civilizations."

2. The "psychological"—"those who stress the importance of the emotions in learning, who are impressed with the influence of the unconscious in human behavior, the powerful educational value of group learning, the role of experience in learning, and the frequent conflict between values and attitudinal systems."[3]

Such a dichotomy has the advantage of giving the analyst an axis around which to arrange his ideas, but also several disadvantages that outweigh this:

1. On several important issues, there are not two but three or four significantly different positions. Collapsing these into a dichotomy, like the right-left continuum in a political analysis, loses more in clarity than it gains in convenience.

2. Very often the distinctions on which the dichotomy is based are false. The experimentation that is usually insisted on in adult education, for example, need not be at the cost of traditional standards. Or: the dispute over methods need not be in terms of absolutes; "it would be as ridiculous to assume that no true learning transpires within the organized study group as it is to hold that no learning occurs outside of it."[4]

3. Some of the issues are false in another sense: a key word is used in several meanings, as in the slogan, democracy in educa-

[3] Birnbaum, "Mind and Emotion," p. 144. For somewhat similar comparisons, see Sheats, "A Middle Way"; Alter, "A House Divided"; Knowles, "Philosophical Issues"; Sillars, "An Approach"; Powell and Benne, "Philosophies"; Schmidt and Svenson, "Methods."
[4] Snow, *Community Adult Education*, p. 64.

tion.[5] Some who advocate this mean that the teacher should try to imbue his subject matter with the values of democracy, others that the teacher should give up his professional authority to student rule. According to one leading figure of the Adult Education Association, for example, "the adult is the one who decides his education, not the educator or the educational agency."[6] Here is a point significant enough to form an appropriate opening theme in a discussion of the principles of adult education.

On "Democracy" in Adult Education

Perhaps the most perplexing question in adult education, as it is ordinarily administered, is how to decide what programs should be offered.[7] With no firm educational principles themselves on what content is appropriate, adult educators generally turn to prospective participants and ask them what they would like. How prevalent customer satisfaction is as a determinant of adult education is indicated by the most extensive survey to date of how programs are established. ·

In 1951, Kempfer analyzed 530 adult-education programs in public schools and community colleges.[8] Arranged in order from most to least "successful" in terms of his criteria,[9] the programs had been established by the following methods:

1. We systematically cultivate a group of "coordinators" in industry, business, and other community organizations and agencies who watch for every opportunity for education to perform a service.

2. We receive requests from business, industrial, labor, and community groups.

3. We study deficiencies of adults (e.g., poor nutrition, low educational level, lack of civic participation, poor methods of child rearing).

[5] For even more egregious examples of multiple meaning of key terms, see the discussion of "needs" and "method" below, pp. 25 ff., 35 ff.

[6] Stensland, "What is Adult Education?" See also Kempfer et al., *Program Evaluation*, pp. 10-11.

[7] In a recent study of a hundred public junior colleges with adult-education programs, for instance, the administrators stated that "their most difficult problem was the lack of criteria to determine need for courses" (S. V. Martorana, "Problems in Adult Education in the Junior College," cited in Kempfer, *Adult Education*, p. 62).

[8] Kempfer, "Identifying Educational Needs," pp. 34-35.

[9] For a criticism of his method of evaluation, see below, p. 41.

4. We maintain an extensive personal acquaintance with a wide range of community leaders and groups.

5. We examine data from the census and similar sources.

6. We make systematic surveys of the industrial, business, civic, and cultural life of the community.

7. We examine published surveys of other communities and similar literature.

8. We examine catalogs, schedules, publicity materials, and programs of comparable institutions.

9. Through "hunch."

10. We try to be sensitive to civic, personal, and social problems of people—problems which can be alleviated by education.

11. We check with other known interests of people (e.g., library reading interests, newspaper and magazine readership surveys).

12. We utilize check lists and other "interest finders."

13. We receive individual requests.

These thirteen methods of establishing the content of an educational program can be grouped into four classes, as follows:

Surveys of various types, either those already in existence (5, 7, 11) or those made specially for this purpose (6, 12). In spite of their limitations, such surveys are obviously one important source of relevant background information.

Requests from groups or individuals, either spontaneous (2, 4, 13) or solicited (1, 4). Again, no one would deny that such requests should be taken into consideration by the director, as well as being solicited by any convenient means. The issue is whether they are taken as absolutes, or fitted into a prior policy that the administrator has set.

Following practices that were successful elsewhere (8) or that the administrator thinks would be successful (9). It is noteworthy that, according to this tabulation, the professional judgment of administrators is restricted to following their colleagues' examples or their own "hunches." Were their knowledge and imagination relatively unimportant in setting up a successful program because of their lack of ability, or because of the criteria by which a program was adjudged to be "successful"?

Remedial education (3, 10), "a negative approach to program planning," which, according to Kempfer, has "long handicapped the full development of adult education."[10] This depreciation of

[10] Kempfer, *Adult Education*, p. 73.

remedial education, usual in writings by adult educators, possibly derives from a comparison with the lofty goals they ordinarily set themselves and the more dramatic activities that these presumably demand.

According to this study, then, adult-education programs are established mainly by what the participants would like. Quite apart from the educational principles on which these procedures are based, it is worth pointing out that most surveys are not very reliable. Even the simplest kind involves all of the weaknesses of public-opinion research.[11] "An extensive personal acquaintance" with leaders and groups, thus, will not be representative unless there is a special effort to make it so. Respondents may be uncertain of their interests and thus inclined to reply to a question concerning them in terms of a momentary whim. Such answers, moreover, will tend to be biased in one direction: when asked whether they are "interested" in fine arts, literature, music, better citizenship, few persons will say No. Replies may be conditioned more by conventional attitudes than by the personal interests of the respondents.[12] According to what seems to be the only check ever made of such a survey (in Radburn, New Jersey, more than twenty years ago), stated intentions do not correspond with later actual behavior:

After the programs were inaugurated, it was discovered that only slightly more than one third of the persons who had indicated interest in a particular activity actually took part in it; whereas nearly two thirds of the total number of actual participants had not previously expressed interest in the activities. . . . Actual participation turned out to be inversely related to stated preferences.[13]

This experience suggests that, at best, surveys can be useful only if they are made in accordance with the best practices of public-opinion analysts—with a carefully selected sample, a professionally constructed questionnaire, well trained interviewers, and coding

[11] See, for example, Cantril, *Gauging Public Opinion*, especially Part I, "Problems Involved in Setting the Issues," and Part II, "Problems Connected with Interviewing."

[12] See, for example, Knowles, *Informal Adult Education*, p. 179.

[13] Beals and Brody, *The Literature*, pp. 67-68. See also Hudson, *Radburn*, pp. 16-63, and Appendix A, pp. 94-95; Ozanne, *Regional Surveys*, pp. 29-31; Brunner et al., *An Overview*, pp. 108-114.

and analysis of the results by persons who recognize the limitations as well as the value of this type of research.

In any case, a community survey should be no more than one criterion out of several in establishing the curriculum of adult education. What "the people" want, even if it were possible to judge this exactly, ought not to be the main determinant, not to say almost the only one, of the content of adult education. According to those who believe differently, "democracy" apparently means that persons must give up their special skills in the economy: the educator must abdicate his professional function of establishing an adequate and balanced curriculum and become "merely a waiter behind a cafeteria line."[14] In the opinion of Nolte, it would be as logical for a physician to demand that his patients themselves prescribe the appropriate medicine.[15] Or, in Houle's words:

> Great courses of study are not enunciated by popular demand. . . . Adults aware of their own need for knowledge and insight rarely can articulate exactly what it is they want to know. If they could do that, the libraries and the museums would already have helped them to know it.[16]

Why do some educators refuse to accept their professional responsibility? The most obvious reason is the notion that this makes their task easier. "The use of the concept of 'needs' for goal defining purposes is . . . an attempt to ease the burden of decision on the educator," who then is "content just to go about sleuthing for 'needs' in the belief that these 'needs' when 'discovered' will relieve him of the leadership task."[17] Moreover, "the altruism" displayed in serving community needs "fools everybody and disarms potential critics."[18] Whether an educator can really make it easier for himself by avoiding his responsibility, however, is another question. "The director is likely to be deluged with requests for all kinds of courses. . . . His life can be made miser-

[14] Blakely, "Adult Education Needs a Philosophy," p. 9. Mr. Blakely argued against this point of view in this address to the Adult Education Association.

[15] Nolte, "The Role of the State University," pp. 64-65.

[16] Houle, "Introduction," pp. 22-23.

[17] James, "Can 'Needs' Define?" pp. 24, 22.

[18] Nyquist, "The Soft Pedagogy," p. 59.

able unless he has a definite set of policies to back him up in screening such requests."[19]

There is a more compelling reason for the prevalence of this type of "democracy" in adult education—that administrators are confronted with the dilemma of running programs that are both educational and money-making, and try to save face by labeling customer satisfaction the "democratic" control of educational policy. Virtually all adult-education programs have to pay their own way to one degree or another. According to Cohen's survey of world-affairs organizations, which may be taken as an example of private adult-education agencies generally, "the need for . . . funds is felt to be so great that many of the existing resources are applied not to education but to the search for new resources."[20] Public schools are generally reimbursed for their adult-education programs on the basis of average daily attendance.[21] Foundations that give support to adult education also, though less formally, tend to measure "success" first by the size of the enrollments and eventually by whether the program becomes self-supporting. And general-extension divisions, unlike any other sector of the university, are usually required to get a large proportion of their income from fees.[22]   .

If the adult educator is forced to regard his students as customers, he must define his program as commodities. Like any other businessman, he tries both to adapt his product to public taste and, through advertising, to induce the public to accept it. The choice between educational offerings is put on the same level as the choice among several brands of breakfast food. A group of evening-college administrators discussed recently "ways in which courses might be attractively packaged and marketed."[23]

[19] Knowles, *Informal Adult Education*, p. 90.

[20] Cohen, *Citizen Education*, p. 58. He continues: "No statement of purposes provides . . . that an organization must replenish its treasury if it is to continue to operate, yet officials are often forced to act as if that were one of their major articles of incorporation" (p. 64).

[21] This is the system in the California adult-education system, for example, where it is a "crucial" factor. "Financing does not merely determine the overall size of activity, but intervenes decisively in substantive matters." However, it is "virtually utopian *not* to expect average daily attendance to be the key concern in administration." See Clark, *Adult Education*, pp. 159-160.

[22] See below, pp. 117-118.

[23] *1957 AUEC Proceedings*, p. 59.

In a chapter of his text entitled "Identifying Educational Needs and Interests of Adults," Kempfer recommends the community survey as the equivalent in education to market research in business.[24]

The notion that in adult education the patients cure themselves is not only professionally degrading but also hypocritical. No one really wants to write himself out of his profession, though he may try to give others that impression. According to Kempfer, for example, "the imposition of goals is authoritarian," but "if the formulation of objectives is left to individuals without control or agreement, on the principle of *laissez-faire*, anarchy is the ultimate result."[25] Similarly, "in a democracy the participants are often the final judges of the worth of an adult-education program," though "few programs should ever be judged solely on consumer satisfaction."[26] If in the opinion of an adult educator a program (for example, on the principles of democratic theory or race relations) would do the community good, he would ordinarily attempt to set it up whether or not anyone had expressed a desire for it.

Needs—Felt, Unfelt, and Other

The conflict between the shibboleth that the content of every program in adult education must be determined by the "felt needs" of the individual or the community, and the actual refusal of educators to abrogate their professional responsibility entirely, has resulted in a remarkable variation in the meaning of this phrase. In most contexts *need* is a good English word with a reasonably precise definition. In the field of adult education,[27] however, the abuse inflicted on it has pommeled this term into a misshapen mess. In order to re-establish a modicum of communication, we shall here replace *need* by the half-dozen nonsynonymous words that it has ousted. Let us begin by breaking down "felt need" into its several component parts.

[24] Kempfer, *Adult Education*, p. 68.
[25] *Ibid.*, p. 402.
[26] *Ibid.*, pp. 416-417.
[27] For a discussion of the meaning of "needs" in education in general, see Tyler, *Basic Principles*, pp. 5-10.

The first recognizable meaning of "need" is *interest*, which we define as a vague, low-level desire to be associated with an activity or subject either for its own sake or for the social contacts it affords:

> The teachers recognized that many students had interests other than information . . . best described as "social" or "recreational." . . . Concerning their own aims as teachers, all of them expressed a strong feeling in one way or another that they should try to meet the *needs* of their adult students.[28]

One of the important criteria defining interest is its low level— needs "best described as 'social' or 'recreational.'" A person who becomes involved in an adult-education program out of loneliness or boredom may become "interested" in painting or ancient history or child psychology and enroll in any one of these courses, but in an educational context it is useful to distinguish the student who does not choose his program merely out of indifference.

The second meaning of "need," then, is *concern*, which we define as a spontaneous, high-level, noninstrumental desire to be associated with an activity or subject for its own sake. A person "concerned" with painting, that is to say, would take the initiative in enrolling in a course in painting, but not in just any subject:

> The people themselves know their *needs*. A careful block-by-block survey of adult education needs in Denver disclosed what 63 per cent found most lacking—an understanding of what is going on in a world at war.[29]

Some "felt needs" are instrumental; that is, the knowledge or activity is desired not for its own sake, as an end, but as a means toward achieving another goal. A woman with her first baby may take a course in child psychology even though she finds the subject boring, or her husband may try to improve his vocational skill. Let us define "needs" in this sense as *wants*:

[28] Zander, "Student Motives," in Sheats et al., *Adult Education*, pp. 324-328. In each of these examples—all taken, by the way, from the same book —we have italicized the word *need*.

[29] Sheats, "Adult Education—A Responsibility of Public Education," in *ibid.*, pp. 146-148.

Sometimes an adult finds that he has prepared himself for a field in which later he discovers himself unhappy or ill-adapted, and so feels the *need* to prepare for an entirely new field.[30]

In seeking to satisfy his "wants," a person retains the possibility of choice, but some vocational "needs" are essentially coercive: a man has been told by his employer that he will be fired unless he improves his level of skill; a public school teacher cannot get an increase in salary unless she accumulates "alertness credits." A vocational "need" with a significant degree of coercion by the employer (or other persons or circumstances) we define as a *requirement.*[31]

There are not only "felt needs" but also, at least by implication, "unfelt needs," that is, "needs" of which the individual is not aware. (It is almost too bad that a Freudian has not wandered into this field, so that the "felt needs" would be interpreted as mere symbols of the individual's unfelt—in the sense of unconscious—"needs." The already unique confusion would then achieve perfection.) But what does this implied distinction between "felt" and "unfelt" needs mean, if not that though adults may know what they want, they are not able to define a sound educational program? However, it is unfashionable, not to say authoritarian, to put this so bluntly; and adult educators ordinarily prefer to say that "the director must understand not only the needs felt by adults but those which they may not recognize" and must be "led to recognize."[32] In other words, adult students must merely be given the impression that they have made a choice on their own.

The first type of communal "need," which may be "felt" or "unfelt" by the individual, comes close to the literal meaning of the word—a functional prerequisite to societal survival or health (or, at the lowest level of intensity, improvement). "Needs" for such institutions or facilities as new school buildings, more industry or retail trade in the community, sanitary programs, various kinds of educational or cultural activities, and the like, we define as *necessities:*

[30] Ralph E. Crow, *Handbook for Adult Education Teachers,* excerpted in *ibid.,* pp. 6-7.

[31] Although this is the type of "need" that motivates the majority of at least the students in credit courses (see below, pp. 68-69), it is apparently not mentioned in the cited volume.

[32] Kempfer, *Adult Education,* p. 62.

Another approach to the problem of more adequately meeting adult *needs* is illustrated by . . . a community-action checksheet . . . as the basis upon which a program of action can be recommended.[33]

A second type of communal "need" relates to the purposes of social life. Necessities have been defined as the means by which democracy, a high standard of living, and other social ends can be achieved. "Needs" in the sense of such ultimate goals we define as *moral imperatives:*

The common man . . . *needs* to understand this life in all its local and remote relationships and he also needs to participate actively in creating conditions whereby democracy has some tangible meaning.[34]

These six separate concepts—interest, concern, want, requirement, necessity, and moral imperative—do not exhaust the range of meaning included in "need," but they are sufficient to demonstrate the utter ambiguity involved in the adult educator's use of the word. It is not merely that "need" can mean any one of several things, but that in many contexts it seems to mean several of them together:

It is always a good idea to start with some planned procedures to determine *needs* and interests. . . . We are all tempted to think in terms of what people ought to have rather than what they *want.* . . . There are several ways of finding out what people *need* and want. . . .[35]

Or, as another example:

The newer type of community or adult-education center program . . . is more flexible and adaptable, covers a broader range of interests, and endeavors to take into account the recreational and cultural *needs* of adults as well as their vocational ones.[36]

This confusion helps the educator in not taking a definite stand for or against anything. In particular, as we have noted, he can both propound the students' "right" to set their own education and also defend his professional prerogative to de-

[33] Sheats et al., *Adult Education,* p. 312, referring to a program of the Agricultural Extension Service at Iowa State College. The examples we have used to illustrate necessities were taken from the sample community-action check sheet reproduced in the cited volume.

[34] McClusky, "Mobilizing the Community for Adult Education," in *ibid.,* pp. 295-298.

[35] Knowles, "Your Program Planning Tool Kit," in *ibid.,* pp. 315-320.

[36] *Ibid.,* p. 312.

termine the best program, without permitting this contradiction to appear above the surface. In part as a result, nothing is too frivolous, too far removed from education, to escape endorsement by some adult educator as a legitimate part even of a *university's* function:

> Courses in ice skating, square dancing, or totem pole carving would certainly be less academic in nature than investment analysis, agricultural mathematics, or construction and maintenance of aircraft; but if the students believe they have some *need* for the training and skill they can secure by doing the work, only an extremely narrow concept of adult education would preclude the possibility of setting up such courses. Although many of the courses that adults require are not of an academic nature, every effort should be made to provide good training.[37]

The educator's canon that he must "begin with people where they are" puts no limit on the legitimacy of the "felt needs" that determine the content of an educational program. Yet obviously there is such a limit—whether legality, good taste, middle-class conventionality, or whatever.

> You have an adult program. It includes classes in bridge. And in how to cheat at bridge? Any in safe-cracking? Seduction? I suppose not; the question is, *why* not? Offered with discretion, they might be both popular and profitable. . . . Your town has a high divorce rate. Should you offer classes in better ways to divorce?[38]

Wherever the line is drawn, the fact that it is drawn is decisive. Since "the people" do not rule absolutely, the limit of their legitimate option might well be set by an *educational* criterion.

The fuzzy thinking typical in adult education touches bottom in the discussion of this crucial issue—to what extent should needs, however defined, determine programs? "Nothing provides such a splendid cover for obscure educational thinking as the underbrush of platitudes that perpetually flourishes about the main moral issues of education."[39] Consider the queer kind of

---

[37] Dugan, "An Extension Class Program," p. 153.

[38] Powell, " 'Where Did You Go?' " p. 261.

[39] James, "Can 'Needs' Define?" p. 24. With a firmness unusual in the literature of adult education, this article states the educator's professional and moral responsibility for setting the content and standards of the programs he administers. Dr. James has since written us as follows: "If I were to do [the

democracy to which this illogical application of political principles to an inappropriate field has led adult educators. Democracy implies not merely the right to choose but the power to make a free choice, and "there can be no free choice unless alternatives are seen and their probable consequences explored. Not to reveal alternatives is to restrict choice."[40] An adult educator who bases his program mainly on surveys and similar indications of students' "needs" deprives them of the possibility of opting for something that, in their relative ignorance, they had never thought of.

Content

The supposed absolute rule of "felt needs" does not apply even in theory. If adult educators took seriously their maxim that "democracy" demands that they give "the people" what they want the way they want it, there would be no point in further cogitation on the matter. Yet there is a good deal of discussion of both the appropriate content of adult-education programs and of the best methods of teaching them.

At the most abstract level, the question is whether adult education ought to benefit mainly the individual participating in it or society as a whole. The aim of adult education, we are told, "is to inspire grown-ups to be something more than they are now and to do their work better than they now do it,"[41] so that they will learn "some content material worth learning and understanding, something that will make their individual lives richer and more meaningful."[42] Other educators insist, on the contrary, that "mere extension of personal knowledge on the

---

article] over I would be more blunt. In my opinion, the present dominant spirit of 'other direction' in adult education is irresponsible. It blocks explicit, open-handed leadership, abets several puerile educational 'philosophies,' and provides superb protective coloration for the man with a hidden agenda. It furthers the sentimental corruption of noble concepts like 'democracy,' reducing them to mean little more than smiling conformity to the 'group.' Meanwhile, the principle of 'meeting needs' has simply turned into a devious rationale for some pretty tawdry commercialism. Unfortunately the ideas behind this sort of thing seem to have lodged in adult education as a last redoubt against the critical reexamination of American educational standards and policy."

[40] Fletcher, *The Battle of the Curriculum*, p. 16.

[41] James E. Russell, "Help to Self-Realization," quoted in Beals and Brody, *The Literature*, p. 18.

[42] McGhee, *A School for Optimists*, p. 23.

part of individual adults does not constitute an adult education movement"[43]; that "the major task of adult education is the reduction of alienation in our society"[44]; that "one of the major areas of adult education is that of training people in the skills of productive group membership."[45]

The difference does not reflect a real dilemma. To the question of whether adult education should benefit the individual or society, the only reasonable reply is: both. In a democracy there is no contradiction between individual improvement and a more viable community life. Where there are rigid class lines, a man can move up from his father's station only by disturbing what is felt to be the suitable relations between himself and his betters. But in the United States, both the democratic credo and in large part actual practice encourage each man to establish himself at the highest level his abilities permit. In a society governed by a totalitarian party, individuals who acquire some uncomfortable facts or, more important, learn to be critical of official dogmas, constitute a danger to state security. But in the United States, again, both theory and practice demand that citizens be taught how to think critically, how to judge political issues objectively; and this educational philosophy has been one basis of what is probably the most stable government in the world today.

The difference over whether it is the individual or society that is to be served by adult education is really one over content. Apart from the thesis that the content ought to follow "felt needs," three major positions are discernible:

1. The content of adult education ought to be whatever is necessary to bring about social reform—to solve "family problems, delinquency, labor difficulties, and national and international problems,"[46] or, in a word, to "help save the world within the next few years."[47] Or, as stated in the guiding principles of

[43] Point 5 in "Principles" stated by the Committee on Social Philosophy and Direction Finding of the Adult Education Association, as reported by Pell, "Social Philosophy," p. 126. See also Sillars, "An Interpretation," which reports a similar consensus among leaders of the AEA's predecessor, the American Association for Adult Education.
[44] Benne, "Why I Ran," p. 7.
[45] Spence and Cass, *Guide for Program Service*, p. 71.
[46] Bradford, "Report," p. 167.
[47] Robert M. Hutchins, quoted in Starr, "Labor's Concern," p. 34.

the Adult Education Association: "*Social action* on behalf of reasoned social change is the functional *raison d'etre* of a modern adult education movement."[48]

There is a basic confusion apparent here. Social reform, in the sense of the establishment and extension of a democratic society, rests in part on popular education. This observation is so obvious at the level of primary schooling that it is generally agreed (though, as has been noted, sometimes with little grace) that one legitimate function of adult education is to remove fundamental educational deficiencies like illiteracy. But those who believe in liberal education maintain that at any level it gives support to democratic society. If a person learns to appreciate a Bach cantata, or to read Catullus in the original Latin, or to use a microscope, his richer inner life will help make him a better member of society. "Should a group of adults appear, asking for a course in astronomy, for example, not because they hope to rearrange the stars and improve the universe, but solely because they are filled with wonder, and would like to know more about the heavens, this is warrant enough."[49] In the last decades of the nineteenth century, when the courts decided in favor of tax support to high schools teaching foreign languages, algebra and geometry, and other "useless frills" previously reserved for the children of the rich, the creed of liberal education became American law.

If in this general sense *all* of education is relevant to the establishment of the good society, in a more specific instrumental sense, very little of it is. There is no evidence, for instance, that the innumerable "marriage and family" courses set up during the past decades have reduced the incidence of divorce; and if

[48] Pell, "Social Philosophy," p. 126; emphasis in the original. Or, as another example: "*Problem-solving* ought to be the preferred *method* of the adult leader. . . . The *end product* of the problem-solving activity ought to be *action*" (Wiggin, "Guide Lines," pp. 14, 16; emphasis in the original). Or, as still another example: "Community self help should be the key strategy of adult education. . . . We became less and less interested in serving groups requesting speeches on any topic from insect extermination to childhood in primitive tribes. If a group wanted only to sit and listen but not think and act, we had more important things to do" (McClusky, "Community Self Help," p. 10).

[49] Browne, "Winds of Doctrine," p. 107. See also McMahon, "Concentric Ripples."

anything we know even less about how to use education to eliminate other "national and international problems." What education can do—and what adult education in particular ought to do—is to give people the basis for understanding, for example, the relation between the United States and the rest of the world.[50] If American citizens acquire such an understanding, and if in part because of their more informed participation in public affairs the United States develops a better foreign policy, and if this policy is successful in maintaining world peace without loss of national honor—then we can say that education helped solve the social problem of war. In this circuitous route, however, many other factors would exert their influence; and educators would play a significant role only to the degree that they stuck to their last and concentrated on transmitting knowledge, ideas, and values to those lacking them.

Education has a function in democratic society, an important but a limited one. This apparent truism is attacked both by educational utopians, who believe that society can be changed only by first changing its system of education, and by educational defeatists, who believe that education can play no significant role until a just society is first established. These extreme positions have in common their extremism.[51]

2. The second important doctrine with respect to the content of adult education is that this is relatively unimportant, or, in an absolutist version, that there should be no content. What matters is *that* a group interacts, not *what* it interacts about.

Democracy cannot be taught by precept, but can only be learned through experience. This means that in the operation of our adult education programs people should always be gaining experience in the democratic process, this means that the way they learn is even more important than what they learn.[52]

If content is unimportant, then it is not necessary to have a teacher.

The focus of adult education is the *local community*. Adult citizens

[50] See below, Chaps. 7 and 8.
[51] Some educators—for example, Robert M. Hutchins—have on occasion upheld both. See Hook, *Education*, pp. 34 ff.
[52] AEA, "Report of the Committee on Social Philosophy," p. 209.

meeting together in face-to-face groups for the purpose of exchanging knowledge and experience constitutes [sic] the sociological nexus of adult education.[53]

In a sense this thesis is a special version of the notion that social reform is the function of adult education. *The* problem in modern society, it is maintained, is the alienation of the individual, and this can be solved only by incorporating him into group life. We comment on this thesis first by questioning its validity and secondly by denying its relevance, if it were true, to adult education.

Any viable society is based on an underlying consensus, and this has been challenged in Western society by the effects of the urbanization, industrialization, and secularization during the past several centuries. The countryman's organic identification with his village cannot be maintained in a mobile urban world; and an attempt to re-establish in the latter setting a feeling of belonging based on mere propinquity results only in a caricature of village life. Too often, in his effort to reduce his alienation from his fellows, modern man has become simply a joiner of groups, a Babbitt of the type that Sinclair Lewis parodied. This is the kind of "education" that the group dynamicists advocate: they seek to dispel one characteristic flaw of "mass society," the alienation of the individual, by fostering another, his other-directed conformity to the current style in faiths, patterns of behavior, or whatever.

It is possible, however, to reduce alienation not by discarding one's principles but by associating with others whose principles one shares. Education in a complex urban society has as one of its important functions the establishment of a common understanding of jointly held basic values. A villager is at ease with his neighbors because he grew up with them and knows them as he knows his family; but a resident of New York or London can feel at home from his knowledge that the rest of his world shares his concept of what fundaments define a good society. To maintain this consensus does not call for crude indoctrination. It is a misunderstanding of democracy to hold that this political system has no place for individualists. It could be one of the

[53] Point 1 in the "Principles" cited earlier, in Pell, "Social Philosophy," p. 124; emphasis in the original.

proudest functions of adult education, on the contrary, to furnish to mavericks—the square pegs who could never fit into the round holes of the standard educational system—the opportunity to develop their potential later in life. Some of the most notable figures in Western society, men like Harry S. Truman or Henry Mencken, have been self-educated; and often their greatness was part of a cantankerous individuality, an inability to adjust to the group.

3. The content of adult education, like that of any other kind of education, ought to be the society's cultural heritage, transmitted for the sake of individual improvement. This third position, to which we adhere, needs little comment—except perhaps amazement that it has to be defended against professional educators. In Powell's words:

> I am . . . astonished . . . that, in discussing a field called "education," it is necessary to argue in behalf of *knowledge*. . . . Adult education, apart from formal courses, has sought to achieve its goals almost wholly through the elaboration of process rather than the enrichment of content. . . . I am quite serious in saying that we are in some danger of leaving "curiosity" to be satisfied by gossip, "creativeness" by a do-it-yourself kit, and "comprehension" by the mere acquisition of tolerance for other people's views.[54]

Method

As this quotation suggests, in adult education the relation between content and method has often been conceived of as an opposition, as content *versus* method. The notion that method is more important than content, to the degree that it derives from similar statements in the works of John Dewey and his followers, is based on a lack of understanding. When a student of Dewey like Sidney Hook writes, "Far more important than knowledge is the method by which it is reached,"[55] he means by this that it matters less, for example, whether a student learns the specific facts of chemistry or of astronomy than that he learns in general terms what constitutes scientific evidence. "Educational institutions . . . must build up in students a critical sense of evidence, relevance and validity against which the multitudinous seas of

[54] Powell, *Learning Comes of Age*, pp. 143-144; emphasis in the original.
[55] Hook, *Education*, p. 94.

propaganda will wash in vain."[56] There is a contrast here not between learning and nonlearning, but between learning matters of first and second priority. When adult educators use the term "method," however, they generally mean "how we may guide the class without dominating it, keep the atmosphere informal without letting it become disorganized, help the student to feel himself a part of the group without feeling submerged in it,"[57] etc. "Scientific method" in the context of adult education designates not a mode of thought and behavior that is taught but an alternative to education in this sense:

> It is [the authors'] belief that an adult-education program should be oriented to meet the felt needs of people and that these felt needs are not generally satisfied by methods designed to pass subject-matter information efficiently from authorities (the textbooks, the reading references, or the instructor) to the student. Felt needs are more likely to be satisfied by methods which involve the use of scientific method—that is, the identification of the problem or the block to needs satisfaction, the gathering of data, the formulation of a hypothesis, and finally, the testing of this hypothesis through an action program.[58]

"Group discussion is the basic method of adult education."[59] This aphorism, repeated so frequently by adult educators,[60] can refer to either of two quite different contexts:

1. *Discussion as a pedagogic device.* Many studies have been made to test whether lectures or discussion (or, sometimes, a combination of the two) is the more effective means of transmitting knowledge and attitudes. A recent survey of this research by Dietrick includes a bibliography of 186 items. Many of these

----

[56] *Ibid.*

[57] Schueler, "The Method of Adult Education."

[58] Sheats et al., *Adult Education,* p. 323. See also Sillars, "An Approach," p. 244; Smith, "Coordinated Community Group Action," p. 114; etc. This is apparently also what a committee of the Adult Education Association meant when it asserted that "adult education . . . should be guided by the truth-seeking disciplines of scientific method" (Point 4 in "Principles," as reported by Pell, "Social Philosophy," p. 125).

[59] Bradford, "Introduction" to "The Dynamics of the Discussion Group," p. 2.

[60] The very same words are also used, for example, by Spence and Cass, *Guide for Program Service,* p. 70.

studies are not wholly comparable, however, since neither "discussion" nor "effective" is uniformly defined. When the amount of information acquired was taken as the criterion of efficacy, most of the studies showed no difference between the two methods; and "where significant differences have been found, they have generally . . . [indicated] the superiority of the lecture method."[61] But adult educators (particularly those who pay lip service to scientific method) have tended to resist this conclusion.[62] The fact that many of the studies were made with college students rather than adults is often used to dismiss the evidence. Let us grant that it is far from conclusive; and for the sake of the argument, let us yield to the bias in favor of discussion. In that case, we must be quite clear what has been accepted. If (a) there is an attempt to transmit a specific content and teach certain facts or attitudes or behavior patterns, and if (b) an expert participates as such in the discussion, group discussion is a valid and often useful pedagogical method. No one would deny this, or even perhaps that discussion may be more important in

[61] David C. Dietrick, "Review of Research," in Hill, *Ways of Mankind Study*, Appendix A at p. A4. The conclusion of Hill's study, similarly, was that "there is no difference in the effectiveness of these methods" (p. 158).

Perhaps the most famous of these studies was directed by Kurt Lewin during World War II. The Red Cross was trying to induce the public to eat more beef hearts, sweetbreads, and kidneys in place of the scarcer muscle meats. Three groups of women from different economic levels were furnished with appropriate recipes and given an illustrated lecture on wartime needs and on the high vitamin and mineral content of variety meats. Three other groups matched in income level were led in discussion by a group leader and a nutrition expert designated as such, who gave them the same facts and recipes; then, at the end of the meeting, these women voted to serve one of these meats during the following week (the "group decision"). According to interviews a week later, a considerably higher percentage of the women in the discussion groups had served these meats. See Lewin, "Group Decision and Social Change" in Sheats et al., *Adult Education*, pp. 463-464; Kempfer, *Adult Education*, p. 416. For a criticism of this experiment, see Dietrick, "Review of Research," in Hill, *Ways of Mankind Study*, pp. A10-16.

[62] For example, Palmer and Verner compared three methods of instruction in Air Force classes—lecture with a five-minute question period, half lecture and half discussion, and only discussion—and found that students attending the lectures learned most. Nevertheless, they concluded that "in most adult education . . . the use of the lecture is less desirable," because, according to another study by someone else in 1925, what one learns in discussion groups is retained longer—a conclusion they themselves did not attempt to test. See Palmer and Verner, "A Comparison."

adult than in standard education. More generally, the efficacy of a teaching method depends mainly on the educational end being sought.

An objective defines the possible processes of education which may be used for its accomplishment. If the presentation of an ordered body of principles is desired, it is necessary to use a lecture, a film, a book, or some other similar approach. If a skill is to be taught, demonstration and practice are required. If a group wishes to examine its existing knowledge to crystallize a set of convictions or principles, it must ordinarily use discussion. To be sure, the objective does not finally determine the means; it merely limits the range of choice.[63]

2. *Discussion as a means of strengthening group feeling.* For group dynamicists, the superiority of group discussion lies not in its effectiveness as a pedagogic device, but in the simple fact that a number of individuals have coalesced into a group. Brought together into a "face-to-face situation," they benefit from the consequent reduction in alienation. Among this kind of advocates of the discussion method, "learning" is good but teaching must be avoided: "It seems to me that anything that can be *taught* to another is relatively inconsequential, and has little or no significant influence on behavior."[64] Subject-matter competence on the part of the discussion leader, if there is to be one, is thus positively forbidden (if such an authoritarian term may be used):

I have often, myself, argued that it is perilous for a man to lead groups in the field in which he *is* expert. As Robert Blakely puts it, "It is harder for a subject-matter expert to keep his special knowledge in check than it is for a layman to acquire the subject-matter orientation and discussion techniques to lead a group well."[65]

[63] Houle and Nelson, *The University*, pp. 148-149.
[64] Carl Rogers, "the University of Chicago's advocate of 'non-directive' counseling," quoted in Powell, *Learning Comes of Age*, pp. 163-164.
[65] *Ibid.*, p. 152. Mr. Powell goes on to say, however, that "a practiced and organized grasp of a recognized field of learning is not, in itself, a handicap to anyone who takes a hand in the learning efforts of others" (pp. 152-153), and he even maintains that "for many areas of adult learning there *must* be content to be learned" (p. 153, his emphasis), and that while "the movement long ago discarded the term 'teacher' in favor of 'leader,'. . . . I am not sure I would go all the way with this notion; it seems to me there is a place for teaching wherever there is a place for learning" (p. 154). Mr. Powell manages thus not only to sit on the fence but to stand firmly on both sides of it as well. He also (p. 164) both agreed and disagreed with Mr. Rogers, cited above.

And when a subject-matter expert is present, he need not—according to the proponents of this view—restrict himself to the area about which he knows something. For example, a man teaching public speaking to members of a trade union discovered that "the fellows who were taking the course were learning speaking so they could throw over the old union leadership." Having discovered their "felt needs," the teacher of public speaking, in Powell's opinion, "should have started a new course on union politics."[66]

Discussion among equally ignorant fellow learners, with no such dangerous expert present, "somehow . . . is more consistent with a democratic philosophy and more conducive to good mental health upon the part of both leader and learners."[67]

The dispute in adult education about group discussion, thus, is not really one over method but rather, like that about whether the individual or society shall benefit from education, a disagreement on content. If content of one sort or another is to be taught, and learned, then no educator would even deny that discussion is one effective means of achieving this end. But to denote mere participation in a group for a therapeutic purpose as "education," and indeed as all of adult education, is "noxious foolishness."[68]

Evaluation

The purpose of evaluation in adult education, it is generally agreed, is "continuous program improvement."[69] It is also an accepted maxim that knowledge of his own progress encourages the student to greater effort. Adult educators agree, finally, that

[66] Powell, " 'Where Did You Go?' " p. 261. Cf. McMahon, "Concentric Ripples."

[67] Bradford, "Toward a Philosophy," p. 93. In a criticism of this view, Dean McGhee wrote as follows: "In the community-centered, action-context, individual-participation, group-decision situation, the teacher is evidently not to be trusted. If he is exposed to a group and is not carefully watched, he will very likely teach someone something. If he is a good teacher, the danger that he will do so is very great" ("Three Dimensions," p. 120). As this example suggests, it is hardly feasible in adult education to argue with sarcasm; for even the most outrageous proposal, proffered ironically, may turn out to be a paraphrase of someone's "philosophy."

[68] Nolte, "The Role of the State University," p. 59. See also Leys, "The Two Rôles."

[69] Kempfer et al., *Program Evaluation*, p. 7.

program evaluation, though of crucial importance, takes place far too infrequently. Beyond these generalizations, the usual confusion reigns.

What is it we want to evaluate? What is "good"? "Unless we know where we are going and what we are trying to accomplish, no design for measurement and evaluation of results can possibly be formulated."[70] Nevertheless, most of the works on adult education that discuss the matter elaborate on *how* to measure educational programs without considering precisely *what* they want to evaluate. This would be legitimate only if programs were established with a clear notion of their specific purpose, but except in credit courses, where evaluation also is less of a problem, the contrary is the typical case. "To educate the community," for example, is much too general an objective for a library to be useful for purposes of measurement.[71]

The questions that the various types of evaluation are designed to answer can be summarized into four basic queries:

A.   Are the consumers satisfied—with the facilities, accessibility, administration, fees, quality of instruction, etc.?

B.   Is the program meeting the "needs" of the community?

C.   Do the participants experience "growth"?

D.   Have the participants acquired new knowledge or skills, or have their attitudes changed?

Each of these will be discussed in turn.

A. CONSUMER SATISFACTION

The usual type of program evaluation is, quite simply, a counting of noses. Most directors of adult education maintain more or less elaborate enrollment records, from which they can tell how many participants they have, how much continuity there is from one season to the next, which are the popular programs, and so on. Additional information is often sought through questionnaires or interviews. At the Rochester Institute of Technology, for example, "it has been the practice . . . to find out what the 'customers' think, on the assumption that nothing is too good to be improved," and students' opinions are solicited on courses,

[70] Sheats et al., *Adult Education*, p. 488.
[71] Houle, *Libraries*, p. 51.

teachers, staff, store, equipment, parking facilities, the catalogue of courses, and registration procedures.[72] Favorable replies to such questions, however, need indicate nothing about educational content. Students' satisfaction with courses may be based on such irrelevant matters as "prices" or the accessibility of the extension center.[73] In general, according to Knowles, students range from "Pollyannas" to "chronic complainers" through a normal distribution curve, like the one that he designed to help directors evaluate this type of evaluation.[74]

Kempfer's "composite superiority ratio," similarly, was based on: size of program, number of population segments served, flexibility of schedule, number of approaches used, number of coordinative practices, number of cooperative practices.[75] The "best" programs, in other words, are those that enroll the highest proportion of the population, that meet at times and places convenient to participants, and that do not conflict with the schedules of other institutions. No reasonable person would challenge the theses that if a program was adjudged "good" by educational standards, generally the more participants it had the "better" it would be, and that such an increase in participation could be furthered, for example, by careful scheduling. But such criteria, while relevant, ought to be subordinate to what Kempfer himself—in a different work—terms "the truest test of the merit of an adult-education program," namely, "the results produced."[76]

Most "evaluation" rests on how many people will "buy" a new program in a certain length of time; and on subjective reports from the participants. But what these "measure" no one knows; *de gustibus non disputandum est*; and an education should have to meet profounder tests than will do for a toothpaste.[77]

---

[72] Stratton and Lipsett, "An Extension Division."
[73] Cf. Thompson, *University Extension*, pp. 86-90.
[74] Knowles, *Informal Adult Education*, pp. 244-245.
[75] Kempfer, "Identifying Educational Needs," p. 33. See above, pp. 20-22.
[76] Kempfer, *Adult Education*, p. 413.
[77] Powell, *Learning Comes of Age*, p. 226. Even if one accepts consumer satisfaction as a legitimate basis for evaluating adult education, the figures are not always unambiguous. For example, junior-college adult enrollments increased in Trinidad, Colorado, by almost two-thirds in a single year, but mainly because the United Mine Workers local there required every member to complete the college's course in first aid and safety for miners (Banta, "Sources of Data," p. 229).

B. ARE COMMUNITY "NEEDS" MET?

Certainly the outstanding example of such an evaluation is the Baltimore Cooperative Survey and Work-Study Conference (1947-1948).[78] This was a joint enterprise of the Baltimore public schools, all other adult-education agencies in that city, and the relevant department of the National Education Association. Eighteen local committees, formed to survey as many areas of adult education,[79] met regularly over a period of seven months and gathered data about local programs and resources. A final committee on coordination and evaluation surveyed the city as a whole and acted as liaison among the other committees. Nineteen parallel committees were set up to survey the surrounding area. All this work culminated in a three-day conference called to discuss the committees' reports. For nearly two years thereafter, an enlarged committe on coordination and evaluation met monthly to plan for further activity and improvement.[80]

It can be assumed that the information accumulated in the Baltimore survey was useful in establishing new courses and eliminating duplications, if only because it resulted in the organization of the Baltimore Association for Adult Education, which provides "some coordinating services for the various participating agencies."[81] More citizens of Baltimore also may have become aware of the adult-education offerings available to them. One might imagine from the enthusiastic appraisal given them, for example by Benne (who participated as a National Education

[78] Van Sant, "A Community Survey." The entire issue of the *Baltimore Bulletin of Education* in which this appears, entitled "Evaluation of Adult Education," is concerned with the survey and conference. For other examples, see Burch, "Evaluating Adult Education"; Jayne and Gibb, "The Mountain-Plains Project"; Sheats et al., *Adult Education*, pp. 488-489. Kempfer discusses this type of evaluation in *Adult Education*, pp. 407 ff., pointing out that the scope of a program is only half of what needs to be measured for a true evaluation.

[79] Library services, recreation, college and university extension, public evening schools, veterans' education, museums, mass media, public and private trade and vocational schools, men's and women's civic and social clubs, PTA's, music groups, materials and instructional techniques, workers' education, industrial arts and crafts, testing and guidance, intercultural education, parent education, religious education (Van Sant, "A Community Survey," p. 163).

[80] Kempfer, *Adult Education*, p. 406.

[81] Letter from Wilmer V. Bell, director of adult education, Baltimore Public Schools, November 25, 1957.

Association expert), that the Baltimore survey and conference had also achieved their stated purpose. He described them as "the marriage of two promising democratic youngsters in the adult education field, . . . the *work-group conference movement* and the *cooperative action research movement*," and thus as "an *historic event in the history of adult education*."[82] We should not be misled by the turgid language into supposing that the survey accomplished what it had been set up to do, the "evaluation of adult education." It was appraised as excellent because of the impressive number of committees created, the many times all these persons met together—in short, because of the process rather than the results. Like the discussion method, the survey is seen less as an effective means toward a worthwhile end than as a good in itself.[83]

C. DO PARTICIPANTS EXPERIENCE "GROWTH"?

According to group-actionists, only the participants themselves, as individuals or preferably as a group, can judge the value of what they are doing.

In every genuine adult education enterprise it happens that the individuals who participate tend to become a *true group*. The principal distinction to be made here, that is, between true groups and mechanical collectivities, pseudo-groups, is this: the former tend always in the direction of fellowship and friendship, whereas the latter tend always to create a semblance of unity through concealed coercions. . . . Only participants will know how true groups come into existence and what dynamic principles they follow.[84]

If "only participants will know," a skeptic might ask, how do

[82] Benne, "The Future of the Work-Survey Conferences," p. 172; his emphasis. See also Sheats et al., *Adult Education*, p. 450.

[83] In 1951, a survey was made of adult education in Springfield, Mass., and its appraisal by the directors constitutes another illustration of this point: "Rigid scientific procedures and statistical analyses of the results, occasionally, fell short of the standards for a pure research project. The limitations of time and the heavy dependence upon cooperating volunteers did not permit the imposition of perfect controls. It is the opinion of the directors, however, that the experience gained and the learning and growth on the part of the persons involved more than compensated for any lack of precision in sampling or analysis" (Kempfer and Deane, *Springfield*, Preface).

[84] Lindeman, "Adults Evaluate Themselves," p. 48. Sometimes the uniquely perceptive evaluation by the group members is supplemented by the appraisals of observers, preferably "participant observers."

they know? It is often admitted that "satisfactory measures of the growth of adult learners have not yet been developed." In general, however, adults' "real satisfaction and that of their teachers comes [sic] when they are aware that the unique personalities are finding ways to express themselves more completely."[85] The path to this awareness is often paved with the most prosaic stones —evaluation questionnaires of various types.

While recognizing that the full evaluation of discussion lies beyond the process of discussion, it is important that a group recognize that they can find intermediate checks on the quality of their discussion by evaluating from time to time their own group process and the difficulties and problems which it presents. It is also true that the latter two objectives of discussion growth of members in insight and skill in managing group participation and the growth of the group as a group may also be well-served by a group's evaluation of its procedures.[86]

One evaluation scale, as an example, ranges from "It was one of the most rewarding experiences I have ever had" to "It was a complete waste of time."[87]

D. RESULTS

The discussion of how to evaluate programs is, thus, largely a dispute over whether there should be any subject-matter content in adult education. If content is irrelevant, then the main question becomes whether the consumers are satisfied, or whether they are experiencing "growth" in a "true group." If, however, education is understood in the usual sense—the transmission of new facts, ideas, and values to persons who lacked them—then evaluation also has a definite meaning. If the goal of a program is to teach the participants conversational French, or to give them a better understanding of American foreign policy, or to change their attitudes toward Negroes, whether

[85] Essert, *Creative Leadership*, p. 275.

[86] Benne, Bradford, and Lippitt, "Stages in the Process of Group Thinking and Discussion," in Sheats et al., *Adult Education*, pp. 334-342 at p. 341. As in a number of the other quotations from this school of adult educators, so also in this passage, the authoritarian dictates of English grammar have been successfully evaded.

[87] See Kropp and Verner, "An Attitude Scale Technique." See also Lippitt, "Group Self-Analysis"; K. M. Miller, "Evaluation."

such a goal has been achieved can be gauged with reasonable accuracy.

Perhaps the main difficulty in measuring the objective results of adult education is that the authority of the evaluator is ambiguous. As we have remarked in several contexts, advocates of "democracy" in education cannot accept forthrightly the dominance of the teacher in any learning situation, and their ambivalence is particularly notable when they discuss evaluation. Thus, according to a committee of the Adult Education Association of which Kempfer was chairman:

> Difficulties often arise when evaluation is made by outsiders. The temptation is great to impose objectives and evaluate the program in terms of them. An outside evaluation can have validity only insofar as it is made in complete harmony with the objectives held by the participants.[88]

The authority of the teacher is further reduced because, we are told, the type of objective tests used in schools cannot be used in adult education:

> To most adults the words "test," "quiz," and "examination" call forth such unpleasant memories that it is often difficult to use them in voluntary adult groups. We have not yet been able to develop satisfactory substitute methods for measuring some kinds of learning.[89]

In most noncredit programs, thus, no attempt is made to measure learning, though sometimes the difficulty has been overcome by calling a spade a shovel: "We find some adult groups filling out 'inventories' or writing 'summaries' or solving 'case problems.'"[90] We doubt whether it is necessary even to disguise a quiz under another name. In a nation where quiz programs are (or were!) used to sell a variety of commercial products, where puzzles are a feature of many newspapers and magazines, we need not take too seriously the dictum that the very word "quiz" turns potential participants away from education.

---

[88] Kempfer et al., *Program Evaluation*, p. 14. Or, in Lindeman's words: "*In adult education, methods of evaluation must exemplify that same sense of freedom which characterizes the learning process itself.* In other words, methods of evaluation should be internal, not imposed from without" ("Adults Evaluate Themselves," p. 46; emphasis in the original).

[89] Knowles, *Informal Adult Education*, p. 53.

[90] *Ibid.*

As examples of both the difficulties and the possibilities in measuring the change in knowledge or attitudes resulting from adult-education programs, several studies can be cited:

Four evening classes were evaluated in terms of "the way in which . . . teachers dealt with the motives of [their] students." While over two-thirds of the students attended the courses for reasons other than content, the teachers apparently ignored these motives. "Although a majority had wanted to learn things about themselves, make new friends or escape their mundane daily life, . . . by the end of the semester they were thinking primarily in terms of the information they had obtained."[91] Similarly, few of the agencies that conduct world-affairs programs "expressed a desire to provide their clients with opportunities for companionship and self-expression," even though they knew that this was at least in part what participants had come for. "Many agencies sought to 'change attitudes,' but the respondents did not indicate that many of the clients wanted their attitudes changed."[92] From the point of view of the participants' expectations, such programs must clearly be evaluated as failures. In an educational rather than "democratic" frame of reference, however, the conclusion might well be precisely the opposite.

About twenty-five years ago, Lorimer compared the occupations and certain leisure-time activities of two Brooklyn samples paired for equivalent juvenile education, one of which had and the other had not taken formal adult courses since leaving school. The differences that this continuing education apparently made in the type of jobs held, recent pay increases, and job satisfaction were significant among grammar school graduates, but less so among high school graduates. For both groups the completion of vocational courses since leaving school was significantly correlated with reading of superior newspapers and magazines and with the use of libraries. Liberal arts courses were also positively correlated with these habits, as well as with interest in the theater and arts.[93] The correlation does not, of course, indicate the direction of the assumed cause–effect relation: we still do not know whether adult courses had subsidiary effects; or whether a larger

[91] Zander, "Student Motives," p. 30.
[92] Sillars, "Education for International Understanding," p. 95.
[93] Lorimer, *The Making of Adult Minds*, pp. 54-59.

proportion of persons who, for example, read better news-papers, also enrolled in courses; or both.

After it was discovered that about 30 per cent of Cincinnati's population knew nothing about "the main purpose of the United Nations," all the city's educational agencies, newspapers, business groups, civic organizations, and church groups cooperated in a concentrated six-month effort to educate the city. Ostensibly the program was intended not to influence opinion but only to present facts, though both aims seem to have influenced some of the campaign's features. In all, 59,588 brochures and throwaways were distributed; 2,800 clubs were "reached" with speakers or written material; club women sent 1,000 letters and 1,350 telegrams; one radio station scheduled spot programs on the United Nations 150 times a week; an archbishop addressed 10,000 members of the Catholic PTA. "Peace Begins with the United Nations—the United Nations Begins with You," the slogan of the campaign, was ubiquitous, printed on trolley cards, on matchbooks, on blotters. The objective was to "reach" every adult among the 1,155,703 residents of Cincinnati and its environs. At the end of this massive effort, the percentage of persons totally unacquainted with the main purpose of the international organization was reduced from 30 to 28.[94] Some adult educators found cause for rejoicing even in this dismal failure (it happened; therefore it was good): "While follow-up studies have found little lasting effect of these efforts in mass understanding of the United Nations, the cooperating educational agencies have learned valuable lessons in discovery and interpretation of new needs that call for educational attention."[95] The fact that these newly discovered needs remained unmet in spite of the agencies' best efforts is apparently irrelevant.

In contrast to these two evaluations of a whole city's adult-education facilities, the following relates to one effort of a single small institution. This school had a parent-education program for members of its mothers' club. Its attempt to measure the effectiveness of the program moved gradually through several of the types of evaluation discussed above. It started with consumer

[94] Star and Hughes, "Report on an Educational Campaign." Houle and Nelson use this Cincinnati Plan to illustrate their contention that broadside campaigns are educationally ineffective (*The University*, pp. 25-26).

[95] Essert, *Creative Leadership*, p. 230.

research: end-of-term questionnaires were given to the participants to find out whether they thought the course had been valuable and the leaders good, and what other problems should be considered in future series. Next it devised an end-of-term "attitude-and-practice test"—a type of self-evaluation. Then one test was given at the beginning and another at the end of the program, in order to measure changes in attitudes as perceived by the individuals themselves. The staff then constructed an anonymous questionnaire for the fathers, in order to find out from a possibly more objective source whether there had been any changes in their wives' behavior toward the children. Results were encouraging, but the staff feared that, as representatives of the sponsoring agency, they were receiving biased answers from the fathers. They then circulated an attitude-and-practice questionnaire among all mothers of the two grades involved in the program, and found significant differences between member and nonmember mothers; but they recognized that the mothers following the more desirable practices might also have been the ones who most frequently joined the clubs. At the time the evaluation was described, they were continuing to experiment with still other methods.[96]

A more complex evaluation was that of an experimental course in social psychology designed especially for adults by the Center for the Study of Liberal Education for Adults. The goals set for the course were: (1) to "sensitize students to the significance of their participating in groups"; (2) to "lead students to understand the base of effective small group action and increase their skill of working in a group"; (3) to "increase their insight into social problems which relate to the interaction of people and groups." Through the use of interviews, a thematic apperception test, and a specially designed problem-solving test, the instructor discovered that the course had produced no change with respect to these three aims. The students, they told him, had enjoyed the course; but one of them, who had "talked enthusiastically to the instructor," when reinterviewed by an outside evaluator said he actually considered the discussion method "a waste of time."[97]

[96] Kempfer et al., *Program Evaluation*, pp. 26-28.
[97] A total of 22 students participated two hours each week for 16 weeks. Miller, *Evaluating Courses*; letter from Roger De Crow, clearinghouse director, Center for the Study of Liberal Education for Adults, May 20, 1958.

Several studies have been made of participants in packaged programs. One of the stated aims of the World Politics Program, for instance, was "the improvement of critical thinking," and one analyst concluded from various before-and-after tests administered to some Los Angeles discussants and a control group that such an improvement had indeed taken place.[98] However, the sample on which the study was based was not only very small but entirely self-selected, and if only for this reason the significance of the results is questionable. Similarly, an earlier study of participants in the Great Books program "demonstrated a positive relationship between the increase in [their] capacity [to think logically] and length of participation in the course," but according to Houle this relation may not be statistically significant, chiefly because the study was limited to the first year's program.[99]

As several of these examples indicate, it is possible to make some evaluation, even if not a wholly satisfactory one, of changes more complex than the mere acquisition of new facts. However, when adult educators try to "measure intangibles such as growth of understanding, insight, 'broadness,' etc.," many "have substituted a kind of intuition as a basis for judging whether a course is effective or not, which means that they have no concrete means of evaluation left at all."[100] "Indeed, most organizations that emphasize . . . indirect services seem to live mostly on faith that their work is producing results."[101] For example, in a survey of 54 communities served by ten general-extension divisions, when some activities proved to have been in existence for too short a time to measure their effects, Thompson concluded with typical optimism that "we may assume some good was performed in each instance."[102] To many adult educators, any attempt to implement the lip service they pay to evaluation is unwelcome, especially if it *is* possible really to measure accurately a program's educational effect. For those who perceive themselves as missionaries, en-

---

[98] Hadlock, "A Study of the Development of Critical Thinking."

[99] Charters, "An Evaluation of the Development of Certain Aspects of the Ability To Think by Participation in an Adult Program," 1948 doctoral dissertation cited in Houle, "The Use of Print," p. 180. In a more recent study, participation in the Great Books program was judged for its effect on changes in knowledge, values, ideologies, etc., but not logical thinking; see Davis et al., *The Great Books Program.*

[100] Miller, *Evaluating Courses,* p. 2.

[101] Knowles, *Informal Adult Education,* p. 241.

[102] Thompson, *University Extension,* p. 228.

gaged in furthering world peace or mitigating human alienation, an assessment of this effort is "a kind of academic impertinence verging on sacrilege."[103]

Summary

Perhaps the most pernicious doctrine in adult education is the notion that "democracy" demands that the educator abdicate his professional authority.

Education is not democratic. It must be directed by those who are already educated, and it is based on the fundamentally antidemocratic notion that some people know better than others what should be done. Student self-government can never be extended to an equal voice in educational policy.[104]

The "right" of participants to dictate educational policy contradicts the effort of adult educators to maintain control over programs they administer. This conflict is half-disguised by a remarkably ambiguous language, which can be illustrated especially in the multiple meanings given the word *need*.

An educator who attempts to manipulate students rather than teach them cannot stop with this initial hypocrisy, for every facet of adult education becomes infected as a consequence of his refusal to accept full professional responsibility. "Democracy" demands that the content of programs be set, at least allegedly, by the "felt needs" of those to be educated. By a "democratic" fetish, the discussion group is designated as *the* method in adult education. Evaluation of programs is principally in terms of consumer satisfaction.

Nothing could be of greater significance to adult education than a method of evaluation of its offerings by which their many deficiencies could be defined, analyzed, and possibly eliminated. Most programs are never appraised, whether in this or in any other sense. The aura of good will that befogs adult education is nowhere more evident than in the implicit axiom that all existent programs are good. Some, of course, are "better," but the criteria by which they are so designated more often reinforce consumer supremacy than help establish relevant educational standards.

[103] C. E. Hendry, "What Price Honesty?" quoted in Miller, "Evaluation," p. 432.

[104] Moore, "The Philosophy of General Education," p. 68.

"Evaluation" of adult education is ordinarily based on one of the following:

1. Questionnaires, interviews, and less directly, enrollment figures, can give an administrator an idea of students' opinions about adult-education services. While students' satisfaction might well be one factor to be considered in judging administrative practices (registration procedure, library hours) or the physical plant (light, janitorial services), teaching methods and the educational content of courses are not within participants' legitimate province.

2. Are community "needs" met? A survey to determine this may, similarly, be used to judge what people say they want and whether this is available to them, but not to set educational policy.

3. Participants' self-evaluations may serve not to set policy but to point up misconceptions about the program's purpose. If a student enrolls, say, in a course in literature and is disappointed in the program because he is no less lonely than before, he might well be advised to join a social club.

4. The increase in knowledge or skill, or the change in attitudes or values, can be measured, and usually is in credit and vocational courses. Noncredit programs, however, generally have no evaluation of this type. Notwithstanding the frequently expressed opinion to the contrary, most adults would probably welcome an objective measure of what they have actually learned, rather than a subjective one of—what they already know—the amount of pleasure they derived from a program.

3

UNIVERSITY ADULT EDUCATION: GENERAL PRINCIPLES

Adult education in universities has grown haphazardly, with little consideration given to underlying principles, with each problem met *ad hoc* when it arose. University adult education, thus, is at least as heterogeneous as American higher education itself; and just as there are few statements that would apply without qualification to Harvard and the University of California, and to small independent liberal arts colleges, and to denominational schools and junior colleges, so also there are few generalizations about university adult education that could not be challenged by citing this or that exception. Since this diversity is combined with a paucity of statistical or other objective data, any analysis of university adult education necessarily reflects, at least in its emphases and overtones, the point of view of the analyst. The reader of this book will not, we think, be troubled by any reticence in our statement of the position we try to defend. Whether or not he agrees with the policy recommendations we offer, we hope at least to be able to convince him that *a* policy is necessary. University adult education "must not be an administrative inadvertance or after-thought."[1]

Ideally, the administrator of university adult education ought to be able to start from a consensus on basic policy. Unfortunately, however, there is little agreement on even the most basic questions. What is "college-level" education? Should the university restrict its extension services to this level, or even to education altogether? Or, most fundamentally, what are the functions of university adult education? Are they the same as those on the main campus, applied to a different population? What is the relevance of the fact that the participants are adults to the kind of program offered, its standards, and so on? Questions of this

---

[1] McGhee, "Higher Education," p. 201.

order of generality, which are dealt with in this chapter, must be answered before we consider the more specific problems of educational and administrative policy.

The Place of the University in Adult Education

University adult education stands with one foot in the university and one in adult education, and many of its administrative problems exemplify the difficulty of maintaining a balance between these two quite different worlds. To understand university adult education, then, we must begin by studying the influences impinging on it from the two larger institutions of which it forms a part.

As was indicated in the last chapter, the number of agencies, institutions, and associations active in adult education is very great indeed. The point is important enough to be emphasized by listing here some of the typical organizations or programs that often have this as one of their major interests.[2] The categories are not, of course, mutually exclusive; and in particular the university frequently overlaps with some of the other agencies.

Educational institutions
    public schools
    colleges and universities
    Cooperative Extension Service
    business, technical, and special-interest schools
    private correspondence schools
    private adult schools
    libraries
    museums
Government agencies and departments
    U.S. Department of Agriculture
    U.S. Department of State
    U.S. Office of Education
    miscellaneous federal agencies that inform the public on their specific fields
    state departments of education
    health departments and institutions
    armed-forces programs
    prison education

[2] With a few changes and additions, this list is from Olds, *Financing Adult Education*, p. 88.

in-service training of government employees
Private health, welfare, and recreation agencies
  health-education agencies
  family counseling and guidance agencies
  community-welfare organizations
  recreation and youth (Y's, settlement houses, etc.)
  civic-improvement groups
  adult-education councils and associations
Business and industry
  trade associations and business organizations
  education of the public about specific commodities and business
    goals
  in-service training of employees
  labor unions
  professional organizations
  farm groups
Miscellaneous organizations
  women's groups
  service clubs
  fraternal organizations
  parent–teacher associations
  alumni groups
  veterans and patriotic organizations
  political associations
  churches and religious groups
Mass media
  newspapers and magazines
  radio and television
  motion pictures and theater

How many persons take part in all these programs? Estimates
are difficult to make, for several reasons: (1) Differences are
great among programs—in level, in duration, in purpose, in cost,
in the work required of registrants; and to add the number of
persons attending a single talk on cancer detection, for example,
to that occasionally participating in PTA projects, to that receiving some instruction on their job, to that taking a correspondence
course for credit over a period of months or years, does not result in a very meaningful sum. (2) Radio and television audiences, and even newspaper and magazine readers, are sometimes
defined as participants in adult education; and estimates of their
numbers, even after agreement is reached on which programs are

deemed educational, can be no more than loose approximations. (3) Some institutions total *students* enrolled and others *enrollments* in courses (without, that is, taking into account the fact that some students take more than one course); and when it is possible to compare registration figures by both procedures, as of the member institutions of the National University Extension Association according to its annual *Proceedings*, the latter figure is frequently more than double the former.

Estimates of the numbers in adult-education programs in the country, therefore, have a wide range. The most restrictive count was by the Census Bureau, which included persons (rather than enrollments) who had met with a group at least three times. Those taking private courses or correspondence courses or on-the-job training were not counted. By this definition, there are some 9.2 million participants in adult education.[3] According to more inclusive estimates, the figure is between 30 million[4] and 50 million.[5] Of a total somewhere in this range, perhaps two or three per cent,[6] or four[7] at the most, take part in university programs. Whatever figures are accepted, it is clear that university adult education constitutes no more than a small fraction of the total effort to educate adults.

Adult education in universities, then, can hardly encompass its whole range and operate effectively. When its special skills are relevant, the university has something that only it can offer; but when they are not, the service to the community might better be given by other agencies, which have both different functions and sometimes easier access to funds. That there should be a rational division of labor in adult education is a dictum most general-extension administrators would support in principle. While all of the general-extension divisions surveyed by Morton, for instance, believed that their programs should be of "significance to 'the public interest,'" there was also "substantial agree-

[3] Wann and Woodward, *Participation*, p. 4.
[4] U.S. Office of Education, *Fact Book*, p. 4.
[5] Knowles, "Adult Education," p. 76.
[6] Calculated from the two preceding sources.
[7] Sheats, "Establishing Priorities," p. 38. However, according to a mail questionnaire with returns from about half the membership of the Adult Education Association, between 14.7 (1956) and 18.7 (1958) per cent of the members worked in university adult education. See Nicholls and Brunner, "Composition of AEA," p. 218.

ment that these services should be of 'college grade.' "[8]
Differences are likely to arise not over the principle but over its
interpretation.

In screening adult-education programs, the university ought to
use a fine mesh. If it exercises a particular, perhaps even an exaggerated, care in maintaining high standards, the consequent
level of its offerings for adults will also facilitate another administrative goal, the closer integration of adult with regular university education.

The central functions of the university have been established
by a long tradition and maintained by a relatively rigid institutional structure. These functions are, in brief, to educate a seg-
ment of the nation's youth in programs leading to one or another
academic degree, and to furnish to the faculty and students the
facilities necessary for scholarly research. It is true that the
charters of many public universities, and even of some private
ones, include a vaguely worded clause enjoining the institution to
render service to the people, and that the public obligation of
land-grant institutions are specified in various acts of Congress.[9]
While this may mean that in some senses public universities have
a greater responsibility to the people than private ones, it does
not mean that they have a greater duty to respond to any demand
from the community. Even the first portion of the statement
might be challenged: private universities also receive public support. The foundations and individuals that contribute to them,
as well as the institutions themselves, enjoy tax exemptions representing in effect substantial donations out of the public treasury;
and many research projects at private universities are financed
through grants from government agencies. In any case, it is poor
policy to control a public institution in such a way as to induce
it to waste its resources on tasks that, however important, do not
lie within its proper function. On the contrary, the "peculiar
duty" that publicly financed universities owe the people is to
avoid accepting too broad a definition of their role. "Always the
obligation must be understood within a complex of limitations as

[8] Morton, *University Extension,* p. 30. This study is based on mail questionnaires returned by 57 of the 76 members of NUEA in 1951-1952, and
on visits to 35 of them.

[9] For a comparison of public and private institutions, see Houle, *Major
Trends,* pp. 11-19.

to provision of facilities, funds, staff-time, scope of curriculum and relative urgency of needs, and in the light of what the university can do well."[10]

The Meaning of "Extension"

None of the important institutions of higher learning in the United States, one can safely say, presently restricts itself to activities precisely defined by the two functions of (1) daytime education toward a degree and (2) research. The supplementary educational effort may now include credit or noncredit courses, in the evening or off campus; lecture series or casual lectures, by faculty or visiting personages, or conferences of various types, on campus or off; mass media and publications; information services; contract research and other aids to business, agriculture, and government; and so on.

The total extension function of the university, thus, is something considerably larger and more complex than what laymen often assume it to be, and this complexity is increased by the facts that the allocation of administrative responsibility varies greatly from one campus to another, and that no standard usage has developed for distinguishing the whole miscellany of extension activities from various portions of it. In this work, we shall use three arbitrary terms to denote successively smaller areas of meaning.

1. The whole of the variegated increment to the university's two basic tasks of education in day sessions and scholarly research (except for Cooperative Extension), we define as its *total extension function*. Cooperative Extension, or the activities of the Agricultural Extension Service, constitutes a special category, which differs so greatly in—among other respects—its legal background, financing, and type and level of education, that we have omitted it altogether from the main text. It is discussed separately in Appendix 1.

2. That portion of the total extension function that is both education and at a college level we term *university adult education*. As will be detailed in ensuing chapters, the university has often taken on functions inappropriate to an educational institution, and within the educational function has often sunk below

[10] Nolte, "The Role of the State University," p. 61.

the standard proper to an institution of higher learning. The term "university adult education," thus, separates out the major portion of what we deem to be legitimate within the total extension function.[11]

3. By *general-extension division*, finally, we mean the formal unit of the university assigned to administer its adult education, or rather a portion of it. Roughly synonymous terms are "division of continuing education," "division of university extension," "evening college," "university college," "community college," and (in England) "extramural department," which are some of the official designations used by various institutions.[12] The fact that a university does not have a separate general-extension division does not mean, of course, that it does no extension work as we use the term. And when an extension division exists, it is never in charge of the total extension function, and sometimes of no more than half of it. Typically it administers the extension of liberal arts courses but often not those of professional schools nor, for instance, the use of the library by the general public, information services, publications, or contract research.

A mere list of universities with general-extension divisions,

[11] Whether university adult education constitutes *everything* in the total extension function that is legitimate depends not only on one's criteria of "legitimate" but also on the definition of the other two terms. For example, we have taken university presses to be part of the extension function, and we believe that they serve a valuable function for the scholarly world; but it would be stretching a point to call their services adult education. A still more difficult case is presented by contract research. Is this one of the two core functions of the university or an extension of "standard" research? It makes some sense to designate it as part of extension, for research for government and business has raised some of the same questions that we will examine in detail with respect to adult education—the danger of perverting the university's resources to alien ends, some of them legitimate in themselves, some parallel to the "tawdry commercialism" of some general-extension programs. In this work, however, we will attempt only to distinguish clearly between the two extremes, university adult education and either nonuniversity education or university noneducation, leaving some of the middle ground for each reader to define as he will.

[12] "For the one hundred members of the Association of University Evening Colleges there are thirty-three different names used. The most frequent one is Evening Division. This is followed by Evening College and this by University College. Some are named for men, such as McCoy College at Johns Hopkins and Millard Fillmore College at the University of Buffalo. Others are named for cities, such as Dallas College of Southern Methodist and Cleveland College at Western Reserve. On the whole, nomenclature is a potpourri, with such names as Intown College, Downtown College, College

thus, would tell us little about how much adult education, or what kind, each university offers; and in any case no complete list is available. Most studies of university adult education are limited either to descriptions of so-called representative programs, "with very little statistical information to show how representative these institutions are and how they compare with other institutions and programs,"[13] or to an examination of the members of one of the two professional associations. These are the National University Extension Association (or NUEA), which in 1959 had 81 members, most of them state universities; and the Association of University Evening Colleges (or AUEC), which in 1959 had 134 members, predominantly private urban institutions but including 34 NUEA members.[14] According to Crimi's study of the 427 accredited private liberal arts colleges in the United States in 1953, slightly more than half (233) engaged in at least some adult education.[15] A survey of all institutions of higher education conducted in 1958 by the United States Office of Education, finally, lists 593 that offered programs other than resident degree-credit work.[16] Combining the data from these several surveys gives a total of 752[17] institutions of higher education (or 748 if the four Canadian members of AUEC are omitted) known to offer programs for adults. This is more than half of all such in-

---

of Adult Education, School of General Studies, Diploma School, Evening College and Graduate Division, Community College, College of Special and Continuation Studies, Division of General Education, and Extension Division. One university apparently doesn't propose to venture far into the dark, for it has a Twilight School" (Dyer, *Ivory Towers*, p. 30).

[13] Harrison, "Analyzing Adult Education," p. 1.

[14] The members of the two associations are listed in Appendix 2, below. For details of programs offered and registration figures, see their annual proceedings. Since the members of the two associations include most of the largest universities, they represent a higher proportion of the total national enrollment than of institutions. Thus, the NUEA institutions covered in Morton's survey included "about 22 percent of the college-grade enrollment throughout the country in November 1953" (Olds, "How Adult Education," p. 232), but only slightly over 4 per cent of all institutions of higher education in the United States. Cf. Harrison, "Analyzing Adult Education," pp. 5-6.

[15] Crimi, *Adult Education*, p. 3. These 233 included 24 AUEC members.

[16] U.S. Office of Education, *Resident, Extension, and Other Enrollments*.

[17] This total includes all members of NUEA and of AUEC (counting dual members only once), the 209 additional liberal arts colleges surveyed by Crimi, and any other institutions of higher learning offering nondegree-credit work, whether the Office of Education classifies this as "resident" or

stitutions in the country. This proportion can reasonably be taken as a minimum, for several reasons: (1) some universities with programs for adults are not members of either NUEA or AUEC; (2) some liberal arts colleges were not included in Crimi's survey, a few of those to which he sent his questionnaire did not reply, and the number with adult education may well have increased in the interim; (3) the United States Office of Education survey did not distinguish between day and evening degree-credit work, so that, for example, 35 AUEC members, 2 NUEA members, and 140 of Crimi's respondents are shown to offer only resident degree-credit work; and (4) many other institutions sponsor activities such as concerts, lectures, etc., that they do not classify as adult education, while we do.

Though the statistics available constitute no more than rough approximations, they certainly warrant the conclusion that programs for adults are a significant and growing element of American higher education. The extension has taken place in several senses.

The first and most obvious one is *in time and place.* In 1906, when President Charles Van Hise of the University of Wisconsin organized its pioneering extension division, he intended to make "the boundaries of the University campus coterminous with the boundaries of the state." The means of reaching the social classes unable to attend the regular sessions have varied according to the circumstances. Courses for adults are now conducted (1) on the

---

"extension." These various surveys are not wholly comparable, partly because of their different dates, but especially because of the variation in definitions of categories.

In 1951 a mail questionnaire was sent to all institutions of higher education in the United States by Leonard and Lowry. It showed 654 institutions, including junior colleges, with some adult education; but since only 56 per cent of the colleges returned the questionnaire, this figure cannot be considered very useful. See Leonard and Lowry, "Continuation Education," p. 235 and Appendix C, p. 388.

Note that junior colleges are not included, either in the total of 752 or in this work as a whole. From 1936 to 1952, while the number of freshmen and sophomores in junior colleges doubled, adult enrollments increased from 20,750 to 321,330, or by approximately 16 times. Of the 660 junior colleges in the United States and territories in 1957-1958, about half had adult-education programs, which in 126 had larger enrollments than the day sessions. See McLain, "The Present Status," p. 81; Gleazer, *Junior College Directory, 1959,* pp. 3, 6-28.

main campus, usually in the evening[18]; (2) in extension centers (also called evening or university colleges, or resident centers)[19]; (3) in schools, libraries, and other widely dispersed public buildings, usually in the evening; and (4) by correspondence, radio, or television.

An extension in time and place does not imply in itself any change in curriculum or standards. An adaptation of courses or methods to the special demands of particular sectors of the population, but still without lowering the standards of higher education, can be termed a *functional* extension.

When the latter change *is* made, in order to carry "knowledge to the masses rather than [extend] the scope of the university along traditional lines,"[20] this can only be termed a *substandard* extension.

In some of the activities in which universities are now engaged, finally, the adaptation to new purposes has been so substantial that the term "extension" seems inappropriate. When only lip service is paid to education or research, so that these purposes are in effect supplanted by others—social welfare, public relations, commercial profit, for example—we can more aptly speak of a *conversion* of the university's function.

Some state universities, believing that they are morally bound to serve all the people of the state, have followed the "Wisconsin pattern" in sacrificing educational standards to this end. Private universities, on the other hand, have tended more toward what has been designated the "University of Chicago pattern" of university adult education: "emphasis seems to be upon academic and cultural subjects and the shaping of adult curricula at the

[18] While summer schools began in the United States as a function of the general-extension division and are still administered by it in some institutions, in most places they are now part of the regular campus program (see Morton, *University Extension*, p. 40) and will therefore not be discussed in this book.

[19] See, for example, the statement of policy and practices at Pennsylvania State University (then College) in establishing extension centers throughout the state, in Pugh, *The Role of Extension Centers.*

[20] Van Hise, quoted in Woods and Hammarberg, "University Extension," p. 131. "Van Hise recognized no sharp distinctions between elementary, secondary, and higher education, or between formal and informal education" (Zehmer, "The Off-Campus and Evening College," p. 130). See also Rosentreter, *The Boundaries of the Campus*; Andersen, "A Study of Discussion," pp. 464-470.

highest university level."[21] These alternative terms, however, are not wholly accurate even of the two institutions chosen as the contrasting types, and we think our designations are preferable. The important thing is to differentiate, in one way or another, university adult education from extension activities that are either nonuniversity or noneducation.

What is "College Level"?

Every discussion of this important question seems to reach the same conclusion: "a set of specific criteria . . . for determining the kinds of services appropriate for inclusion in extension programs . . . [has] yet to be defined."[22] There are several, not necessarily mutually exclusive, ways by which the standards appropriate to an institution of higher learning can be indicated approximately.

1.   What is meant by the phrase "college level" can be spelled out at greater length. University adult education, thus, "should concentrate on the qualitative and relatively complex, on programs and courses that emphasize ideas and provide intellectual stimulation,"[23] those "requiring familiarity with broad fields of knowledge and the exercise of mature judgment in their organization and interpretation."[24] These paraphrases of "college level" are useful to some degree; but since they also have to be interpreted, there must still be an administrative policy to implement the intent of the expanded definition.

2.   By rigorous admission requirements and/or by stipulating a general examination as a prerequisite to graduation, the university as a whole can maintain at least a partial control over standards. When it exists, this is usually confined to credit courses.

3.   Entrance requirements may be set for particular programs. Certain credit courses, thus, typically are restricted to students with a given number of completed credits, and sometimes certain other courses are prerequisites. Similarly, many conferences and

[21] Woods and Hammarberg, "University Extension," p. 132.
[22] Morton, *University Extension*, p. 32. See also Hunsaker, "What Are the Responsibilities?"
[23] Chamberlain, "Should Our Colleges and Universities?"
[24] Morton, *University Extension*, p. 32. For the best statement, in our view, concerning the meaning of this term, see Gordon, "The Meaning of University Level."

other noncredit programs are so specialized or at so high a level that they appeal only to those with an appropriate background.

4. The various academic departments on the home campus can be made responsible for curricula, texts and other reading material, teaching personnel, and academic standards generally.

Most university extension directors [surveyed by Morton] believed that "college level" courses are those (1) "equivalent to resident courses offered for credit," (2) "with standards of information and attainment and inclusion of subject material fully equal to resident courses and would be so recognized by 'usual catalogue descriptions of universities,' " or (3) "which colleges and universities usually provide and which would be recognized by university faculties as being of college grade."[25]

The control by the faculty that these recommendations imply has the obvious advantage of vesting the discretionary power in the carriers of the academic tradition, who have themselves undergone the discipline of attaining advanced degrees. To point out that standards on the home campus are not very high, while often true enough, is not too relevant; it would be utopian in most institutions to expect the quality of extension programs to be higher than that in the university as a whole. Some degree of faculty control is usual, and is especially appropriate, over credit courses. For it to be effective, however, it has to be part of an administrative arrangement by which faculty members become fully involved in the general-extension division's welfare. And their intrinsic competence to determine the content of the much more heterogeneous noncredit program is not so obvious.

5. The dean of extension can be given full control. This system, which has the advantage of focusing responsibility on the one person most directly associated with the program, is that most used with noncredit programs. "That responsibility for non-credit courses rests solidly in the hands of evening college deans is apparent from the fact that of the 82 schools offering such work, only seven place the responsibility elsewhere."[26] Similarly, in 33 out of 39 general-extension divisions surveyed by Dugan, the deans exercised "complete administrative control over non-credit

[25] Morton, *University Extension*, p. 32.
[26] Neuffer, *Administrative Policies*, p. 21. This study is based on replies to a mail questionnaire from 84 AUEC members in 1953.

classes."[27] General-extension administrators, however, cannot be expected to have subject-matter competence in all areas of their programs; and many of them are under heavy financial pressure to increase enrollments. If some deans have used their discretionary power to improve on the curriculum of the day campus,[28] others have perpetrated courses in driver-training, conversation, and so on.

6. The extension dean and the appropriate academic department can be given joint responsibility. Such a system is apparently seldom used, though when either the dean or the department has sole control, this is usually exercised after consultation with the other.

7. One way of setting standards for noncredit programs, finally, is to maintain that all courses, credit or noncredit, should be of equal quality and that the same control should apply to both. If "universities will husband their resources for education that comes within the meaning of the term 'higher,' . . . . there is no good reason why anything that a university is willing to offer at all should not carry credit if students wish it."[29]

In sum, we must distinguish both between worthless and worthwhile activities and between the broad genus constituting the second group and, within it, that smaller species appropriate to a university. To do this, we must ask several questions:

1. Is it education or research?
2. Is it at college level?[30]

[27] Dugan, "An Extension Class Program," p. 81. This study is based on 44 replies to a questionnaire sent to 71 of the 76 NUEA members in 1951, and on visits to five or six of them.

[28] See, for example, the communication from Dean McGhee cited below, p. 137.

[29] Beals and Brody, *The Literature*, p. 338. In a similar vein, Dean Nolte has suggested that "perhaps our greatest work lies in the patient offering of the best opportunities for adult learning, even the good old-fashioned laborious kind, the kind of learning that demands unremitting attention, close analysis, hard work, the kind that is handled by a subject-matter expert rather than a clever emotion-broker" ("The Role of the State University," p. 69).

[30] According to some adult educators, the university ought also to undertake education below college level when it is necessary to get a new type of program under way; once it is successful, it should be turned over to another agency to administer (Houle and Nelson, *The University*, pp. 56-57, 100-101). We do not think it likely that a program, particularly a successful one, once established in the university's bureaucratic structure, would ordinarily be relinquished easily; cf. Kidd, *Adult Education*, pp. 71-72. The uni-

3. If so, would the program duplicate activities that either are already in existence or could be undertaken by other institutions?

4. Within the class of nonduplicating college-level programs, is this one more significant than alternative ways of using the money, personnel, and facilities it will require?

The principal difficulty in defining "college level" is not in saying *what* it is—there is really no great mystery here—but in designating *who* shall decide in doubtful cases. So long as the responsibility is left vague, it helps little to specify criteria. As we have seen in the preceding paragraphs, different universities have established a number of administrative structures by which the responsibility for quality has been specified. Which arrangement is most likely to continue from the nineteenth century the tradition of democratizing educational opportunities without vulgarizing this mission? In abstract terms, that which combines real control over academic standards with an incentive to use it in order to establish and maintain a high level. What particular division of responsibility will lead to this end in any particular case would depend in part on local circumstances, but we believe that an arrangement that encourages the executive, administrative, and teaching personnel to cooperate is usually better than full control by any one of these.[31]

Since the matter is of considerable importance, the reader may find it useful to compare this set of guides to programing in university adult education with one other that has been drawn up. According to Kidd, five criteria have won general acceptance among Canadian universities, several of which believe that "every course offered should be subjected to this kind of enquiry by some committee once every year."[32]

1. Will the program meet the demonstrated demand of a sizable number of people? (Our comment is that this seems to smack too much of customer sovereignty, by which "felt needs" take precedence over educational policy.[33] Even if an administra-

---

versity's proper role in education below the level of the college is to teach the teachers (in the broadest sense of this word), and if this were well done, not merely public schools but an array of other institutions could benefit from its instruction and guidance.

[31] This question is discussed at length in Chapter 6, below.

[32] Kidd, *Adult Education*, p. 57.

[33] See above, pp. 25 ff.

tor is limited by his budget, as he almost always is, should his creativity be restricted to programs for which there is not a probable, but an already "demonstrated" demand?)

2. Will it contribute to the "economic, social or cultural well-being of the people?" (Our comment is that if the program is educational in a true sense, the answer to this question is Yes in all instances; and if the program is not educational, then the university has no business in it, whether or not other benefits might ensue.)

3. Do participants care enough to "support it with intellectual effort as well as with fees?"

4. "Is the subject matter of the course on a level that is suitable for the university?" (These two questions, we feel, might be improved by specifying how, and by whom, the answers would be given.)

5. "Is any other agency in a position to provide the service at least as well as is the university?" (This is one of the best ways, though not sufficient in itself, of specifying "college level.")

The Teaching of Adults

One excuse frequently offered for the low level of university adult education is that the participants constitute, in one sense or another, so special a group that ordinary standards do not apply. It is true that students in extension differ in some respects from their regular-session counterparts, but there are no intrinsic reasons excusing systematically lower standards.

First of all, by definition, participants in adult education are considerably older on the average than those in the regular day session. The physiological relevance of this age difference, however, can easily be exaggerated. While it is true that the ability to learn—particularly if "learning" is defined as memorizing—reaches a peak before thirty, deterioration thereafter is very gradual, so that "at least well beyond the age of fifty there is ample ability to learn far exceeding the limits attempted by most individuals."[34] Though not for physiological reasons, adult students do

[34] Buswell, "Conditions for Effective Adult Learning," p. 16. See also Thorndike et al., *Adult Learning,* the classic work on this subject; Brunner et al., *Overview,* Chap. 2, and Siegle, "The Adult Learner," two summaries of more recent research findings; McGeoch, *Psychology of Human Learning.*

have certain special handicaps. If they have been out of school for a long period, they may well have lost the habits of study established there. Adults are less malleable than adolescents; they tend to be more set in their ways, less inclined to assimilate new theories and abstractions.[35] While such an "attitude is often a serious limitation, it is also their great strength, for it disciplines any instructor who would move their minds with a jejune preoccupation with a fact or a principle. They insist, to the perpetual vexation of teachers and the eternal enrichment of subjects, upon wedding their own knowledge of things to the generalizations of learning."[36] Among the adults who are likely to take courses, moreover, such a resistance to instructors' generalizations is likely to be based on at least as sound a general factual background as the average day undergraduate has mastered. Groups of day and evening students matched for sex, high-school scholastic record, and the number of college credits completed, were given three-hour tests in history and social studies, fine arts, and science and mathematics; and the evening students did as well as the day students in one case, and better in another.[37]

The one really significant deficiency of adult students derives not from their age but from the related fact that education is for them a secondary part-time activity, undertaken usually after a day's work. In that case, they may well be less able to concentrate on a lecture or discussion than when they are fresh,[38] and they generally have less time to study at home. Their education is usually spread over many years, often with long gaps and little continuity from one course to the next.[39]

[35] Sorenson, *Adult Abilities*, pp. 83-85.

[36] Demarest, "Faculty Organization," p. 16.

[37] "Soft Pedagogy Study," Center for the Study of Liberal Education for Adults, *Eighth Interim Report*, Appendix D. While these findings are interesting in themselves, they have only a peripheral relation to the study's purpose, which was to disprove the charge that academic standards are lower in evening classes. The fact that adult students have as good an over-all cultural background as adolescent undergraduates suggests that standards in extension *need not* be lower; but unless we assume that no learning takes place except in the classroom, it tells us nothing about whether standards *are* lower.

[38] See, for example, Morton, *University Extension*, p. 72; Dyer, *Ivory Towers*, pp. 11-12.

[39] Thompson found that two-thirds of general-extension students had been unable to complete college without interruption, requiring from five years

The point is often made that such handicaps are offset by the generally high level of motivation of extension students. They demonstrate by their very presence in the program that they are willing to work hard to learn what they deem to be useful or necessary. That they are highly motivated is patent, but motivated in what sense? According to the studies summarized in Table 1, two-thirds to four-fifths attend classes, whether for credit or not, mainly in order to improve their occupational efficiency.[40]

Table 1. Proportion of Extension Students Taking Classes
in Order to Improve Their Occupational Efficiency

Date	Sample	Percentage Vocationally Motivated
1956	University College, Syracuse University[1]	75
1953	8 universities in the Chicago area[2]	78
1951-1952	57 NUEA member institutions[3]	more than 80
1951	University of California at Los Angeles[4]	66
1948	Rochester Institute of Technology[5]	73
1939	10 NUEA member institutions[6]	63
1937	6 universities[7]	about 75

[1] Knox, "Adult College Students."
[2] Carey, *Why Students Drop Out*, p. 25.
[3] Morton, *University Extension*, p. 93.
[4] Lawrence K. McLaughlin, "Student Population in University of California Extension Classes," excerpted in Sheats et al., *Adult Education*, pp. 182-183.
[5] Stratton and Lipsett, "An Extension Division," pp. 240-241.
[6] Thompson, *University Extension*, pp. 94 and 308.
[7] Sorenson, *Adult Abilities*, p. 25.

(22.7 per cent) to over ten years (27.5 per cent) to do so (*University Extension*, p. 304). This book is based on an intensive survey of ten representative NUEA members.

[40] See also Lorimer, *The Making of Adult Minds*, pp. 51-54, for a discussion of adult students in Brooklyn, including but not limited to university-extension students; 66 per cent of the men and 50 per cent of the women had vocational aims.

Certainly a much smaller proportion of the students in regular daytime classes are so directly focused on future professional needs. The reasons for taking extension classes are often compelling, if not coercive. Not only do degrees lead to better jobs, but in a number of professions the accumulation of college credits (not necessarily degree-credits) is required even in order to maintain one's present status.[41] According to one survey, many of those in credit classes had enrolled because their employers (who occasionally also paid the fees) urged them to do so or even set studying as a prerequisite to promotion.[42] Extension students, then, are very often a captive audience in almost the same sense that school children are; and the frequent statements to the contrary[43] hardly apply to credit courses and are not wholly valid concerning noncredit programs. Many extension students, on the contrary, are in a hurry to acquire credits, or at least to master a technical field; and very often the instructor will need to make a particular effort to explain why the seemingly extraneous liberal arts courses required for a degree are also useful to them.[44]

[41] This is particularly true of teaching. "In certain states the credit-hunting motive is especially prevalent among teachers as a direct result of the law which requires them to earn certain credits in order to maintain their teacher's certificate" (Sorenson, *Adult Abilities*, p. 27).

[42] The survey was made in 1949 at the University of Maryland; see Deane, "Who Seeks Adult Education." Powell estimates the number of students attending McCoy Evening College under "employers' incentive plans" at over 10 per cent (*Learning Comes of Age*, p. 48). For the students at the ten institutions he surveyed, Thompson reports this figure at 16.4 per cent— 28.9 per cent for noncredit, 11.4 per cent for credit work (*University Extension*, Table A 19, p. 305).

[43] See, as three examples, President's Commission on Higher Education, *Higher Education for American Democracy*, I, 98, excerpted in Sheats et al., *Adult Education*, p. 324; Smith, "Improvement of Instruction," p. 12; and Lindeman, "Adults Evaluate Themselves," p. 45, referring to *all* of adult education. But see H. L. Miller, "Comments," for a contrary view.

[44] Indeed, the pressure to rise, and specifically to rise by mean of an education suitable to a more advanced position, is so strong that it has frequently brought about a strange inversion of this cause-effect relation. If occupations low on the status scale can be restricted to persons with a college degree, even though this is no more relevant now than it ever was, such an upgrading may raise the prestige associated with the job. Everyone interested in the matter has heard of fantastic instances—the salesgirl in a department store, even the usher in the most ostentatious movie palace, who must have an A.B.; but to our knowledge there has been no systematic general study of this practice. A related trend is the establishment of special schools in, among other fields,

It is true that some participants in noncredit programs are not captive, but it does not follow from this fact that academic standards ought to be lowered, not even if the administrator's main desideratum is to maintain a large enrollment. Take a noncredit class, say, in American history. Some joined it out of what we have termed an "interest" in the subject—that is, either partly or wholly for social or other noneducational reasons. Others joined it out of a "concern" with American history; they are serious in their intent to learn something of this field. So long as both types of motivation are called "felt needs," one cannot distinguish between them; but now that a distinction has been made, what follows from it? To some degree, a choice must be made between the "interested" and the "concerned": the same course will not necessarily appeal to both. If some of the "interested" drop out, this may be all to the good; they may not have belonged in a college program altogether. Others, if they have the ability, may be stimulated by a good course. Though they joined it for reasons irrelevant to the function of the university, they stay in it in order to get an education. A person "concerned" with the subject, on the other hand, will drop out of a program if it is watered down; having come for bread, he will not be satisfied with pap. The irregular attendance, the high drop-out rate in some noncredit programs, thus, are not—what they are too often taken to be—compelling arguments to reduce the academic level. It may be that some participants had a "felt need" for high standards and therefore quit a program conceived in the "philosophy" that no adult can become seriously involved with truly intellectual questions.

Summary

University adult education constitutes no more than about 4 per cent of the whole adult-education movement. This fact reinforces what would be true in any case: the proper role of the university in adult education, no less than in any of its other

education, journalism, library practice, business administration, public health. On principle, we are inclined to be skeptical of the alleged value of such schools, although the technical skills they stress are often useful and a course or two might well be included in a liberal arts program for potential teachers, journalists, and so on. This is a difficult and polemical area, however, that we will stay out of.

activities, is to educate by standards appropriate to an institution of higher learning.

The prerequisite to intelligent administrative policy is a precise definition of the organization's purpose. The purpose of a university's adult-education program, we believe, should be to conduct college-level education. Of the four types of extension that we have defined, that in time and place generally and correctly forms the basic fare. Given a population of potential participants much more heterogeneous than college students, however, the administrator of university adult education ordinarily seeks a greater variety of content and method than on the day campus —what we have termed functional extension. While this is usually a smaller element than the first type of extension, it is no less important for that reason. What we have termed substandard extension and conversion, we deem to be illegitimate—not because high-school education, recreation, and social welfare, for example, are reprehensible in themselves, but because the university's reservoir of scarce skills and facilities should be used exclusively for the highly important tasks that only the university can perform.

Many adult-education programs lack a traditional guide to either content or method, and thus offer the university administrator the opportunity either to experiment truly creatively, or to sacrifice educational quality to commercialism, public relations, or social welfare. If he is to distinguish between novelties that are appropriate to an institution of higher learning and those that break completely with the scholarly tradition, the administrator must be very precisely aware of what he means by "college level." Ideally, noncredit courses in particular ought to have as their primary function the education of adults seeking learning for its own sake, helping them find new meaning in life after they have been jolted out of their routine sufficiently to go back to school. If this ideal has sometimes been approached, in many programs the content has been set without any regard for this or any other educational goal, simply in response to the "demonstrated needs" of the participants.

Adult students are different in several important respects from their counterparts on day campuses. Their participation is ordinarily a part-time venture, secondary to other activities. They are more mature, and thus more critical and less flexible. About three-quarters attend general-extension courses in order to improve their earning capacity, and they are thus hardly less a captive audience than regular daytime undergraduates. Those who stray into university programs with no understanding of their purpose ought to be seduced, if they have the ability, into learning something at college level, but they should not be permitted to pervert the program.

4

EDUCATIONAL POLICY

The first two types in our proposed classification, extension in time and place and functional extension, might appear to be paraphrases of the more usual designations, credit and noncredit programs. While there would be some truth in this supposition, it is better to restrict "credit" and "noncredit"—like "general-extension division"—to formal descriptions of actual programs, and substitute other terms in an abstract analysis of university adult education. Moreover, practice varies so much that the meaning of "credit," even in this limited sense, is somewhat ambiguous.

At one time courses accepted toward a higher degree were "credit," and all others were not. Today, this dichotomy has spread out into a continuum, with a variety of intermediate types between the extremes. Often no more than a stipulated proportion of the semester-hours required for a degree may be taken in extension, and sometimes extension credits add up only to an Associate degree or a certificate rather than an A.B.[1] Some credit courses can also be taken without credit, though often the fee and requirements are then lower. And sometimes no credit is offered for the most advanced programs, such as a review of recent developments in a professional field for persons with graduate degrees, for whom more academic credits would be pointless. Yet while there is a large overlap in all respects, the typical participant, his motives for enrolling, the subject matter and teaching method, the maintenance of standards, all still differ to some degree between credit and noncredit programs. Most obviously, the student in a credit course wants some formal recognition of the work he has completed, while in a noncredit program

[1] Until recently, the extension division of the University of Wyoming carried the devaluation of "credit" to its logical if somewhat ridiculous conclusion, and granted a "certificate" for any course completed.

the participant may not. This means that those who attend for no credit are sometimes more interested in the content itself, rather than in pursuing a course of study for its instrumental value; sometimes they are interested only or mainly in meeting people. It means, also, that better records are ordinarily kept of credit courses and that more studies have been made of credit students; and much of the discussion in this chapter, willy-nilly, will reflect this imbalance.

"Credit" and "Noncredit" Courses

There is a broad consensus among university administrators that both credit and noncredit offerings are appropriate to its adult program, though some exceptions to this rule can be noted. In 1958, a faculty committee at Columbia University recommended that all students in its School of General Studies "be required to take full programs leading to a degree of Bachelor of Science," and when the administration put this new policy into effect, Dean Louis Hacker resigned his post in protest.[2] The contrary position, that credit work be abandoned, has seldom been defended, except by indirection:

[A] director of an extension organization offered the opinion that the real purpose of a university extension program is to provide opportunities for any learning important to the problems and the lives of people. He expressed the belief that the greatest opportunities are in the area of non-degree-credit specialized college level courses and that these should be offered whenever and wherever a real need and demand exist.[3]

Given the typical shortage of funds, personnel, and facilities, setting this priority would probably lead to skimping degree-credit courses.

In any case, in view of the varying proportions of the total extension function that are defined by different universities as "extension," it is difficult to say what the relation between credit and noncredit work is in actual practice, as opposed to stated

[2] *New York Times*, February 9, 1958. Of the 6,663 students enrolled in these evening courses in that year, only 1,397 were working toward a degree.
[3] Morton, *University Extension*, p. 29. He adds that the director "did not specify what a 'college level' course is nor what represents a 'real need.'" See also Dugan, "An Extension Class Program," p. 59.

policy. While a few universities in addition to Columbia, as well as a larger number of liberal arts colleges, restrict their general-extension *course* work to degree-credit classes,[4] probably all also sponsor some sort of noncredit or "informal" activities.

Responsibility for the content and teaching of degree-credit courses usually but not always rests with the corresponding subject-matter department of the university, either directly or through a committee.[5] Which courses are offered is usually determined by student demand, the requirements of the various degree-curricula, and the availability of teachers, rather than by any policy of the administration.[6]

As can be seen from Table 2, over the past two decades the increase in general-extension activities for degree-credit has been very much faster than that in day colleges, rapid as their growth has been. Whether one compares the number of institutions or the enrollments, the contrast is striking. If one could include in extension the university credit courses over radio and television, for which no separate data are available, the difference would be still greater.

One step below degree-credit courses are the so-called certificate programs. The number of institutions offering this kind of credit has risen markedly in recent years; among NUEA members, for

[4] According to the *1958 NUEA Proceedings*, only three universities in this association restrict their courses to degree-credit work (pp. 92-93), and it is not clear whether they permit students to enroll in them also for no credit. The *1958 AUEC Proceedings* gives no information on programs. According to the *Proceedings* of the previous year (pp. 100 ff.), 39 out of the 70 AUEC respondents offered no noncredit work *on campus*, and six of the 39 accepted only students matriculated for a bachelor's degree in their on-campus evening classes. Of the 233 liberal arts colleges with adult-education programs investigated by Crimi, 48 offered only degree-credit courses.

[5] This was true of 69 per cent of the 77 AUEC institutions reporting on this point to Neuffer. In about a third of the remaining institutions, credit courses had to be approved by some university administrator not connected with the evening college (*Administrative Policies*, p. 3). At all the universities that responded to Dugan's questionnaire, "all courses and instructors were approved by the respective department heads and deans; . . . in some classes it was necessary that the instructors be recommended by one of the resident deans" (Dugan, "An Extension Class Program," p. 67). Morton's figures on the subject do not distinguish between degree-credit courses and other services (*University Extension*, Table 69, p. 127).

[6] But see, for example, Schwertman, "General Extension," and Woodward, "The Evolving Mission," advocating an emphasis, respectively, on liberal arts and on vocational subjects.

TABLE 2. Degree-Credit Courses in Some General-Extension Divisions and Daytime Colleges, 1930-1952

Activity	Number of Institutions					Students Enrolled				
	1930	1940	Increase over 1930	1951-1952	Increase over 1940	1930	1940	Increase over 1930	1951-1952	Increase over 1940
Extension classes	18	23	28%	57	148%	50,558	53,140	5%	325,220	512%
Extension centers	7	9	29	23	156	28,758	34,185	19	480,506	1,306
Correspondence	27	33	22	44	33	36,826	53,887	46	133,223	147
High-school correspondence	12	23	92	27	18	2,005	11,037	450	22,666	105
Regular Daytime Courses — Public Colleges		1,708		1,832*	7	532,647	796,531	50	1,155,557*	45
Regular Daytime Courses — Private Colleges						568,090	697,672	23	1,146,327*	64

* 1952.

Sources: Calculated from Morton, *University Extension*, Table 25, p. 46; and from U.S. Census Bureau, *Statistical Abstract*, 1955, Table 145, p. 124, and Table 147, p. 125.

instance, there was an increase from twelve in 1951-1952 to 23 in 1956-1957.[7] The meaning of "certificate," however, varies considerably from one university to another. The 642 certificate programs at 66 AUEC institutions in 1952 ranged over the following areas: business administration (most frequent), liberal arts, science–technical, home economics, and agriculture. Of the sixty AUEC members that responded to Neuffer's questionnaire on this point, seven required a minimum of 16 to 30 credit hours for a certificate, eight 30 to 40, and ten 40 to 50; the maximum was 90.[8]

One meaning of a certificate, thus, relates to technical, business, and professional education. If a person follows courses in a well defined technical subject such as air-conditioner installation, or a similarly narrow area of business administration, the university gives him a formal certificate upon their completion. The distinction between this and a degree is feasible in such fields, because one can specify with equal precision what an electrical engineer, for instance, should know at one level and a television repairman at another. Certificates in liberal arts, on the other hand, are in principle more dubious. The education that one receives through four years in a liberal arts college cannot so easily be divided into parts that are meaningful in themselves. To what degree do the first two years of college (the portion taught in junior college) constitute more than preparation for the upper-division courses?

Among certificate programs in liberal arts, perhaps the best known is the one at New York University. The course of study leading to the certificate in general education "offers the mature student an opportunity to develop his educational talent and interests under the guidance of the faculty of the Division of General Education." All courses are open to the general public with no prerequisites, and none carry degree-credit. To obtain a certificate the student must have worked out a program approved by a faculty representative and the administrator of the certificate program, but there are no required courses. He must complete 48 semester-hours with a grade of "C" or better and complete a

[7] Morton, *University Extension*, p. 122; *1958 NUEA Proceedings*, pp. 92-93.

[8] *1952 AUEC Proceedings*, p. 88; Neuffer, *Administrative Policies*, p. 21.

personal project, which is understood as the "directive goal in planning the student's individual program."[9]

The College of General Education of Boston University, to cite another example, has developed a two-year curriculum taught off campus. If the student goes no further, he is given an Associate in Arts degree, but he may also transfer with junior standing to any one of the other colleges of the university. This policy, thus, sets half as the maximum number of extension courses that may be applied toward a bachelor's degree, and it also gives formal recognition for the successful completion of the first two years of college work.[10] In both respects, this extension division is analogous to a junior college.

Brooklyn College has gone farther. Under a program established in 1953 with a grant from the Center for the Study of Liberal Education for Adults,[11] mature persons are permitted to obtain college credit for equivalent experience outside the formal academic environment. Many of the goals of a liberal education, according to the assumptions underlying the program, "can be so defined" as to make them equivalent to informal nonacademic experience. It is still too early to judge this program in terms of its results: the first bachelor's degree under it was granted in 1956, and there were only sixteen by 1958. An average of 32 hours, and a maximum of 68 hours, were granted toward a degree. Up to 1958, 1,100 persons had applied for admission to the program, and of these some 200 had been evaluated with oral and written examinations. Credit for "adult experience" is given in humanities (English, art, music, philosophy) and social sciences (economics and sociology), but not in physical sciences, and the

[9] *New York University Bulletin,* LVII:31 (June 17, 1957), 77. There were 21 such students enrolled in the Division (out of a total of about 8,000) in 1957-1958; see *1957 AUEC Proceedings,* pp. 52 and 53.

[10] Siegle and Whipple, *New Directions in Programming,* pp. 61-62. In 1956-1957, 21 members of the AUEC offered credit work toward an "associate" degree; six of them had enrollments of 400 or more, and three had 1,000 or more students matriculated for an associate degree; see *1957 AUEC Proceedings,* p. 99. The many different certificate programs offered by institutions in the AUEC sometimes permit transfer of some or all credits to a degree program, sometimes are terminal (*1952 AUEC Proceedings,* p. 89).

[11] The Center was established in 1951 with a grant from the Fund for Adult Education to the AUEC; see Siegle, "Liberal Education."

various professional schools have not accepted the program at all.[12]

The value of such a program must be judged principally in terms of how it is administered. If an adult is able to demonstrate by a test the equivalent ability in a clearly defined subject matter such as a foreign language, it is at least arguable that he should be exempted not only from the ordinary requirement in this subject but also from the number of credits toward a degree that it represents—in effect, the same as advanced placement of freshmen in daytime colleges. If this equivalence in competence is loosely defined, however, the concept is obviously capable of gross abuse.

Included in the usual adult-education program, finally, is a large number of noncredit offerings. An illustrative list, quoted from Morton,[13] suggests their diversity better than could any description.

Air Conditioning and Heating	Health Problems for Social
American Foreign Policy and the	Workers
Far East	Income Tax Changes
Art Appreciation	Industrial Safety
Meaning of Atomic Energy	Insurance
Cost Accounting	International Relations
Creative Writing	Interior Decoration
Current Affairs	Landscape Gardening
Economics of Collective Bargaining	Management of a Small Business
ing	Merchandising
Employee Selection	Problems of the Small Investor
Engineering Mechanics Review	Retail Sales
Family Life Problems	Soviet Imperialism
Geology of our National Parks	

Conferences

The university frequently acts as host to what are variously known as conferences, institutes, short courses, lecture series,

[12] Stern, "Evaluation"; *How Much Does Adult Experience Count?*; *Adults Grow.* See also Siegle and Whipple, *New Directions in Programming,* pp. 62-64. Evening students may pass examinations and thus earn a certain number of credits toward a degree at several other institutions, such as George Washington University and Trinity University (*1952 AUEC Proceedings,* pp. 87-88).

[13] Morton, *University Extension,* p. 113.

clinics, forums, seminars, panel sessions, round tables, work conferences, or workshops. While there are slight differences in meaning among these terms, they are generally used as alternative designations for the same type of activity,[14] often approximating what we have termed a functional extension. Perhaps the most common term is *conferences,* which are defined as "short periods of study on questions of importance to the participants at the university campus or at other suitable locations, arranged for the purpose of using university facilities and staff and other appropriate leadership to gain new insights or skills."[15] It is usually difficult to differentiate sharply between "conferences" and "noncredit courses," or even courses for credit. Participation may bring credit toward a degree, "professional-advancement" credit, a special certificate, or no credit, depending on the circumstances or on someone's arbitrary decision.

Conferences are usually set up on request from a particular group or groups, especially such professional societies as those in business administration, engineering, medicine, dentistry, industrial relations, law, education, public health, social welfare, public administration. The task of arranging a conference may be undertaken by either the appropriate academic department or the extension staff, or the two in combination.[16] During the academic year 1951-1952, 38 of the institutions included in Morton's survey acted as hosts to some 3,500 conferences on 300 topics ranging

[14] "There appears to be little or no uniformity among the responding institutions relative to the terminology applied to their short intensive programs. . . . Perhaps this is a problem of sufficient merit for continued study" ("Report of the Division of Conferences and Institutes, 1955-56," *1956 NUEA Proceedings,* pp. 34-35). For one educator's attempt to differentiate among some of these terms, as well as a useful summary of problems and practices in scheduling noncredit programs of various kinds, see Hammarberg, *Informal Adult Education,* pp. 8-10 and *passim;* see also London, "Program Development," pp. 70-71.

[15] Morton, *University Extension,* p. 54. See also Fisher et al., *Adult Education,* p. 17.

[16] Among Morton's sample, 13 per cent of the conferences were sponsored by the general-extension division alone, 14 per cent by general extension together with one or more instructional departments, 41 per cent by extension together with one or more groups outside the university, 20 per cent by extension with one or more departments plus one or more outside groups; only 12 per cent were held without general-extension participation (*University Extension,* p. 125).

from aeronautics to wild life, and attended by a total of 402,848 persons.[17]

More than fifteen years ago, the University of Minnesota set aside for resident conferences a special building, complete with its own seminar and classrooms, library, dormitory, dining hall, and chapel. "In its first 12½ years, the . . . department conducted 812 'schools' or courses for a total of 40,252 persons. The courses varied in length from two days to a month, with the average seven days." The participants were educators, physicians and surgeons, public employees of professional standing, engineers, social welfare workers, dentists, pharmacists, lawyers. Civic or cultural courses, "although they have been conducted upon a professional level, have been attended by many who took them less from a professional interest than from the equally keen interest of the enlightened amateur."[18] In recent years, several other universities have set up similar centers, most notably Michigan State University and the University of Georgia. According to a 1958 survey of NUEA institutions, there were sixteen continuation centers in operation and eleven more planned.[19]

A common educational device, perhaps better classified under conferences than anywhere else, is the special "courses" or "institutes" established to refresh professionals' knowledge of their field and to keep them abreast of new developments. Examples of such programs are the Continuing Education of the Bar, at the University of California; the Conferences on Business and Tax Policy, originally offered jointly by the University of Miami and New York University; the Advanced Management Program, at Harvard; and similar programs for physicians, engineers, social workers, nurses, librarians, and other professional groups.[20]

[17] *Ibid.*, pp. 115-118, 125, and Table 25, p. 46. For a tabulation of conferences held during 1956-1957 and the names of the sponsoring member institutions of NUEA, see *1958 NUEA Proceedings*, pp. 96, 101.

[18] Unpublished statement by J. M. Nolte for the Carnegie Study of University Extension, quoted in Sheats et al., *Adult Education*, pp. 193-194. See also Price, *The Center for Continuation Study.*

[19] Division of Adult Education and Extension Services, University of Washington, *Continuation Center Survey.* For a history of resident adult schools in America—not including, however, these university centers—see Pitkin, *The Residential School.*

[20] For an article listing some areas in which such courses are or can be offered, and discussing some of the administrative problems involved, see Woods, "The University."

A more recent trend has been to establish liberal arts programs for professionals and businessmen. The fees and expenses in most of these programs are paid by the employers, for according to the view of a number of large corporations, their executives need an understanding of society and skills in human relations beyond those provided by the technical and professional curricula they followed in college. The first firm to set up a program to repair these deficiencies was the Bell Telephone Company, and its resident Institutes of Humanistic Studies for Executives for one academic year at the University of Pennsylvania, one semester at Swarthmore, or eight weeks at Dartmouth, Williams, or Northwestern, are still the most ambitious. Some other examples are the one-semester Institute of Liberal Studies for Executives at Clark University, a nonresident program; the two-week resident institute for professional secretaries at Vassar College; various part-time programs at the Universities of Akron and Denver and Southwestern University; and the International Harvester Corporation program offered in cooperation with the University of Chicago.[21]

A special type of composite university activity—part conference, part course, and part institute—is related to business and trade unions. Programs in industrial relations, which began to be set up in the mid-1930's, are now fairly well established. Their purpose has been to provide for the joint training of labor and management representatives, so as to facilitate cooperation and reduce industrial strife. Institutes of Industrial Relations are usually associated with one or more of the departments in social sciences (political science, economics, sociology); in some cases, especially at state universities, they have extension programs either of their own or as part of the general-extension division. At Cornell University, for example, the New York State School of Industrial and Labor Relations has offered both undergraduate

---

[21] For a description of these and similar programs, see Siegle, *New Directions in Liberal Education*; Siegle and Whipple, *New Directions in Programming*. The Bell Telephone Company's program is also sympathetically described by one of the company's officers in Gillen, "The Institute of Humanistic Studies." The vice-president in charge of industrial relations of the International Harvester Company has described its program in Willis, "Industry's Concern." For a discussion of the institute at Vassar, see Vaughan, *The Vassar Institute*; Miss Vaughan acted as "participant observer."

and graduate resident courses and, through its own extension division, tuition-free noncredit courses to members of labor, management, government, and civic groups. At the University of Illinois, as an example of a different pattern, the extension division of the Institute of Labor and Industrial Relations, operating through general extension, has offered credit and noncredit courses and administered such services as conferences and libraries.[22]

While these programs in industrial relations were ostensibly planned as much on behalf of labor as of management, trade unions were generally suspicious of them and demanded special programs in workers' education parallel to those provided for management in schools of business administration.[23] Among the twelve university programs in workers' education that could be cited in 1951,[24] the best known was at the School for Workers of the University of Wisconsin.[25] In October 1957, L. H. Adolfson of Wisconsin's general-extension division was listed as one of the directors of the newly established National Institute of Labor Education, "a national vehicle for labor-university cooperation" with headquarters in Madison. Among other functions, the institute was to solicit funds from foundations, unions, and business, and to make grants to nonlabor educational agencies.[26]

When a university enters the field of workers' education, how should it avoid duplicating the educational functions of the trade unions themselves?[27] The education that ought to be available to workers can be divided into the following four categories:

[22] Ely, *Handbook*, pp. 378, 379.
[23] Kaplan, "Labor-Management Programs." See also Hollander, "Higher Education"; Fernbach, *University Extension*, p. 7.
[24] Alabama, California, Chicago, Harvard, Illinois, Indiana, Cornell, Penn State, Rhode Island, Roosevelt, Rutgers, Wisconsin (Grattan, *In Quest of Knowledge*, p. 255). For both workers' education *and* industrial relations, the figure was given as 75 programs for 1957 (Hollander, "Higher Education"). For a discussion of the field and descriptions of programs offered by trade unions, universities, and other agencies, see Mire, *Labor Education*; Barbash, *Universities and Unions*, which is an evaluation of the program of the Fund for Adult Education's Inter-University Labor Education Committee.
[25] The school's activities are described briefly in Ely, *Handbook*, p. 500, and its ideology is stated by Ernest E. Schwartztrauber in Sheats et al., *Adult Education*, pp. 230-231. See also Fernbach, *University Extension*, pp. 8-19.
[26] *New York Times*, October 13, 1957.
[27] For a discussion of this question by a former union official, see Mire, "The University and the Union."

1. "Bread-and-butter" union courses, such as shop-steward training, grievance procedures, contract negotiations, union administration, etc. This type of training ought to be undertaken by the union's own educational department.

2. Remedial, in the usual limited sense of this term. Since remedial courses are ordinarily in subjects taught in primary or high school, in accordance with our proposed rule that the university restrict itself to college-level material, the adult-education program of the public school system should offer them.

3. Professional—time and motion studies, job evaluation, economics, health and welfare, journalism, etc.

4. Cultural—foreign affairs, community relations, art, etc. Courses in these two categories might well be provided by the university, as long as they are at college level; but in that case there would seem to be no good reason for segregating union members in special courses.

The NUEA has attempted to establish more general standards for deciding whether a university ought to sponsor any given conference. In 1951, a committee of this organization proposed the following criteria:

1. Sponsorship that cannot be better done by nonuniversity agencies.

2. Sponsorship or cooperation with related academic departments.

3. Must be educational.

4. Universities must play active role in planning the conference or institute, not just provide facilities and prestige for "canned" program.

5. University must have financial control of institute.[28]

Two years later, most of the member institutions indicated that they generally used such standards to decide on conferences, though some also accepted canned programs under pressure. In 1957, the NUEA's Division of Conferences and Institutes set "appropriate procedural channels" for the "three major categories of programs"—"Institution Sponsored," "Request from Within or from Outside the University," and "Programs without Formal University Sponsorship." The proposed rule against providing

[28] "Report of the Committee on Conferences and Institutes," *1953 NUEA Proceedings*, pp. 81-89. See Kidd, *Adult Education*, pp. 23-24, for similar rules formulated by the general-extension directors of the four western provinces of Canada.

university facilities for canned programs had apparently been
abandoned.[29]

The relevance of a campus setting lies mainly in the easier contact it provides between faculty (together with advanced students) and the outside world. At these conferences, not all
learning is in one direction; in Dean McGhee's words—

Consider the most modern developments, new techniques and problems arising in manufacturing, in management, and in legislation.
Perhaps General Electric and I.B.M., the American Management Association and the American Law Institute *would* do the job better.
But how does that benefit the Colleges of Engineering, Business, and
Law? Where is the feedback into the curricula for preparing tomorrow's engineers, businessmen and lawyers?[30]

In setting policy concerning conferences, thus, the university
ought to consider carefully their educational value in either
direction. In particular, it ought to make sure that its facilities
are not being used as a cheaper and more convenient substitute
for a hotel or other meeting place.

Methods and Technical Facilities

The developing shortage of even regular university instructors
means that those available for university adult education will increasingly be too few in number to enable it to fulfill its task
satisfactorily. Against this background, the experimentation with
various methods and supposed aids to teaching acquires especial
importance. The effects of most of these on the learning process
have not been adequately tested,[31] and no implication is intended
here that they are, or are not, suitable to university adult education. This is merely a list (and not an exhaustive one) to exemplify what has been done in either credit or informal programs
of various types.

As we have pointed out at length, we do not agree with those
devotees of group discussion who regard the absence of a subject-

[29] "Report of the Division of Conferences and Institutes," *1957 NUEA
Proceedings*, pp. 49-54.
[30] Letter from Dean McGhee, July 21, 1958.
[31] There have been many analyses, of course, of some of the established
methods, such as correspondence or television courses, and even some of the
packaged programs, for instance. Many of these analyses were made, however,
without adequate controls, in order to prove a point. See above, pp. 35 ff.

matter expert as a good thing in itself. But it is reasonable to suppose that if, say, several persons read a number of college-level assignments and come together regularly to discuss them following a discussion guide, they will learn more than from reading on their own; and in many situations this is the realistic alternative to no program at all. Given adequate controls and tests, such teacherless courses might even be offered for credit.

Regular discussion groups are frequently based on so-called *packaged programs,*[32] or selected readings on a specific topic, usually but not always from previously published sources, assembled into a series of pamphlets or a book. Before each session the participants read one assignment and then convene in one of their homes or at a public building. Sometimes films or records are then used to supplement the readings. Discussion is led by one or two participants, who in some cases have been briefly trained in discussion techniques but not in the subject matter. A few of the better known programs of this type are the "Great Books" courses of the Great Books Foundation; "Economic Reasoning," "Ways of Mankind," "Introduction to the Humanities" of the Fund for Adult Education; "World Politics," "American Foreign Policy," and "Russian Foreign Policy" of the former American Foundation for Political Education[33]; "The American Heritage" of the American Library Association; and "Freedom Agenda" of the League of Women Voters. The "Great Decisions" of the Foreign Policy Association and "Challenge to Iowa" of Iowa State University combine packaged readings and discussion guides with a correlated information campaign in the mass media.

Over the past several decades the development of new communication media has made possible a still greater proliferation of adult-education programs. Teaching by *correspondence,* one of the oldest activities of universities, has remained an important and growing part of their extension programs.[34] Most corre-

[32] Houle prefers to term them "coordinated courses." For a short history of such programs and a discussion of their value and limitations, see his "The Use of Print," pp. 169-186.

[33] Its successor, the American Foundation for Continuing Education, prepares adult-education materials that are published commercially.

[34] For figures on past enrollments, teachers employed, etc., see Morton, *University Extension,* pp. 43-49. The best known book dealing with the sub-

spondence courses attempt to duplicate for individual students some of the regular campus offerings. Of the 76 member institutions of the NUEA in 1957-1958, 45 reported that in the preceding year they had had correspondence courses, of which 42 carried degree-credit, 10 certificate-credit, 34 high-school credit, and 23 no credit.[35]

Teaching by mail was supplemented by *radio courses* shortly after this became technically possible. As early as 1924, about half a million adults were participating in educational programs over the radio.[36] Some twenty-five years later there were more than two dozen university radio stations broadcasting both regular classes and many more informal courses and public-service programs.[37] By 1956, 99 institutions of higher education, including 39 state colleges and universities, held licenses to operate educational radio stations. Some broadcast over both AM and FM, or from several locations in the state. One license is held by the general-extension division of a state university (South Carolina).[38]

The Canadian Farm Radio Forum consists of weekly *radio* broadcasts of panel *discussions* by experts on issues of current interest to rural audiences. Participants are organized into discussion groups, which meet at the home of one of them. All are sent a discussion guide and supplementary facts. After listening to the panel, each group discusses the issue, and at the end of the session a secretary records its decision on a Findings Sheet and mails it to the provincial Farm Forum office. There all opin-

---

ject is by the former long-time secretary-treasurer of the NUEA, Bittner, with Mallory—*University Teaching by Mail.* See also Rowbotham, *Correspondence Instruction.*

[35] *1958 NUEA Proceedings,* pp. 94-95.

[36] Essert, *Creative Leadership,* p. 37. Tyson, *Education Tunes In,* gives an account of the early days of educational radio in the United States. In Australia, the *two-way radio* has been developed as a technique especially adapted to areas of low population density and great distances. In the outlying districts almost every ranch home has such a radio, which is used not only as a means of communication but also for education. "School is taught through this device, involving teacher-pupil conversations and recitations. Specific curricula and lesson assignments have been designed" (Kraenzel, *The Great Plains,* p. 345).

[37] McCarty, "Radio and Understanding." See Ely, *Handbook,* pp. 425-429, for brief descriptions of the educational broadcasting programs of fifteen colleges and universities, mostly state institutions.

[38] Broderick, "List of Educational AM and FM Radio and Television."

ions are collated and summarized, and eventually reported back
to the participants.[39]

The considerable experience with correspondence and radio
courses has laid a base for teaching by *television*. With this new
medium, some of the advantages of classroom teaching can be
made available to a mass audience. Though it has developed
rapidly during the past several years, television teaching is still
in an experimental stage, and current practices are only indicative of probable future developments. In 1959, New York University used a grant from RCA to institute a Center for
Instructional Television, whose purpose it is "to develop effective
techniques for television teaching."[40]

At present, closed-circuit television is used by some 93 universities, including 43 state institutions, mainly in order to pipe
lectures by master teachers to several daytime classes, which
sometimes also have junior faculty members to direct the discussion developing out of each lecture.[41] The Oregon State System
of Higher Education, with a grant from the Fund for the Advancement of Education, is experimenting with closed-circuit
television over several campuses. In 1957-1958, courses in history,
chemistry, and education taught at the University of Oregon,
Oregon State College, and Oregon College of Education were
broadcast to students at the other two institutions and at Wil-
lamette, a private university.[42] Starting in the fall semester of
1957-1958, the University of New Mexico has offered courses in
biology, anthropology, English, and mathematics to evening students over closed-circuit television. The same courses on 16-mm.
film are made available off campus in eight New Mexico com-

[39] For a history of this program and a discussion of some of its accomplishments and failings, see Sim, *Canada's Farm Radio Forum*.

[40] *Adult Leadership*, 8:4 (October, 1959), 129.

[41] For reports on the use of closed-circuit television at various institutions,
see American Council on Education, *Teaching by Closed-Circuit Television*,
pp. 4-34; Siegle and Whipple, *New Directions in Programming*, pp. 74-81;
Dunham, "List of Closed-Circuit Educational Television." Classroom use
of closed-circuit television was called "a costly failure" at the Los Angeles
City College (*New York Times*, April 27, 1958).

[42] Letter from Glenn Starlin, director of the Inter-Institutional TV Teaching Project, University of Oregon, January 31, 1958.

munities, where students can attend them and earn residence credits.[43]

Television classes are presently given over both commercial stations and educational channels. As early as 1951-1952, Western Reserve University had degree-credit offerings in psychology, child psychology (with elementary psychology a prerequisite for enrollment), elementary economics, geography, and comparative literature.[44] Of the 46 educational television stations on the air in January 1960 (four of them on non-reserved channels), 15 were operated by universities, of which 14 were state institutions. In addition, commercial stations were operated by one private and three land-grant universities.[45] Educational stations licensed to councils, associations, or foundations, moreover, often have one or more universities as participating agencies. By fall of 1957, 77 universities, including 34 state institutions, were offering or planning to offer "telecourses" for credit in a great variety of subjects.[46]

In the fall of 1957, when New York University introduced a television course in comparative literature at the rather discouraging hour of 6:30 A.M., the bookstores and libraries of this metropolis were unable to meet the extraordinary demand for Stendhal's *The Red and the Black,* the first work the instructor

[43] *Denver Post,* October 14, 1957; letter from M. H. McMichael, assistant director of the Division of Extension, Summer Session and Community Services, University of New Mexico, March 5, 1958.

[44] Stromberg, "College Credit."

[45] The 15 institutions were the universities of Arizona, Florida, Illinois, Michigan State, Nebraska, New Hampshire, New Mexico, North Carolina, Ohio State, Miami (Ohio), Houston, Utah, Washington, Wisconsin; and the Oregon State Board of Higher Education. In addition, Florida State University and the university system of Georgia were expected to start telecasting soon, and plans for an educational station were more or less advanced at Arizona State University, Ball State Teachers College, Southern Illinois University, the University of Kansas, Kansas State College, the Universities of Maine and Michigan, Central Michigan College, the University of the State of New York (8 stations), and the University of South Dakota. The commercial stations were operated by Iowa State University, the Universities of Missouri and North Dakota, and Loyola University (New Orleans). See Joint Council on Educational Television, *Educational Television Directory,* January 1960.

[46] Michigan State University, *Telecourses.* For a year earlier, another source had given 400 as the number of telecourses, both credit and noncredit; see Dunham and Lowdermilk, *Television,* pp. 19-20.

discussed. There were 177 enrolled for degree-credit in this course, and the total audience was estimated at 120,000. In early February, 142 of the former took a final examination at the university, and all but 10 per cent passed the course and gained three credits toward a college degree. By the instructor's estimate, the final showing of his television students was as good as that of the campus students, if not better.[47]

The major advantage of television instruction is, of course, that the number of potential participants is large,[48] particularly if it is supplemented by the use of kinescopes, which make it possible to serve areas not reached by the station's own transmitters. It is possible to follow a course at any one of three levels. To take a course for degree-credit, the student enrolls with the university, pays a fee, and purchases the syllabus and texts; he sends in periodic examination papers for correction, and comes to campus at the end of the course for his final examination. (Given the demand for such an arrangement, it would be possible to have students' final examinations administered throughout a large area by various cooperating institutions, as is sometimes done with final examinations in correspondence courses.) Those with a high level of interest but no desire for college credits can purchase the syllabus and texts but need not submit examination papers. A much larger audience can follow the course at the level of observers. This combination of audiences, however, suggests an implicit invitation to try to appeal to the largest one.

There is a danger of becoming so fascinated with the medium as such that we might be trapped into becoming pseudo- or semi-tele-

[47] *New York Times*, September 24, 1957; January 19, 1958; February 12, 1958; *New York Times Magazine*, November 17, 1957, pp. 74-76. The second semester's credit enrollment was 113, of whom 93 took the final examination (*New York Times*, May 11, 1958). In Chicago, open-circuit television classes were given by the Chicago City Junior College to 7,239 students, of whom 1,511 enrolled for credit (*New York Times*, May 11, 1958).
[48] In October 1959, Purdue University filed applications with the FCC proposing an experimental project with airborne transmitters that would provide television coverage over an area with a radius of 150 to 200 miles. The potential audience would include approximately 5 million students in some 13,000 schools and colleges. See Joint Council on Educational Television, *Factsheet*, November 1959.

vision-professionals and forget our goals and missions as educators. Our role in television is that of the educator.[49]

Audio-visual kits were originally developed by Dr. Robert S. Warner, with a grant from the Kellogg Foundation, as part of a program of postgraduate medical education. Each of his kits consists of a recorded discussion on one of a number of medical topics, a set of 35-mm. slides correlated with the discussion, a viewer, and a script. The kit can be used by one isolated physician or by a group with a projector. Dr. Warner later developed a similar kit for the American Heart Association, and this "Cardiac Clinic" is used by local branches of the association in their program of professional education.[50]

In sum, recent experimentation in teaching methods in adult education has been even more striking than the great variety in subject matter. Supplementing classroom lectures, and discussion groups, and correspondence courses, there are now radio, television, and film programs; audio-visual aids; and various combinations of these. With these methods, faculty participation in the program is reduced or even, in some cases, dispensed with altogether. Unfortunately, the educational effects of most of these methods have never to our knowledge been adequately tested, and before adopting them it would be important to know how much is lost by the attempt to preserve faculty time.[51]

Standards in Degree-Credit Courses

There is no reason, apart from the lack of data, why a discussion of standards should be limited to those in credit courses.

[49] Ralph Steetle, executive director of the Joint Council on Educational Television, in American Council on Education, *Teaching by Closed Circuit*, p. 37. See also University of Chicago, *Television*.

[50] Letter from Dr. Robert S. Warner, November 11, 1957; Warner and Bowers, "Program of Postgraduate Medical Education"; Christensen and Warner, "The A-V Lecture Kit"; letter from Miss Beatrice Schenk, educational materials director, American Heart Association, December 16, 1957; American Heart Association, *Publications and Teaching Aids* and "Educational Materials."

[51] The Fund for the Advancement of Education has been sponsoring a number of experimental programs to develop ways by which colleges could "better teach more students without a proportionate increase in size of faculty." For a tentative evaluation of the 1956-1957 experiments, see Paschal, "What New Developments."

High quality, we feel, should be a routine characteristic of every university product; and if more university administrators agreed with this dictum, in fact as well as in principle, recommendations for experimentation in methods and techniques would more frequently include some evidence of their educational value.

However, even the relatively simple case of credit courses, which are closest to traditional disciplines in content and are controlled by regular examinations, must be examined with care if we are to judge their standards accurately. There is, it is true, a general feeling among university faculties and administrators that credit courses in general extension, no matter in what subject, are not typically at the level maintained on the home campus.[52]

Many sincere and dedicated university leaders . . . regard adult education with uneasy suspicion. They dread the possibility that the hordes of new claimants on their time and service may finally destroy the university itself. The university, such observers fear, may grow to be like the lumbering behemoths of prehistoric time, whose bodies grew too large for their brains to integrate and who thereby failed in the struggle for survival. This fear of size is paralleled by a fear of cheapness and vulgarization.[53]

In order to refute such sentiments, several studies have been made comparing extension and day students. Dugan, for example, compared the grades *in the same courses*, taught by the same instructors, earned by 499 extension and 2,330 resident students at the University of Wyoming, and on this basis concluded that extension students did better.[54] From this finding, one might conclude (1) that, indeed, extension students do better work, or (2) that instructors find extension teaching more stimulating and consequently do a better job of teaching, or (3), most plausibly,

[52] In 1955, the executive secretary of the NUEA declared that it was necessary for extension divisions to begin to stress standards (McCurdy, "Report of the Executive Secretary," p. 90). See also, for example, Crimi, *Adult Education*, p. 14; Morton, *University Extension*, p. 45; Dugan, "An Extension Class Program," p. 123; Houle, "Community Educational Services," p. 10, and *Major Trends*, pp. 43-44; Bray, "Extension Credit," p. 62.

[53] Houle, "Introduction," p. 13.

[54] Dugan, "An Extension Class Program," pp. 126-127. See also the several earlier studies cited in Thompson, "Quality of Correspondence," pp. 140-142; Bittner and Mallory, *University Teaching*, Chap. VI and Appendix XIII.

that grading in extension is more lenient. Dugan's study does not refute this third alternative, and several others confirm it.

McMichael, for instance, compared the grades earned at the University of New Mexico by *the same students* who had taken courses both on campus and in extension (either by correspondence or in extension classes, or both). The mean grades earned by this sample of 380 students were 1.41 in residence courses, 1.65 through correspondence, and 1.70 in extension courses.[55] From a number of studies at several other universities, Sorenson concluded that instructors generally mark extension students a half to a full grade higher than their regular campus students, and he concluded that "it is therefore unsound to evaluate the quality of extension work by comparing extension and residence marks."[56] Instructors in extension are under pressure to be generous to their highly motivated students, who are often in a minority ethnic group, or who depend on the credits earned to keep their jobs. They "seem to grade with their hearts rather than with their heads, . . . [and this] soft grading practice . . . is one way by which an objective observer can detect dissimilar standards."[57]

The lower standards in extension, whether or not they are admitted in words, are often given at least informal recognition in a number of administrative procedures. For example, admission requirements for evening students are sometimes lower; and on some campuses students who flunk out of the regular day college are permitted to make up the courses in extension.[58] Or, most strikingly, only a certain proportion of the credits required for a degree may generally be earned in extension. It would seem logical to allow a student to earn a degree in extension if the courses are at the same level as those on the home campus; and, if they are not, not to permit *any* extension credits toward a degree. If the lower quality of extension courses is not frankly admitted, and the number of extension credits acceptable toward a degree is nonetheless limited, what reason can be cited for this

[55] McMichael, "A Comparison," p. 29.

[56] Sorenson, *Adult Abilities*, pp. 97-98. For a list of the 18 institutions included in this study, see *ibid.*, pp. ix-xii.

[57] Nyquist, "The Soft Pedagogy," p. 61.

[58] This policy prevailed at 47 per cent of the evening colleges surveyed by Neuffer (*Administrative Policies*, p. 15). Comparable data for NUEA institutions are not available.

differentiation? It may be, for example, that certain required courses cannot be given in extension because of the lack of library or laboratory facilities, or of qualified teachers; but such a limitation, while it would force the student to take a required course given only in the regular day session on campus, would not justify a residence requirement as such. Or the point is made that extension students lack counseling[59]; but "mature persons . . . would greatly resent a requirement that they interview a counselor at periodic intervals."[60] The occasional problem that really requires special attention, particularly at registration time, is often given it no less in the case of extension than of regular campus students.[61] Arguments about counseling, thus, "often fall very flat," especially with students who have attended both regular and extension classes and can compare them in this respect.[62] Or the point is made that the informal life on the campus—for example, clubs and bull sessions—is as educational as classes; but even if this unproved thesis were to be accepted, it would hardly apply to the older, often married, sometimes commuting, *part-time* student, whether he attends classes in extension or on the regular campus.[63] Setting an arbitrary limit to the number of extension credits that may be applied toward a degree, thus, can reasonably be interpreted as a covert recognition that standards in extension classes are generally lower.

How prevalently is this differentiation made? In extension *centers*, "usually no distinction is made between the degree credits earned in their programs and in campus classes,"[64] and this

[59] See, for example, Thompson, *University Extension*, pp. 130-133; Nyquist, "The Soft Pedagogy," p. 63; see also statements by Rev. Richard T. Deters of John Carroll University, Willis H. Reals of Washington University, and R. C. Young of the University of Georgia, in *1952 AUEC Proceedings*, pp. 95, 194-209. One administrator has even found "some justification" for the low salaries paid extension teachers in the fact that they are not called on for counseling and committee work (Strickler, "Financing Evening Programs").

[60] Burns, "Self-Evaluation," p. 28.

[61] See, for example, the statement by Gurth I. Abercrombie, of Northeastern University, in *1954 AUEC Proceedings*, p. 14.

[62] Bray, "Extension Credit," p. 60.

[63] See Burns, "Self-Evaluation," p. 30.

[64] Morton, *University Extension*, p. 58. But see Bray, "Extension Credit," pp. 61-62.

seems also to be so of independent liberal arts colleges that offer degree-credit extension courses[65] and the evening colleges of urban universities.[66] However, university extension *courses*, including those by correspondence,[67] usually have a lower status than nominally equivalent ones on the home campus. Among the members of the NUEA who replied on this point to Dugan's questionnaire, thus, the maximum credits that might be earned in extension toward a bachelor's degree ranged from 20 to 100 per cent, with the median at 42 per cent.[68] Similarly, of the 46 universities that replied to this question in Morton's survey, all set a limit on the number of extension credits applicable toward a degree except two, which took

the position that provision of any courses by them was a guarantee, at least insofar as an institution can guarantee quality, of the worth of these offerings, and that if a high quality of educational service could not be maintained, none would be offered. These institutions make no distinctions between "residence" and "extension" credits.[69]

This, we believe, is the correct policy.

The same difficulties as in extension generally have been encountered in setting criteria for degree-credit in telecourses. At a 1955 meeting of universities offering such courses, one participant maintained that the credit that can be earned should be limited to a maximum of twenty-five hours, while others de-

[65] Crimi, *Adult Education*, p. 15.

[66] Of the 70 members of AUEC that replied to the association's 1956-1957 questionnaire, 57 had students enrolled in a four-year program leading to a bachelor's degree (*1957 AUEC Proceedings*, pp. 101 ff.). Concerning AUEC institutions, Dean Neuffer has written us: "To my knowledge, the credits earned in evening colleges are in all cases applicable to degrees offered by that particular institution. There is no limitation concerning the number of hours that an individual can complete in an evening college toward the bachelor's degree and I believe in most cases the master's degree. Any deviation from this I would believe to be a local situation. I have no specific statistics but this is a conclusion that I would reach as a result of my conversations with evening deans around the country" (letter from Frank R. Neuffer, July 11, 1958).

[67] Morton, *University Extension*, Table 31, p. 49.

[68] Dugan, "An Extension Class Program," p. 75. He recommended that the University of Wyoming extension division use "at least 35 to 40 per cent" as its own limitation, "on the basis of national practice" (p. 139).

[69] Morton, *University Extension*, pp. 45-49; Table 30, p. 48.

clared that no courses should be offered for credit over television unless approved by the faculty and administered in such a way as to be acceptable without limitation.[70]

Community Services

Universities perform a great many services for the community, often though not necessarily always through their general-extension divisions. The diversity of these services, which vary considerably from one university to another, can be indicated by an illustrative list:

The broadcasting of cultural and scientific programs by radio or television; or the maintenance of an educational station.

Lectures open to the public, on or off campus.

Concerts, plays, motion pictures, art exhibits, readings of poetry, etc., open to the public.

A speakers bureau.

The printing of publications for use also off campus.

A lending service of library materials, to individuals or groups off campus.

The circulation of audio-visual aids.

Consulting services to business, industry, municipal or state governments, public schools.

Social welfare services.

Placement services for persons other than students and graduates.

Testing services for persons other than students.

Participation in community improvement projects.

Information services to the general public or to special groups.

Recreation, sports, etc.

Some of these types of services—lecture tours, library extension, etc.—are obviously educational; others have only a remote relation (if indeed any at all) to the main functions of an institution of higher learning. All reflect the alleged duty that universities owe the community, but we feel that this is a somewhat overworked theme, and that it would be well if administrators took a long, hard look at this shibboleth. Fifty or seventy-five years ago, in a near-frontier area like the Middle West, the state

[70] American Council on Education, *Credit Courses*, pp. 2-3.

university was *the* harbinger of urban culture; and if the people there were to hear concerts and lectures, or have access to adequate libraries, it usually had to be as a consequence of the university's effort to provide them. Today, the situation is reversed. As we pointed out in the introductory chapter, we are now faced with a tragic paradox: a great, rich nation is skimping badly on its educational system, one of the important historical bases of its greatness and wealth. The main problem has become how to induce the community to serve the university.

In terms of this perspective, what criteria can be set for judging which community services are *now* suitable, and which not, for an institution of higher learning? Let us begin by classifying some of the activities according to the amount of additional money, time, and personnel they are likely to cost.

1. The first and simplest type of community service is rendered when the general public is given access, at no great additional cost to the university, to an existent facility or to a special event planned primarily for the student body. For example, university *libraries* may often be used by local residents; and *television* courses, as was noted in an earlier section of this chapter, are usually followed by a very much larger audience than those who enroll.

2. It is often difficult to draw the line between such instances, where the public is permitted access to university facilities, and those where the extension administration has planned for a joint student–public participation. For example, most of the universities surveyed by Morton declared that the purpose of their *broadcasting* facilities is "to allow the university to contribute directly and continuously to adult education,"[71] and this vague formulation permits them to avoid setting a clear policy on how far into the community this service should reach, and at what level. *Concerts, recitals,* and *special lectures,* similarly, are ordinarily not merely open to members of the community, but also organized, at least in terms of the size of the hall and publicity, with both the campus and the general audience in mind.[72] *Uni-*

[71] Morton, *University Extension,* p. 59.
[72] For brief descriptions of recent lecture programs at a number of state universities, see "Report of the Committee on Lectures and Concerts," *1957 NUEA Proceedings,* pp. 68-69.

versity presses, as another example, publish not only the works of their own faculties but also those of other scholars, and also books of a broader appeal.[73]

3. Certain university facilities are not merely made accessible to the public but taken to it. *Library services*—not only books and periodicals but also pamphlets, clippings, plays, art exhibits, etc.—are often made available throughout the state, either through a special division in the library or through the general-extension division.[74] The university assists public schools, organizations, and individuals with programing, book lists and bibliographies, specially prepared packets of materials, etc. At the University of Wisconsin, for example, the Bureau of Information and Program Services has a special staff and separate collections of materials, including plays, reproductions, music, and magazines.[75] *Art exhibits, theater* productions, and *concert* groups are taken to rural areas of Nebraska, Washington, and North Carolina, for example, by the general-extension divisions of these state universities.[76]

In many localities, *audio-visual teaching aids* are regularly distributed to schools, organizations, and individuals; and sometimes instruction is given to educators on how to prepare and use them.

[73] Beals and Brody, *The Literature*, p. 341. For a short account of the development of university presses in the United States and some figures on titles and sales, see *Time*, October 5, 1959, pp. 85-87.

[74] One of every three library-extension services surveyed by Morton was administered by the university library and two by the general-extension division (*University Extension*, p. 50). In 1951-1952, the 17 institutions that provided these services reached 305,320 persons (*ibid.*, Table 25, p. 46).

A new technique for extending library books is being tested at the University of Virginia, with a grant from the Council on Library Resources of the Ford Foundation. Students at branch libraries on campus can telephone their requests to the main library, have the book they want reproduced on a television screen over a closed circuit, and turn the pages by using a remote-control gadget. If the distance over which it can operate, originally limited to about 4,000 feet, can be increased substantially, this device may help to correct one of the most serious deficiencies of extension courses—the usual lack of adequate libraries away from campus (*New York Times*, October 13, 1957; letter from Roger P. Bristol, deputy TV grant director, Alderman Library, University of Virginia, November 5, 1957).

[75] Leaflet, *Bureau of Information and Program Services*, University of Wisconsin Extension Division. For a history of Wisconsin's "package library," see Andersen, "A Study of Discussion," pp. 478 ff. See Thompson, *University Extension*, p. 163, for a definition of "package library."

[76] Broady et al., "Three Arts Go on Tour."

Some audio-visual departments make their own films. Among the institutions surveyed by Morton, the 25 audio-visual departments serviced nearly 28 million people, principally through public schools.[77] According to a 1956-1957 survey of these institutions, audio-visual services of one kind or another were offered by 53 members of the NUEA.[78]

4. The faculty of a university is often approached by business firms, private organizations, and government bureaus; and professors are usually expected to respond to such requests for *consultation* or *lectures* in their spare time and frequently without remuneration. In some universities the general-extension division has acted as liaison between the public and the faculty, channeling inquiries to the appropriate department, institute, or person.[79] We have no information on how well this system works.

These four types of community services—university facilities and special events (1) made accessible to the public, (2) set up in part for public use, or (3) distributed to the public; and (4) consultations and lectures—are in principle unexceptional but secondary to the university's main functions of teaching and research. Several guide lines are suggested to define which services are suitable:

1. They should be related to college-level education or research. To sponsor a concert series, for example, would be appropriate, but not to set up a mimeographing service for the community.

2. The university should not compete with other agencies in providing services. It "should confine its activities to those for which it has *unique* resources."[80] In particular, it should not do gratis what commercial firms do for a charge. Here is an especially striking instance of what in our opinion is illegitimate:

[77] Morton, *University Extension*, Table 25, p. 46 and pp. 51-52.

[78] *1958 NUEA Proceedings*, pp. 97-100.

[79] According to a report for 1947-1948, this was the role of general extension at, for example, New Hampshire and Kentucky with relation to government research; Kentucky and the State University of Iowa—business research; Kentucky—taxation; Virginia—population and economic research; New Hampshire—biology; Pennsylvania State University—engineering services to small industries; etc. See Fisher et al., *Adult Education*, p. 21.

[80] Gordon, "The Meaning of University Level," p. 24; emphasis in the original.

A member of the staff of the Department of Physical Education at Massachusetts State College has given valuable service to communities throughout the State by giving information on the construction, cost, and maintenance of swimming pools. The College, largely through the work of another member of the Department's staff, has given outstanding services in the field of winter sports.[81]

On the other hand, university presses, which perform a unique and valuable service by printing nonprofitable scholarly books, complement rather than compete with the commercial publishers. The distinction is in many cases a fine one, but we believe that usually any doubt should be resolved by restricting the university's role. Such a rule of thumb would counteract to some degree the bureaucratic expansionism of the ambitious administrators who in universities, as in other types of institutions, tend to confuse increase in size with progress. And as we pointed out, it is an especially fit rule at the present time: since the university's resources will be increasingly strained in carrying out its main functions, subsidiary tasks should not be undertaken unless these cannot reasonably be avoided.

3.   To the degree that it is feasible, community services should pay their own way.[82] A counter argument is often made that fees discourage community groups and individuals from turning to the university for such services. Though there is little evidence to support this contention, it seems reasonable and we can accept it as at least probable. The question still remains, however, whether the money spent on free services is better so used than for the education of students and for research. Finances are never adequate to provide for *these* services, and in principle money should not be spent freely on peripheral matters, however useful they may be. Thus, it is quite reasonable for even a public university to charge a fee of townspeople or organizations for the use of the library or other facilities, or for a lecture or concert.[83] Or, as another instance, it is neither reasonable nor just that university faculties, an occupational group grossly underpaid for performing essential services, should be expected to respond gratis

[81] "State Universities," p. 128.
[82] For some figures, see below, pp. 116-117.
[83] See, for example, Van de Water, "Supplementary Summary," p. 4, with reference to the services of university film centers.

to taxpayers' requests for consultation. Nor should they be paid for such services out of the university's own budget or—what in monetary terms is the same thing—be excused from regular duties in order to do research for others on university time.

Summary

Just as the available data make it necessary to analyze university adult education largely in terms of what general-extension divisions actually do, even though the portion of the total extension function that they administer varies greatly from one institution to another, so it is necessary in a discussion of the educational range of the offerings to retain the ambiguous, and partly obsolescent, distinction between "credit" and "noncredit" programs. Since on the daytime campus, academic credits are one important means of maintaining academic standards, the blurring of this distinction in extension is an important trend. What are the reasons for it?

1. In extension courses (though not usually in extension centers), credit is generally rated lower than that for ostensibly equivalent courses in the regular curriculum. That is to say, even within the class of degree-credits, those earned in extension are typically one step down, one step closer to no credit.

2. On the other hand, there has been a contrary, upward trend, in response to the demand that formal recognition be granted for completion of a program of less than the four years ordinarily required for a degree. Thus, we have "associate degrees," "certificate-credit," credit for "nonacademic experience," "professional-advancement credit," "alertness credit," and so on.

3. The subject matter of adult-education programs ranges widely over areas too new or recondite, or sometimes too peripheral or insignificant, to have been included in the regular curriculum; and in such cases there is no precedent to denote what credit is appropriate.

4. The range of participants, similarly, includes persons who have no interest in credit—because they are looking mainly for social contacts, because they are interested in the content of the program per se, because they already have an advanced degree and need no further formal recognition.

While credit courses do not necessarily impose higher standards than informal programs,[84] the fact that some control is exercised is important. Probably the best and the worst in university adult education are to be found among the noncredit programs, the lively innovations that are the product of true creativity and, at the other extreme, the flagrant caricatures of education, devoid of content, sometimes of taste, in fact of anything except commercial profit. Between these extremes lies the credit program, solidly based on academic tradition but often taught with no hint of how exciting learning can be.

During the past several decades, educators and particularly adult educators have become increasingly aware of "the community."[85] That the university should serve its community in an appropriate fashion is axiomatic. "But where does a reasonable recognition of the claims of the community end and community-worship, a fetishism as disastrous as state-worship, begin?"[86]

The extension of the university has made available to a larger sector of the population not only courses but also such other facilities and services as, among others, radio and television programs, concerts and lectures, library facilities, audio-visual aids, and faculty consultation. Conferences are arranged for a wide variety of professional, business, labor, and other groups. With no principle to guide in their selection, such activities can be almost indefinitely expansible. We hold that university services ought to be related to college-level education or research and ought not to overlap with other agencies' programs.

Parallel with the experimentation in content there has been one in methods. In an earlier chapter, we tried to deflate those enthusiasts who hold that the discussion group is the best, or even the only valid, medium of education. But if competent subject-matter experts are not available as instructors, then a self-administered discussion group that reads significant works and talks over their implications may be an acceptable substitute in noncredit programs and possibly even in credit courses. Dis-

---

[84] Cf. Houle, *Major Trends*, pp. 34-36.

[85] The index to Beale and Brody's survey of the literature of adult education (1941) has one single entry under "community" (referring to community centers and schools), while that by Sheats, Jayne, and Spence (1953) has forty-four. For a discussion of the "community approach" in public schools, see Julian L. Woodward, "Is the Community Emphasis Overdone?"

[86] Grattan, *In Quest of Knowledge*, p. 298.

cussion groups based on packaged reading programs, the mass media, or a combination of the two, have been sponsored by a number of adult-education organizations, often in collaboration with a university. New methods of teaching have been made possible by various technical developments over the past several decades. Of these, the most important are educational films, audio-visual aids, and, of course, television, whose potentialities for education have hardly begun to be exploited.

If it is true that the level in extension classes is lower than on the main campus, one reason is the distinction between residence and extension credits, for such a compromise helps to maintain the difference in standards by recognizing it as quasi-legitimate. The administrative structure, which half isolates the general-extension division from the rest of the university and forces it to pay its own way in a unique proportion, has of course an important effect on educational standards. Under the usual financial arrangements, it is inevitable that general-extension administrators should constantly be tempted to lower standards—either to branch out into popular and therefore profitable fields, or to ignore educationally valuable new programs because they will not pay for themselves, and in both cases with little regard to what activities are appropriate to an institution of higher learning. Unfortunately, this temptation may sometimes be encouraged by the main-campus administrators, who too often believe that the university's public reputation can be improved if general extension caters to every "felt need," however irresponsibly. These are some of the topics that we will discuss in the next chapter.

5

ON UNIVERSITY NONEDUCATION
FOR ADULTS

The term "community services" is ambiguous. We have used it to designate a great number of extension activities, useful in themselves, that are only loosely related to the education of students or research. Our contention is that the greatest service a university can offer to the community is to perform these limited tasks well. That some of the peripheral activities are worthwhile in themselves is true—and irrelevant. The university, to repeat, is a reservoir of rare and expensive resources, assembled to perform a crucial function. Particularly in the years before us, with the already great strain on institutions of higher education bound to get worse, increasing the burden still more is socially irresponsible. It is as though in the middle of an epidemic the ground floor of a hospital were cleared to make room for fire engines. An argument that the community needs fire-fighting equipment, though often made in the context of university adult education, is not convincing. And it is even less so if not fire engines but gambling tables are substituted for the hospital beds. Our partial, contingent rejection becomes a total one with respect to those "services" devoid of educational content. The distinction must be made sharply, particularly since the terminology is not consistent and "community services" are not always differentiated from "community development."[1]

[1] Some universities term their community services "community development," while others call their community development "community service" or "community organization." See, for example, the description of leadership training, institutes, broadcasting, etc., at the Universities of Alabama, New Mexico, Texas, and Michigan under the heading of "community development" rather than services in "Report of the Committee on Community Organization," *1954 NUEA Proceedings*, pp. 86-102. Even the word *community* has a confusing variety of meanings; see Shannon, "A Study of Objectives," pp. 71-79.

Under the direction of several international agencies, community develop-

Community Development

Community development is the attempt on the part of universities—

to discover ways for helping communities to help themselves through the study and efforts of their citizens. The projects. . . . point in the direction of a new kind of extension education—education for all, education for action on a wide front, education that is democratic in nature and education that comes to grips with the realities that people have to face daily in the homes and communities in which they live.[2]

In other words, community development is an attempt to make over the community and the people in it; to seek out and eliminate any and every deficiency from inadequate sewers to juvenile delinquency, from unemployment to a lack of square dancing; and thus to strengthen again the social cohesion of the citizenry and promote personal and community "growth." In greater detail, the aims of community development can be spelled out as follows:

1. The first goal is to strengthen the "community," identified by some community developers as the village or small town, by others[3] as the neighborhood in a larger city. In either case, the community is a group of persons who interact on the basis of personal, familylike knowledge and sentiments, rather than the businesslike relations of the metropolis. The community, this "backbone of American democracy," has been markedly weakened by the migration of America's population to the anonymous city; and the university, instead of doing something to improve "the quality of living in the small towns and communities from which many of their students are taken," has actually been one of the main offenders in furthering this shift. "The general effect of college life is to withdraw American youth from their

ment is being carried on in a number of under-developed areas of Asia, Africa, the Americas, and Europe. The programs in India and Pakistan have been particularly well publicized (see, for example, *Community Development Review*, No. 6, September 1957). We take no stand on the merit of these programs. For the definitions of community development as used by the Community Development Division of the International Cooperation Administration and by the United Nations, see *Community Development Review*, No. 3, December 1956.

[2] NUEA, *University Extension Experiments*, p. 5.

[3] See, for example, McClusky, "Community Development," p. 246; Sheats, "Present Trends," p. 559; Jones, "Neighborhood Council."

home communities, train them for a specialized, individual-centered career as contrasted to a family-centered or community-centered life, and send them off into the impersonal crowds of a great city."[4] One of the main objectives of the Montana Study thus, was to inhibit the migration of young people from small towns to the city, and this is presently one of the aims of the Department of Community Development at Southern Illinois University.

2. In order to reduce the incentive to leave small towns or in order to convert areas of a city into real neighborhoods, one must improve their physical facilities and social life. The community's problems are discussed in an open meeting, which decides which "needs" are most pressing. This very discussion, culminating in a community decision to act, is seen as an enhancement of the democratic process. In the words of the Ogdens, pioneer community developers in Virginia, "the philosophy on which the program was based was an honest belief in the democratic way of life."[5] Or, in more effulgent prose:

> The community organization movement. . . . is the sole, indispensable, not-to-be-escaped, channel through which freedom of the individual and the "right to life, liberty, and the pursuit of happiness" can be realized.[6]

3. Following the decision to act, the "action-solution" can consist in almost anything. Community developers

> focus directly on the improvement of the immediate conditions of community life. The citizenry must be aided to achieve anything it thinks it needs: a sounder economic structure, health, better sanitation or schools or recreation, a deeper appreciation of the arts, or a more effective political structure.[7]

The way these goals are sought by community developers can

[4] Poston, *Small Town Renaissance*, pp. 23-24. See also Brownell, *The College and the Community*, p. 24; "The College and the Community."

[5] Ogden and Ogden, "Special Projects," p. 118. But in a community-development project in Louisa County, with over 5,000 Negroes, membership was "open to all *white* citizens" (Ogden and Ogden, *Small Communities*, pp. 123, 126). Similarly, Poston and his staff are strengthening segregated communities in southern Illinois.

[6] Rogers, review of the Ogdens' *Small Communities*. The whole sentence is italicized in the original.

[7] Houle, "The Energy of Local Liberty," p. 9.

be described most effectively in terms of an example, and our choice to illustrate the pattern is the well publicized Montana Study. In 1944, the Humanities Division of the Rockefeller Foundation made a $25,000 grant to initiate this program and to support it on a decreasing scale for three years, with the University of Montana providing the balance of the budget each year.[8] According to the application to the foundation, the Montana Study was to be a "research program to determine the contribution of the humanities to a program of higher education designed to improve the quality of living in the State of Montana."[9] Its director was Baker Brownell, whom Poston describes as "the father" of the best type of community development.[10]

The staff began by preparing a discussion outline listing ten topics, one for each meeting, with detailed suggestions and discussion questions; and each meeting of each group was usually led by a member of the staff.[11] "Brownell said he wanted the group to be completely informal, so they refrained from a regular election of officers and everyone just decided to make Free Halverson chairman."[12] The meetings supposedly enable the participants to get to know their community and to identify its most pressing problem or problems.

After their use in the application to the Rockefeller Foundation, the words "higher education" do not appear again in Poston's book, which has Brownell's endorsement. The "humanities" are mentioned frequently, in the sense of "everything from having

[8] According to Poston, the study received only partial and reluctant cooperation from the six institutions that make up the University (*Small Town Renaissance*, pp. 118-119 and *passim*).

[9] *Ibid.*, p. 20.

[10] Poston, *Democracy is You*, p. ix. Poston wrote this book while he was director of the Bureau of Community Development at the University of Washington; in October 1957 it was still in use there as a study guide for communities being developed, according to a letter from Frank Anderson, Poston's successor.

[11] Brownell, "The Montana Study."

[12] Poston, *Small Town Renaissance*, pp. 41-42. We are reminded of Houle's comment in "The Development of Leadership," p. 57: "For the old rigidity of content, there is imposed a new rigidity of method. For forced formality, there is substituted a forced informality. . . . As one examines the excess of zeal to which some of the leaders of antithesis have gone, one is compelled to conclude that they have no more real respect for the dignity and maturity of their students than do those who would insist that adults must learn by the same patterns and processes as do children."

a good time to making a living."[13] A tentative program for "one year's community cultural events" was drawn up as part of the "renaissance"[14]:

January—New Year's Celebration and Winter Sports Day
February—Washington-Lincoln Dinner and Home Orchestra Concert
March—Community Drama Day
April—Singing Night
May—Garden Day
June—Graduation Day and Chorus
July—Community Picnic
August—Ice Cream Night
September—School and Teachers' Night
October—Hunter's Day and Game Dinner
November—Harvest Festival and Thanksgiving Dinner
December—Christmas Chorus and Community Tree.

The accomplishments claimed for the Montana Study include fourteen discussion groups set up in three years, several recreational programs, new small businesses, health services—even one small library,[15] as though as a partial concession to learning, if not to higher education.

While the Montana Study has had an important influence, there have been various patterns of community development. In the early days the extension division "offered its services rather insistently"[16] to communities considered by the staff to be in need of improvement; and once a program was started the professional organizers also carried the major responsibility for its continuation. While the extension division now usually waits until the community invites it in, this invitation is frequently solicited or contrived.[17] "Sometimes it is hard to find a felt need for the community to rally round."[18] Extension personnel call the first meeting, or are present at one organized by a community group. They encourage more meetings, with if possible more participants, who

[13] Brownell as quoted by Poston in *Small Town Renaissance*, p. 40. See also Brownell, "The Value of the Humanities."
[14] Poston, *Small Town Renaissance*, p. 208. This is an excerpt from Poston's condensation of the study guide prepared by the Montana Study staff for use throughout the state.
[15] Brownell, "The Montana Study."
[16] Ogden and Ogden, *Small Communities*, p. 129.
[17] Orcutt, "The Role of the College," pp. 68-69.
[18] A community-development consultant quoted in *ibid.*, p. 79.

discuss the problem and decide what needs to be done about it, under the "nondirective" guidance of the general-extension division.

What has been accomplished by community-development programs? To what degree were the stated goals achieved? Most of the reports have been written while the programs were still in progress, or shortly after their completion; and they overflow with optimistic statements about "new creative relationships," "growth," "added insight," "action programs for better living," and sometimes even the expectation of new interest in educational activities. In the large literature on community development there appears to be no mention of a discussion that, at least after the first warming up, did not go well. There is no suggestion that some discussion may be nonproductive or that any action program resulting from such discussions may not always be an unqualified success.

The universal approbation with which its proponents view community development suggests that they have no standards by which to judge what is worthwhile. Any program that materializes is *ipso facto* good. One reason a more critical evaluation is not attempted is that so many of the goals of community development are defined too vaguely to be measured. Its proponents generally maintain, for example, that they are more interested in the "personal growth" of the individual participants and in "community growth" than in the achievement of material goals.[19] This disclaimer of interest in the physical results of action programs, however, is neither consistent nor unanimous. While all the university consultants on community development that Orcutt interviewed agreed that "working together has an impact upon the community and individuals that is more important than any other results," they all also said that the problem picked by the group must not be too difficult, for otherwise the resulting action will not be successful.[20] "The ultimate test

[19] See, for example, Houle, "The Energy of Local Liberty." Characteristically, the list of "needed research" at the end of Orcutt's thesis does not include examining the meaning of "growth" resulting from community development, or ways of measuring it; nor does he, in 171 typewritten pages on "The Role of the College or University Consultant in Community Development," raise the fundamental question of whether this role is legitimate.

[20] Orcutt, "The Role of the College," pp. 77, 90-91. He interviewed 19

of discussion which focuses upon devising action-solutions to problems always lies beyond the process of discussion itself in the consequences of action undertaken."[21]

Even when a goal is one that can be precisely defined, success in reaching it is not necessarily evaluated. For example, one of the objectives of the Montana Study, as has been noted above, was to halt the cityward migration of young people; but apparently none of the many works appraising this program—neither Poston's book-length study nor several articles by Brownell and members of his staff—ever state whether this goal was attained nor even refer to it in the so-called evaluations.[22]

Long before community development was established in university adult education, innumerable agencies existed whose specific function it was—and is—to encourage citizen groups to cooperate in getting better community services, or a library, or folk-dance groups, or whatever. Many such programs have been carried out by social welfare agencies, both private[23] and public; industrial concerns; chambers of commerce; various government bureaus[24] and the Cooperative Extension Service. None of these agencies, it should be noted, have as their primary function college-level education and research. This includes even the Cooperative Extension Service, though it is attached to universities.

---

persons in all, whom he considered to be about 20 per cent of the country's university consultants on community development, but since the 19 were chosen mainly on the basis of their proximity to New York, they were not a "statistical sampling" (*ibid.*, pp. 60, 63).

[21] Benne, Bradford, and Lippitt, "Stages in the Process of Group Thinking and Discussion," in Sheats et al., *Adult Education*, pp. 334-342 at p. 341.

[22] See, for example—in addition to Poston's book—Brownell, "The Montana Study," "The Montana Project"; Hansen, "An Evaluation of the Montana Study," "A Project in Community Education," "Darby, Montana, Looks at Itself." Mr. Hansen's special responsibility on the study staff was "community pageant-dramas."

[23] For example, the National Conference on Family Life, the Conference on Children and Youth, the Conference on Citizenship, the American Council on the Community, the Advisory Committee on Citizen Participation, the Regional Planning Association, the National Commission for the Public Schools (Spence and Cass, *Guide for Program Service*, pp. 22-24).

[24] Some of the government agencies active in community development are the Home Economics Department of the U.S. Office of Education (see, for example, Brown, *With Focus on Family Living*); the Department of Commerce (see, for example, *Small Town Manual for Community Action!*); state planning boards with projects in, for example, Iowa, South Dakota, and Tennessee (Manny, *Rural Community Organization*); state economic councils

Under the various laws by which it was established and defined, it has a specific mandate both to convert the findings of university research into education assimilable by the whole of the general public, and to assist the people of the area in many other ways. Neither function can be properly ascribed to the university itself. Cooperative Extension, moreover, is financed not out of the university budget, but out of federal, state, and county appropriations.[25]

The dimensions of the work done by these various agencies can be illustrated by discussing very briefly some of the activities of the Cooperative Extension Service. Many of its 9,000 county agents and some of its state specialists, assisted by many more volunteers, are engaged in various community-improvement programs. "Throughout the country, extension agents assisted 34,100 communities with their recreational facilities, 57,600 community groups with organization problems, nearly 7,000 communities in obtaining library facilities, and 2,266 communities in building community houses."[26] Together with other federal and state agencies, the Cooperative Extension Service is currently expanding a federally financed "rural development" program on a community, county, and regional basis.[27]

It would be impossible to maintain realistically that community development is a neglected field, or even that the particular emphasis of university community developers has been bypassed. It is simply not true that "unless adult educators see to it that it happens, there will not be citizen participation in community development programs." In replying to this allegation, one social worker referred to his own profession, which "over a period of decades has developed the professional practice of 'community

---

(see, for example, "Government by the People"); departments of public instruction (see, for example, Gucky and Corey, "A Community Organizes to Help Itself"); and public high schools through their Citizenship Education Projects (see, for example, Johnson and Harless, "Implications of the Citizenship Education Project").

[25] See below, Appendix 1.

[26] Matthews, "The Cooperative Extension Service," pp. 68-69. Reports for Alabama, Arkansas, Georgia, Illinois, Iowa, Kentucky, Louisiana, Mississippi, North Carolina, Oklahoma, South Carolina, Tennessee, and Texas are listed in Manny, *Rural Community Organization*, pp. 36-49. See also Garrett, "The Influence of Extension," p. 5.

[27] See *Extension Service Review*, Vol. 29, No. 3, March, 1958.

organization for social welfare.' "[28] Nor have adult educators brought a higher level of competence to the well staffed field of community development. And it has even happened that citizen groups have accomplished a limited objective without outside organizational help.[29]

Many adult educators are neither for nor against including community development in their field, but merely skeptical: the effectiveness of action projects and "the extent to which the university should participate in them are still open to discussion."[30] Others, however, deny the relevance of community development to adult education. At the 1955 national meeting of the Adult Education Association, according to Powell, "a threatened split over 'community development' and 'education' was averted . . . by the statesmanlike persuasions of Cyril Houle, Kenneth Benne, and Howard McClusky."[31] In reply to strong statements denying that community development is a legitimate function of adult education,[32] its advocates assert their cause with the fervor of missionaries.[33] Democracy, they say, is doomed unless adult education comes to its rescue. A university-inspired, locally implemented revival of the neighborhood is urgently needed to counteract the "malevolent influences of rampant urbanism."[34] Community development, according to one community developer, "has the potential to bring a rebirth of spirit in America and to

[28] Albert G. Rosenberg, executive secretary of the Area Councils Project, Dayton, Ohio, in "The Role of Adult Education in Community Development," p. 18. The adult educators participating in this symposium, on whose point of view Mr. Rosenberg was commenting, were Otto G. Hoiberg (at the time Coordinator of Community Service, University Extension Division, University of Nebraska), H. Curtis Mial (at the time executive director, New York State Citizens' Council), Eugene I. Johnson (then coordinator, Community Education Program, San Bernardino Valley College), Watson Dickerman and staff (Community Adult Education Department, Extension Service, University of Michigan), and Weldon R. Oliver (director of Adult Education, Niagara Falls, New York).

[29] See, for example, the description of the Sycamore Court Block Group in Thelen and Sarchet, *Neighbors in Action.*

[30] Siegle and Whipple, *New Directions in Programming,* p. 50.

[31] Powell, *Learning Comes of Age,* p. 204.

[32] See, for example, Gruen, "A Pragmatic Criticism"; McGhee, "Adult Education."

[33] Shannon, after reviewing the literature on community development from 1940 to 1955, also comments on the "hortatory quality" of statements by its advocates ("A Study of Objectives," p. 276).

[34] *Ibid.,* p. 130.

eliminate war and starvation from the earth."[35] "Survival of the university depends upon survival of the community. Unless the university dedicates itself to the support of the community, both will perish."[36]

The disagreement over the propriety of including community development in a university's program has not, however, prevented its expansion.[37] Whether one measures the influence of community development by the number of universities with such programs, by the recognition of the professional societies of adult education, or by its literature, it is manifest that this field has grown rapidly during the past two decades. According to a 1956 survey of community-development programs in NUEA institutions, most of them were less than ten years old.[38] As far back as 1951-1952, Morton found that 43 per cent among his sample of NUEA general-extension divisions were engaged in community development.[39] In 1955, the NUEA replaced its *Committee* on Community Organization, which for some years had been at least partly concerned with community development, with a *Division* of Community Development.[40] Michigan State University has recently appropriated $1.5 million for a community-development program in suburban areas. Among 2,000 members of the Adult Education Association, almost a third denote community development as one of their three major areas of interest within adult education.[41]

There are various indications that this rapid growth will con-

[35] Poston, *Democracy is You*, p. ix. See also Poston, "The American Community in Trouble"; Sheats, "The Responsibility of the Evening College."

[36] Shannon, "A Study of Objectives," pp. 280-281.

[37] While some ambiguity remains concerning the meaning of "community services" and "community development," the two terms have been differentiated enough to make it possible to discuss trends in the latter. In each of the examples we cite, the meaning given to "community development" was clear from the context.

[38] Shannon, "A Study of Objectives," p. 22.

[39] Calculated from Morton, *University Extension*, Table 21, p. 41. See Hunsaker, "What Are the Responsibilities," p. 88, for the names of some of these institutions.

[40] "Report of the Division of Community Development," *1956 NUEA Proceedings*, pp. 42-43. For activities of the earlier committee, which had been set up in 1948, see, for example, its "Resources for Community Development Programs," prepared under the chairmanship of Hoiberg. See also Lackey, "Eight Communities in Action."

[41] Nicholls and Brunner, "Composition of AEA," p. 220.

tinue. "At least one major university is now planning to establish a five-year degree program in this field."[42] Professor Poston sees it as his function as chairman of the Division of Community Development of the NUEA to spread this type of program as widely as possible through universities. He succeeded in getting the Sears Roebuck Foundation to finance a two-year project in which NUEA universities will cooperate in training members of the General Federation of Women's Clubs. As he put it—

I was impressed by the almost unlimited potential for community development throughout the world if these 11,000,000 women [the world membership of the Federation] could have the benefit of the necessary training and field consultation that could be provided through university extension if our NUEA member institutions either could or would see fit to equip themselves to provide such training and field consultation. And, in this possibility, I saw what I believe could be one of the greatest opportunities of this century for university extension to contribute toward the enrichment of American life and the preservation of free society.[43]

A meeting held to plan further steps in this project included representatives of the following universities: New York State, Utah, Washington, Virginia, Maryland, Kansas State, California, and, of course, Poston's own bailiwick, Southern Illinois. Not all of these institutions had the necessary staff, but this lack could be remedied.

In our opinion, community development is not only not college-level education or research; it is not these at any level. It is not research: community developers do not even pretend that they go into a community, as anthropologists or sociologists would, in order to study its workings; and in any case it would be an empty pretense, for they are not trained to make empirical studies of any scientific value. And it is not education.[44] Indeed, some of

[42] Hiett, "Community Organization," p. 57; he may be referring to Southern Illinois University, where Poston directs a department of community development.

[43] Poston, "Report of the Chairman," p. 26.

[44] An adult educator who was kind enough to comment on the first draft of this work challenged this point. One learns from the experiences that the community developers arrange; therefore they are "educators." By a similar logic one might argue that a traffic policeman who teaches us to stay within the speed limit, and the judge who fines us if we do not, and the scores of other occupational types whose authority gives them a measure of social control, are all "educators."

the attacks on education that community developers have made are as strong and as Philistine as one is likely to find in print. A commentary on a group sitting around exchanging funny stories, for example:

> Lonepine was participating in a form of culture that certain intellectuals might not appreciate, but to these people it meant more than tea at the Metropolitan or a course in the classical works of art.[45]

Or, as another instance:

> Teaching, particularly at the university level, has emphasized the giving of information. The man whose gizzard is chock full of facts and who scratches diligently for more facts is honored; the practitioner is not. . . . To talk learnedly about juvenile delinquency in a class or institute on the campus is easy compared to helping John Doe and Rachel Roe do something about juvenile delinquency in the town of Crossroads. There the scholar is often at a discount and what counts is know-how in human relations, . . . and maybe a good hand at poker or a guitar.[46]

Community development is a social-welfare—or, better, a social-reform—movement. That its aims may be worthy is not relevant.[47] There are many other institutions designed and financed to perform these functions; and the fact that even Cooperative Extension engages in community development is another good reason why general extension should not. A university's decision to use money for community development means, in effect, a decision that in some way, in quality or quantity, the adult education offered shall be less. Community development does not come "anywhere near paying for itself" in any part of the country.[48] Writing about the Department of Communitiy De-

[45] Poston, *Small Town Renaissance*, p. 47.

[46] Unpublished report, Carnegie Study Committee on Community Development, Hugh G. Pyle, chairman, excerpted in Sheats et al., *Adult Education*, pp. 195-196.

[47] If it were appropriate here, we would challenge at length the ethical worth and empirical validity of many of the basic tenets of community development; see above, pp. 33-35. In Crabtree's words, "In a society that presupposes the dignity and identity of the individual, we cannot proceed on any premise that prescribes his total absorption into the group" (comment on Poston's article, "The Relation of Community Development to Adult Education").

[48] Unpublished report, Carnegie Study Committee on Community Development, Hugh G. Pyle, chairman, excerpted in Sheats et al., *Adult Education*, pp. 195-196. See also "Report of the Committee on Community Organization," *1950 NUEA Proceedings*, pp. 197-198.

velopment at Southern Illinois University and similar activities at the University of Washington, Poston asserted that their "increase in budget and the spread of the work have been effected in the face of economy measures in virtually every other area of adult education."[49] This boasting is particularly distasteful when we contrast this "increase in budget" with the finances of other extension activities.

Extension as a Money-Maker

Too many universities regard their general-extension divisions as commercial rather than educational ventures. Among the evening colleges surveyed by Neuffer, only 11 per cent were permitted to retain any excess of income over expenses; that is, 89 per cent of these evening colleges refund to their parent institutions a part of the funds allocated to them, whenever they show a profit.[50] About three-quarters of the independent liberal arts colleges with adult programs studied by Crimi said "that they are realizing a direct financial surplus from their adult work."[51] "Because of the complexities of accounting systems it is difficult to estimate the amount of this contribution but in many institutions it will range as high as 40 per cent of the evening college's income."[52] In Canada, "in all but a few universities, the entire service 'pays its way' and in some it turns back a substantial cash surplus into the general revenues of the university."[53]

Where does extension income come from?[54] Miscellaneous sources do not ordinarily amount to much. Some general-extension divisions have a small profit from the sale of materials and of tickets to lectures and similar events.[55] Services to industry,

[49] Poston, "The Relation of Community Development," p. 196.
[50] Neuffer, *Administrative Policies*, pp. 4-5; see also Reals, "The Evening College," pp. 48-49. See Dugan, "An Extension Class Program," pp. 89-91, for a discussion of the management of fee income at NUEA institutions.
[51] Crimi, *Adult Education*, p. 33.
[52] Bell, "Finance," p. 146.
[53] Kidd, *Adult Education*, p. 99.
[54] Once again, this discussion pertains almost entirely to that portion of the total extension function administered by the general-extension divisions. The financial arrangements of other portions seem not to differ very greatly, but there is no systematic study to back up this supposition.
[55] Thompson, *University Extension*, p. 245. Except for the last sentence, the data in the rest of this paragraph are from Morton, *University Extension*, pp. 96-104.

government agencies, other colleges, hospitals, voluntary health agencies, and miscellaneous organizations are sometimes the source of a substantial income; but this is the exceptional case. Conferences, on the other hand, are run at a loss: of the annual average of $50,000 spent on them, the participants furnished only $46,000. Libraries incur a much greater deficit: total library income from fees ranged from $325 to $4,000 per year, as compared with library expenditures of from $2,000 to $55,000. Film and audio-visual services are given at a deficit of between 25 and 60 per cent. Funds for university broadcasting come almost entirely from state and institutional appropriations, except for a few intermittent and occasional gifts. Community development, as we have pointed out, is an expensive boondoggle.

The major source of extension income is student fees, as can be seen from the data compiled in Table 3. Since no two of the studies cited include the same institutions, the figures are not wholly comparable. The range is wide: in 1954, four general-extension divisions were *wholly* supported by student fees, and three not at all.[56] Nevertheless, there is in general a sharp contrast with both Cooperative Extension[57] and regular daytime sessions.[58] If we take 60 per cent as the average proportion of general-extension income derived from student fees, this is more than three times the comparable figure for the regular campus. Most of the balance is allocated—at least in bookkeeping terms—from the over-all university budget, only about 4 per cent of which goes to support the general-extension division.[59]

An unofficial but important source of income is the preposterously low salaries paid to general-extension faculties. Some universities do not pay faculty members at all for participating in their conferences or giving evening or off-campus lectures as part

[56] See Association of Land-Grant Colleges and Universities, *A Study of Problems*, Table II, p. 33; III, p. 34; V, p. 36. These tables are based on questionnaires sent to 73 of the then 93 members of the association, and returned by 60.

[57] *Ibid.*, Table I, p. 32.

[58] In 1952, a date comparable with that of most of the studies cited in Table 3, only 17.4 per cent of the total current income from the regular sessions of all 1,832 institutions of higher education in the United States, both publicly and privately controlled, came from student fees (calculated from U.S. Census Bureau, *Statistical Abstract, 1955*, Table 147, p. 125).

[59] Morton, *University Extension*, Table 56, p. 97.

TABLE 3. Median Percentage of General-Extension Division
Income Derived from Student Fees

Sample	Year	Median Percentage
8 land-grant colleges[1]	1954	52-58
7 state universities[1]	1954	57
22 land-grant colleges combined with state universities[1]	1954	73-75
47 NUEA members[2]	1952	78
46 NUEA members[3]	1951-52	61-70
7 state universities[4]	1949	45
36 NUEA members[3]	1940	71-80
10 universities[5]	1939	50*
28 NUEA members[3]	1930	51-60

* Average rather than median.

[1] Association of Land-Grant Colleges and Universities, A *Study of Problems*; calculated from Tables II, III, and V, pp. 33-36.

[2] Dugan, "An Extension Class Program," p. 88.

[3] Morton, *University Extension*, Table 57, p. 98.

[4] Quoted in Sheats et al., *Adult Education*, p. 435, n.

[5] Thompson, *University Extension*, p. 245.

of the general-extension division's program.[60] And whatever the rank of those who teach in extension, they usually get paid for this less than the lowest rank of instructor on their home campus.[61] A disproportionate number of extension teachers are either full professors, who can lay claim to a greater share of the small plums that become available, or beginning instructors, who must take these assignments if no one else wants them. This bimodal distribution may be one reason for the sharply opposed views about extension teachers. According to one survey, they are "somewhat above the average of the faculty in their respec-

[60] "Report of the Division of Conferences and Institutes, 1955-56," *1956 NUEA Proceedings*, pp. 38-39; "Report of the Committee on Lectures and Concerts," *1957 NUEA Proceedings*, p. 69. See also the recommendations of Workshop Group 2 in *1954 AUEC Proceedings*, p. 119.

[61] Calculated from Morton, *University Extension*, Table 52, p. 85, and Council for Financial Aid to Education, *Backing Up Brains*, p. 5. Whether there has been a change in this situation in the last two or three years, parallel with the upward trend in regular faculty salaries, is difficult to establish. The *1958 NUEA Proceedings*, for instance, contains information on this matter (pp. 72-73), but the questions on faculty salaries were answered by only slightly more than half of the 66 institutions to which they had been sent—generally those, one can reasonably presume, that pay more.

tive departments both in scholarship and in teaching ability"[62]; according to another, "in general, an insufficient number of instructors, poorly qualified instructors, and a limitation of the extension class program tended to be the consequence of low stipends."[63]

The rank of extension teachers is in any case less important than the quality of extension teaching. Faculty members who receive their status and income from their position on the main campus understandably expend most of their thought and effort in their teaching, research, and writing there; and if because of their low salaries they are induced to teach also in general extension, many do this reluctantly and undoubtedly devote less effort to what is—according to the catalogue listing—an identical course.[64] Where the income of part-time faculty depends on the number of students in their classes, as it still did in nearly one-fourth of the extension centers surveyed by Morton,[65] the instructors are given a direct money incentive to make their courses popular. A popular course may be one in which the teacher makes a special effort to be well prepared, to make his classes meaningful; and in that case teaching can "evoke the highest level of his abilities as a teacher." Or it may mean a class whose teacher goes "overboard in the direction of showmanship and cheapens the experience for himself and for his students."[66] In the abstract, one might say that either possibility is equally likely; but under the actual administrative conditions that generally prevail in extension courses (though not in evening colleges), it is

[62] Sorenson, *Adult Abilities*, p. 117.
[63] Dugan, "An Extension Class Program," p. 95. In his survey of more or less the same institutions, Morton found a higher proportion of faculty in the upper academic ranks teaching correspondence classes than in the parent institution, but a lower proportion of full and associate professors teaching extension classes, and a still lower percentage on extension-center faculties (*University Extension*, p. 81).
[64] See Houle and Nelson, *The University*, p. 152.
[65] Morton, *University Extension*, p. 84. For part-time instructors of extension classes, as differentiated from those teaching in extension centers, the equivalent figure was about 10 per cent (Table 50, p. 84). While all 62 members of the AUEC that replied on this point to the 1957 questionnaire stated that the number of students enrolled is not the basis on which faculty pay is determined, 25 institutions did not answer at all and 24 others omitted this question (*1957 AUEC Proceedings*, p. 95).
[66] Letter from Dean McGhee, July 21, 1958.

more probable, as Sorenson indicates, that academic standards are sacrificed to the customers' satisfaction.[67]

Many spokesmen for general extension have deplored the fact that it is required to be self-supporting to so great a degree.[68] Indeed, as extension divisions are presently financed, the inadequacy of funds affects everything in university adult education, from organization and administration to faculty and courses.

In some institutions, the criterion of financial success appears to be more highly regarded than is the principle of educational effectiveness. This emphasis on profit is typically imposed upon, rather than willingly accepted by, the dean or director. Regardless of where the responsibility lies within the university, however, it is clear from repeated testimony that many institutions place adult education at a distinct disadvantage in comparison with other university functions, requiring of it a budgetary performance that would be considered an absurd criterion of success if applied to other educational activities. To the extent that money-making becomes paramount, education must become subordinate.[69]

Extension as a Public-Relations Activity

The debasement of extension prevails also in another sense. From the point of view of the president's office, one of the important functions of the division is to develop a positive attitude toward the whole institution among voters and legislators, or among potential donors.[70] By extending itself into the community, in part by welcoming citizens to attend events on campus, the university hopes to establish a greater understanding of both its achievements and its problems. Such a favorable climate of opinion with respect to education is, of course, especially important to public institutions. No reasonable person would challenge this purpose. While in theory all Americans favor a good educational system, in fact they are notoriously penurious whenever they are asked to support it, and an effort to bring the fact closer

[67] Sorenson, *Adult Abilities*, pp. 97-98.
[68] As two examples out of many, see Keller, "What Should We Expect," p. 28; Godard, "Relation of Academic Standards."
[69] Houle and Nelson, *The University*, p. 154.
[70] See, for example, Meder, "The University Providing Service," p. 91; Crimi, *Adult Education*, pp. 30, 34. See also Kidd, *Adult Education*, pp. 94-95, for statements to this effect by the presidents of several Canadian universities.

to the ideology is both legitimate and worthwhile.

There is a tendency, however, for universities to equate good public relations with customer sovereignty. The school in educational philosophy that has misinterpreted the meaning of "democracy"[71] has its counterpart in educational administration.

The university wishes to cement the bonds between itself and its public. It therefore—often with the statement that it is "meeting needs"—attempts to enrol as many adults as it can, preferably adults holding some key place in the social hierarchy, in any sort of course of study for which it can find a market. . . . The programmes thus lose all intellectual responsibility, because they are not designed to help adults solve an intellectual problem or explore a new field of interest.[72]

In a recent debate among several deans representing member institutions of the AUEC, John S. Diekhoff, then professor of education at Hunter College, argued that programs be offered even if "stimulation may be required to attract" participants; while Alfred C. Nelson, dean of Community College, University of Denver, favored solely those set up in "response to felt needs" and as "a reflection of public demand":

If institutions did not set out to offer broad offerings in response to demonstrated need, these individuals would be lost to higher education . . . and . . . would consider colleges and universities as available to only the few. . . . [Moreover] taking them where they are and directing them where they should be . . . [is] far more enjoyable to both students and faculty than the more restricted accomplishments with "captive audiences" fettered by the limitations of credit work.[73]

The moderator of the debate made the peace "by stating that most schools of his acquaintance operated uneasily somewhere between the two standards."[74] According to the editor of the *Proceedings* in which this exchange appears, the audience did not dispute this "no-decision," as he calls it.

[71] See above, pp. 20 ff.
[72] Houle, "Introduction," p. 19. Cf. Cohen, *Citizen Education*, p. 59, for a similar comment concerning some foreign-affairs programs of private organizations; Fernbach, *University Extension*, p. 7, concerning the influence of this factor on university-sponsored workers' education.
[73] *1957 AUEC Proceedings*, pp. 55-57.
[74] Harry L. Miller of the Center for the Study of Liberal Education for Adults, in *ibid.*, p. 57.

The notion that university educators should begin with their charges "where they are" is a recurrent theme; but the road from *Kitsch* to art, from lack of interest to involvement, from lackadaisical pottering to academic disciplines, or, most typically, from noneducation to education, has not been mapped by Dean Nelson or any other ideologue of the "soft pedagogy." "A course in sanitary engineering may finally bring the students to an understanding of the glories of Shakespeare, although I must confess that the intermediate steps are hazy in my mind."[75] Education is a process (the literal meaning is "a bringing forth"); and a good teacher is one who begins—and stays—not where his students are but ahead of them, inducing them to move toward him.

There is no evidence, moreover, to support the notion that abandoning standards *does* improve a university's public relations. Some of the public, on the contrary, might resent paying taxes (or making donations) to help support such courses as one in wrapping Christmas packages, or in "Charm,"[76] or in fishing.[77]

A number of . . . public institutions which formerly felt that political pressure required that they accept all high school graduates have now stiffened their entrance requirements and discovered, to their surprise, that by doing so they have won almost universal approbation. Is there a lesson here for higher adult education?[78]

In other words, the best way for a university to maintain a good reputation is to deserve it. "The first prerequisite for good public relations is to be sure that you have a good product to sell,"[79] and the definition of a "good product," while it may be influenced by the public's demands, is in the domain of the professional educator. The legitimate functions of a public relations office are to

[75] Houle, "An Appraisal of the American University's Role in Adult Education," quoted in Kidd, *Adult Education*, p. 105. Cf. Miller, "Group Discussion."

[76] The general-extension divisions of the Universities of Colorado and New Mexico, respectively, actually did offer these courses in 1957.

[77] At the same meeting of the AUEC, Dean Nelson suggested that, if he changed the title of his course in "Fishing" to "Piscatorial Science," critics might well find it acceptable as a university course (*1957 AUEC Proceedings*, p. 60).

[78] Houle, *Major Trends*, p. 8.

[79] Holt, "Extension's Role," p. 51.

explain to the people why policies that have been adopted are necessary and in their interest, and thus to develop a greater understanding of the true purpose of a university.

Summary

The extension of the university to other regions of the state or sectors of the population, with new areas of learning and methods of transmitting them, has included also functions— recreation, social welfare and reform, commercialism, and public relations—that do not jibe with the purposes of an institution of higher learning. Community development, a relatively recent interest of universities but one that has grown rapidly in the postwar period, is a prime example of university noneducation. According to a good deal of evidence, the adult educators in community development have gone into an already well staffed field, to which they contribute nothing that is new and little that is useful. We believe that community development has no place in the program of a university.

A British adult educator, after visiting a number of American campuses and encountering in their general-extension divisions courses in bridge and golf, wrote:

> There seem to be only two major arguments in favor of the practice. One is the hope that a student once attracted to the programme by such an interest will come into contact with more genuinely educational ones, and proceed to take them up. Our own experience is that this hardly ever happens, and that the non-educational activity may even tend to draw students away from educational ones and develop a centrifugal tendency in relation to the educational centre of the programme. . . . The other argument is much more practical: pure entertainment dressed up as classes is a sure money-spinner and provides a welcome subsidy for genuinely educational activities. The question is whether its effect on the rest of the programme and the spirit of the institution is worth risking.[80]

In most cases adult education has the status of a poor relation to other university divisions, "like Lazarus, stand[ing] waiting to catch the crumbs that fall from the degree tables."[81] The share of the university's budget allotted to the general-extension

[80] Elsdon, *Reality and Purpose*, pp. 4-5.
[81] McGhee, "Higher Education," p. 201.

division is ordinarily determined less by its requirements than by what is left over when all other demands have been met. Very often, this arrangement is by the common consent of both university and general-extension administrators. The former too frequently perceive the adult division as a means of buying good will (and perhaps even of making a bit for the university on the side). And the latter so frequently lack a clear idea of either their educational objectives or the organizational means to achieve them that their divisions have been shaped to an inordinate degree by their chronic need to produce income.

Good educational policy cannot be effected merely by reforming the usual financial arrangement, but if this remains the same no other change is likely to be significant. Under the present system, about 60 per cent of extension-division income is derived from student fees, a relatively inelastic source. In effect, most of the balance comes from the faculty, who are generally paid less than beginning instructors on the home campus. The only way to meet the problem is to view adult education within the context of an educational institution, and not as a commercial venture, a social gathering, or a general means for doing good, and to bring it meaningfully within the university's organization. This is the subject of the following chapter.

6

RECAPITULATION: A GUIDE TO POLICY

The word *policy* has two meanings, either the sum of administrative decisions or the general principles from which these decisions flow. We use it in the second sense, to denote the relation between abstract statements of what is desirable and the specific applications of these to particular conditions. As we have already noted, policy in the deductive rather than inductive sense is a rather rare commodity in university adult education.

Every college and university in the nation is in one way or another engaged in adult education activities. These activities have grown so rapidly and institutions have been so busy responding to these demands that relatively few have had the time or the resources to examine the implications of this development.[1]

Adult education is at best a poorly charted sea, and the "creative challenge" of unexplored areas has induced many a captain of extension to sail his ship on the reefs of triviality and sloth, where its standards break up one by one and the vessel finally sinks into the murky depths of commercialism.

Setting policy is necessary, but it is not so simple a matter as in what we have termed standard education (that is, all but adult education). Educational philosophies differ, but with respect to the primary and secondary schools or colleges, the framework of the differences is set by the relative homogeneity of a student body of about the same age and with more or less the same educational background and goals. A discussion of standard education can begin, thus, without having first to define the institution, the student, the degree, the period of residence, and so on. In adult education, on the contrary, each of these axiomatic categories is an object both of dispute and, more often, of obfuscation. We found it necessary, therefore, to include a section,

[1] Hunsaker, "What Are the Responsibilities," p. 87.

125

Chapter 2, in which we attempt to define some of the most important terms used in adult education.

If in this volume we have often taken a negative stance, it is because we accept university adult education as an institution good and valuable in itself. Its functions, in the words of John S. Diekhoff, are as follows:

1. The primary aim of evening colleges should be learning, not social reform, recreation, or therapy.
2. [Their] objectives should be to offer opportunity to students to acquire new knowledge, new skills, and [to] develop the capacity for self-education.
3. This kind of learning should be appropriate to the university: intellectual, dignified, and leading to interest in the latest research.
4. Colleges should thus recognize their special mission and their special clientele; i.e., people of intellectual competence and prior knowledge, and leave the lesser tasks to other agencies.[2]

The reader of this book knows by now that in this statement Diekhoff was not speaking for the whole of his profession and, even more, that much of university adult education deviates greatly from the standards he suggests. For when the intention is to offer programs of such quality, this high purpose is frequently frustrated by, for example, the necessity of mixing commercialism with education. In short, to be effective policy must guide not only the educational ends but also, and equally, the organizational means by which they are presumably to be achieved.

How are general-extension divisions—or, better, all of the facilities for university adult education—organized; and how does this actual structure compare with one best suited for their purpose? What of their staffs, their administrative rules, their relation with the rest of the university? These are the key questions, and in order to discuss them in full context we shall summarize relevant portions of preceding chapters.

Should the University Engage in Adult Education?

The answer to this question, the most fundamental in setting extension policy, is not obvious. It has become axiomatic in the United States that free public education should be available through high school, and this principle has been extended also

[2] *1957 AUEC Proceedings*, p. 56.

to include the regular day curriculum of public colleges. Whether tax money should be used to support adult education, however, is still a moot issue, which includes questions more basic than the manner in which the institution should be financed. Opposition to the general-extension division among main-campus administrators and faculty is often related to their fear that its low level will come to pervade the whole university, but this again does not touch on the most essential question. Supposing an administrative system could be established by which the quality of extension work could be guaranteed, should the university then divert some of its scarce faculty and facilities to the education of adults?

It is arguable that the answer to this question should be No, at least for noncredit programs. Even those who believe that learning should be a life-long process might well hold that, from a certain point on, organized education is no longer necessary. Should not adults who have been taught to read—particularly those qualified to enroll in a university program—be able to use, for example, the country's public-library system and thus continue to learn on their own?

There is something pathetic in the mature adult still dependent on a school for intellectual stimulus and intellectual security. . . . At some point schooling should be terminal. "Terminal schooling" should be a self-explanatory phrase: it is the schooling which leads not to more schooling but to self-education.[3]

We also would disagree with adult educators who believe in life-long enrollment, ranging from programs in vocational improvement or marriage guidance during early adulthood to, finally, those designed to help one adjust to widowhood or retirement.[4] This is the perspective, we believe, of one or another type. There is first the "educator" who views education less as a learning process than as a way of combating alienation and loneliness. One can also become a life member of Arthur Murray's dancing schools: the number of dances to be learned each year may be limited, but it is always pleasurable to meet congenial people

---

[3] Diekhoff, *Schooling for Maturity*, pp. 5-7. See also his "From the Cradle to the Grave."

[4] See, for example, Burkett, *Comprehensive Programming*.

and do with them the things one enjoys. Then there is, second, the "educator" who refuses on principle to admit that there is a limit to the educability of anyone. Given the very great differences in innate ability, home environment, and interest, such a misconceived "democracy" can be applied only by abolishing standards, catering to those who attend a program for the wrong reasons.

In spite of these strictures, we believe (as does Professor Diekhoff) that university adult education has an important place in present-day American life, and we devoted the first chapter of this volume to an extended argument for this position. Many adults are less well educated in the formal sense than would be desirable for both their own and society's welfare, and while they may know how to read they have not learned what is worth reading. One reason for this is that public education in the United States has developed over the past generation or two, with the consequence that many gaps have been left. In any case American society is changing so rapidly that even an adequate education can become dated very quickly. Engineers, physicians, accountants, and other professionals find it convenient to keep up with the latest developments in their specialties through courses, which represent only the most obvious kind of educational adaptation to social change. The American population is highly mobile in every sense. Each year one out of every five persons moves to a different home, and many of these removals are combined with a change of job or even of occupation. This high rate of social mobility is at once one of the most valued features of the democratic system and an important reason for the country's high level of technical and economic efficiency. To move up in the social scale, however, is generally possible only if one is able to acquire basic knowledge in a formal college education, if not as an adolescent then later in life in adult-education programs. And moving up need not be interpreted merely in occupational or monetary terms; it is no less important that Americans acquire a liberal education—the knowledge and understanding by which their increasing leisure could really enrich their lives.

Ever since the struggle in the last century to establish first free primary, then free secondary schools and colleges, the principal argument in favor of this gradual extension of public education has been that in a democracy, where the people exert an important control over the government, they must understand public issues in order to carry out their civic duties adequately. With the growing complexity of our urban society, the ideal of a town meeting has become more and more a meaningless slogan, but it is still true that a representative government requires an informed citizenry.

For all of these reasons, we believe that a university, if it has or can acquire the necessary facilities, faculty, and other resources, should engage in adult education. We also believe, however, that adult education of poor quality is worse than none, and that the university's decision to extend its services to new age groups, social classes, and areas of knowledge should not be taken lightly.

University adult education constitutes no more than about four per cent of adult education as a whole. It is one sector of a vast, amorphous institution, in which universities, junior colleges, public schools, government bureaus, community agencies, and private organizations engage in recreational, vocational, remedial, cultural, and educational activities of every type, at every level, for every purpose. Within this all but infinite range, university adult education can play a meaningful role only by rigorously defining its distinctive place, by setting a limit to the tasks that it will undertake and an order of priority among them. Thus, many of the current extension activities are out of place in an institution of higher learning, in our opinion, and should be transferred elsewhere or abolished altogether.

The function of university adult education is education (and, legitimately, though usually to a small degree, research); it is not making money or public relations or social service or therapy or recreation. While no one, at least to our knowledge, has challenged in so many words the truism that the university's function is education, many define this term so broadly as to include these other activities, all of which are commonly associated with adult education. Even more frequently, general-extension administrators fail to think through the implications of contradictory purposes. In setting any kind of policy, accepting A means that B is inevitable, M likely, and Σ impossible. A university that tries to be both educational and commercial (with detours, say, into social work) succeeds only in being a monster.

The function of university adult education, to define it more narrowly, is *college-level* education. Once again, the truism that a college should offer college-level programs is ordinarily disputed not in words but by defining the term so loosely that it lacks any effective meaning. College-level means, very simply, the standard maintained in the traditional academic disciplines of the day campus, or in programs with a content of comparable or greater difficulty and complexity. Considering the heterogeneity of present-day curricula, such a definition is broader than an educational purist would like, but also certainly broad enough to include all of the legitimate purposes of extension. To designate the persons responsible for maintaining college level and to establish the kind of organizational structure that would motivate them to uphold standards are more important, we believe, than to attempt to spin out longer paraphrases of this self-explanatory term.

From the very beginning of university adult education in the United States, as in the philosophy and practice of President Van Hise of the University of Wisconsin, the "extension" of the university had several meanings. In order to discuss the issue, we found it useful to designate four types of extension. The simplest type, extension in time and place, consists in making available to persons other than the regular day students catalogue courses and other university services with no change in their content or quality. Since this type is of college level by definition, it is in principle a legitimate activity for the university. A second type of extension, consisting in the adaptation of college work to the particular needs of subgroups in the adult population, we have termed a functional extension. A large portion of noncredit programs and community services would be included in this class. It gives an opportunity for creative administration, but unless the limitation to college-level education is followed, this deviation from the traditional academic disciplines diverts the university from its proper course. The attempt to take over all of education and to teach subjects below college level, thirdly, we have termed substandard extension. While this may have been a legitimate activity of the university fifty years ago in a semi-frontier state like Wisconsin (we do not think so), it is certainly not so today anywhere in the United States. To undertake an educational task below college level, a dozen agencies are available; for higher education there is only the university. The fourth type, the extension out of education altogether into recreation or social service or whatever, we have termed conversion. We deem this to be an illegitimate practice of the university under all circumstances, though the line may be difficult to draw in particular instances. With a good teacher learning is not a dull experience, but having fun or mitigating alienation should never be more than subsidiary by-products of the essential process of education. Similarly, we judge the main purpose of the community-development movement to be social improvement, and we believe that it has no legitimate place in the university.

The Dimensions of the General-Extension Division

As we have noted, the very concept of "total extension function"—that is, the whole of a university's activities in addition to its two core purposes of scholarly research and the education of young people toward a degree—is not ordinarily to be found either in the minds of university administrators or in abstract discussions of administrative policy, not to say in the records of extension activities as compiled by such an organization as the NUEA. Some elements of the total extension function are typically administered by a general-extension division (for example, correspondence courses) and others more often by a separate office (for example, university presses); but with respect to most activities, practice varies a good bit from one campus to another. No organizational principle seems to be involved, but more probably the interest or ability of one rather than another person in having developed a particular activity some time in the past, or in maintaining it now. Perceiving the total extension function as a unit is important, thus, because it can stimulate thought on questions that to date have generally been settled *ad hoc*, with no consideration of underlying principles: Under what circumstances is a general-extension division useful? When it exists, ought it to administer all or only some of the university's total extension function? And if the latter, what should be the basis for distinguishing one from the other type of activity?

In any field, a prerequisite to the formulation of intelligent policy is accurate and complete information. Amazing as it may appear, it seems that even top-level university administrators are often not aware of the adult education offered by their own institutions. The dean of faculty of one large state university, for example, stated verbally that unfortunately it had no adult education (apart from that offered by Cooperative Extension); actually, 40,000 persons had attended short courses on his campus during the past several years. At another state university (not a land-grant institution, and thus with no Cooperative Extension), the vice-president recently had a survey made of all extension activities and found, somewhat to his surprise, that the general-extension division administers less than half of the total. We suspect that this ignorance is typical, and wherever it exists it constitutes a block to intelligent policy.

Every institution ought to establish an accounting system capable of measuring the portion of its budget that goes into adult education, as well as the allocation within this among various types of programs. Unless this is done, there is no possibility of real control, either in the sense of banning unsuitable types of activity or of setting a schedule of priorities among those that are suitable but of greater or lesser importance. The office assigned to maintain such a record could also serve as a central information bureau, both for administrators and those faculty members interested in keeping informed on what is being done supplementary to regular teaching and research. Whether this minimum degree of coordination ought to be exercised by the president's office, the general-extension division, or a special center, is not a principled question. In any case, it would supplement the general-extension division as it is presently constituted.

The actual range of control of general-extension divisions varies greatly. For example, among 51 universities surveyed by Morton, in 10 the responsibility for off-campus work was divided between academic departments and the extension division; in one the faculty of each school could operate any such program it chose; in 22 all off-campus activities had to be administered by the general-extension division; and 18 had no policy on this matter.[5] Like all such statistics, however, these pertain mainly to formal course work and similar programs. If we had full informa-

[5] Morton, *University Extension*, Table 22, p. 43.

tion on *all* extension activities, the picture would change considerably.[6]

There is an equally great variety in the organizational relation between general extension and the rest of the university, as can be seen from a few examples:

At the *University of Chicago*, "in addition to Committees, Institutes, Centers, there are eleven divisions and schools. University College is one of these. But unlike the other ten, it is merely an administrative adjunct of the Office of the Chancellor, is not under University Statutes a 'ruling body' and has no relationship to the Faculty policy-making body, the Senate. Hence it is not represented in the Council of the Senate, which legislates academic policy."[7]

The *Pennsylvania State University* has one extension director, who is advised by an administrative committee comprising the assistant deans for continuing education from the undergraduate colleges and the graduate school, representatives of the admissions office, and the director and two associate directors of continuing education. The state is divided into three regions, each with a regional director and assistant director of continuing education as well as district administrators in the principal population areas.[8]

The *University of California's* statewide general-extension division is headed by a university dean of extension, and the Agricultural Extension Service by a director under the university dean of agriculture. All extension activity is coordinated through a university extension advisory board, of which the university dean of extension is chairman. Its members comprise the director of agricultural extension and faculty representatives from the several campuses.[9]

At *Michigan State University*, the various off-campus programs

[6] For example, according to Houle and Nelson, no state university has its general-extension director administer *all* educational services for adults (*The University*, p. 76). This inconsistency with Morton's findings illustrates the importance of differentiating the total extension function from the general-extension division.

[7] Maurice F. X. Donohue, dean of University College, University of Chicago, in *1957 AUEC Proceedings*, p. 42.

[8] Letter from E. L. Keller, director of Continuing Education, Pennsylvania State University, November 25, 1959.

[9] Letter from President Clark Kerr of the University of California, November 20, 1959.

are coordinated through the provost. The continuing Education Service, the Labor and Industrial Relations Center, and the Highway Traffic Safety Center report directly to his office, and the Cooperative Extension Service to it through the dean of agriculture.[10] As of the beginning of 1960, according to a prior announcement by the presidents of Michigan's nine state universities and colleges, a coordinated system of extension courses went into effect.[11]

Oregon has a state system of higher education, with the director of the Division of University Extension responsible to the chancellor.[12] *Florida* also has a unified system of higher education, with the dean of the single general-extension division serving the entire state and responsible to the president of the University of Florida.[13] The Agricultural Extension Service has a separate director responsible to the provost for agriculture.[14]

What impressions do such illustrative organizational systems make on the observer? Within the continuing great variety, there seem to be a great proliferation of titles and a certain tendency toward statewide centralization. Whether these are altogether healthy trends we do not know, and a good case can be made for either side.

The central administration of all off-campus and evening activities seems, at least in the abstract, to be a good thing. It is desirable as a means of "conservation of planning, funds, and energy,"[15] since the "elimination of conflict and confusion" makes for greater efficiency.[16] There is a "need to coordinate the work . . . so that the resources of the institution will be used carefully and economically."[17] For example—

[10] Letter from Provost Paul A. Miller of Michigan State University, November 12, 1959.

[11] *Adult Leadership,* 7:8 (February, 1959), 245. Earlier, Wayne State University and the University of Michigan set up a joint Division of Adult Education in Detroit under a single director. At first, because of its small staff, it administered only some of the noncredit programs of the two institutions. See Stillwell, "Detroit's Merger."

[12] Houle and Nelson, *The University,* p. 76; letter from Chancellor John R. Richards, Oregon State System of Higher Education, November 24, 1959.

[13] Houle and Nelson, *The University,* p. 77.

[14] Letter from F. W. Parvin, Assistant to the President, University of Florida, November 11, 1959.

[15] Thompson, *University Extension,* p. 273.

[16] Morton, *University Extension,* p. 140.

[17] Houle and Nelson, *The University,* pp. 75-76.

The president of a southern university, on a recent visit to a county-seat town, encountered five members of his staff, each one of whom was working in the community with no knowledge that anyone else had any contact with it. Even worse, five university cars had been used for transportation![18]

On the other hand, the unified administration of such variegated activities as off-campus courses, noncredit programs of several types, concerts and lectures, conferences, the university press, and so on and on, is inherently difficult. Centralization of control can result in bureaucratic waste almost as easily as in greater efficiency; and in the best case "efficiency" is perhaps more likely to be defined as carrying out established routines well. This danger is particularly great in university adult education, since its purpose is often ill defined, the means of achieving it are a matter of dispute, and neither administrative structures nor any other variables are generally evaluated for their educational efficacy. If the measure of "efficiency" is to be set in an educational framework, there must be concern for "the careful preservation of the right of the respective departments and schools to establish and maintain . . . standards."[19] Moreover, "by far the majority of [general-extension] directors expressed themselves as not at all alarmed" by the fact that they were not administering all adult-education activities; they had more than enough to do without trying to add to their responsibilities.[20]

We do not believe there is any resolution of this dilemma that will fit every institution. Within the framework set by certain general principles, which we believe to be applicable to all adult education in an institution of higher learning, many different organizational structures are possible. The goals appropriate and the means and personnel available are different for a large or small university, a public or private one, a rural or urban one, and so on. We do think, however, that a good deal of the existent variety is the consequence of historical accident, of irrelevant precedent, or of lack of policy—and that little, if anything, in the typical organization need be regarded as sacrosanct.

Indeed, the crying need for reform is in itself a relevant factor

[18] Houle, "Community Educational Services," p. 12.
[19] Houle and Nelson, *The University*, p. 75.
[20] Fisher et al., *Adult Education*, p. 28; this booklet is based on the "combined thinking of extension staffs in practically every institution that has membership in the NUEA." But see Houle, *Major Trends*, p. 33.

in setting the future organizational structure, and in some instances perhaps a more important one than any other. An attempt to tighten standards would undoubtedly be welcomed by some extension administrators and faculty. But the group therapists, the mongers of better bridge, the community developers, the advocates of the soft pedagogy—these would regard any reform as an attack on themselves, to be answered with a counterattack. Where such types are well entrenched in a university's adult-education program, no abstract argument that centralization effects greater educational efficiency would justify bringing a larger share of the total extension function under their control. A university president interested in fostering significant adult education in his institution might be able to do this, at one extreme, by facilitating the work of a competent dean; but at the other extreme he might have to resort to the device (familiar enough in bureaucratic manipulation) of building a second adult-education section of the university, designed eventually to undermine and supplant a general-extension division that he considers beyond repair.

Relations between Extension and the Main Campus

It is the task of the general-extension division to administer a given portion of the university's total extension function, but what is meant by "administer"? Here, once again, we find no agreement on fundamentals. According to Dean Morton—

> An extension organization . . . can and should be only an agency for interpreting, promoting, organizing, and financing the types of educational services desired by the deans and department heads of the various instructional divisions of an institution of higher learning. It is, however, the duty of the staff of the extension organization to see that the deans and department heads understand the alternatives they face in making these choices.[21]

According to the no less authoritative view of Professor Houle, however, while the general-extension division is in part "a facilitating organization through which the other departments operate in the field"—

> It is not . . . merely their instrument but attempts to survey the

[21] Letters from Dean Morton, October 28, 1957 and June 2, 1958. See also Thompson, *University Extension*, p. 256.

community, organize and develop new programs of educational activity, call needs to the attention of the regular instructional departments, and, in other ways, see that the community's needs and interests are represented within the institution.[22]

In another publication, Houle goes farther and asks under what conditions the person in charge of extension merits the title "dean." "Only if," he replies, "in addition to or *in place of* the service functions he may have to perform, he accepts the responsibility for being creative in the construction of . . . programs . . . appropriate to the mature students he serves. . . . Even if the university has a vice-president in charge of extension, it will still need a special officer acting as dean, to arrange the unique programs of adult education."[23]

The issue, in other words, is whether the "extension division" ought to be merely an extension or at least in part a division of the university. How one resolves the question affects a wide variety of policy decisions. An extension administrator operating under the first principle is likely to make fewer mistakes. The educational quality will be set, at least in theory, by main-campus faculty, who tend to follow the academic disciplines. If they sometimes perform their role of guardians of traditional standards somewhat stolidly, and if these courses—particularly as presented under the conditions prevalent in extension—are sometimes rather dull, their subject matter nevertheless includes the significant core of our higher culture. Some of the wider-ranging, more experimental extension administrators have deviated from tradition with tawdry programing, but others with true educational creativity.

The alert extension department will often have organized lectures on Internal Auditing, Electronic Data Processing, and Zen Buddhism long before the "academic department" head has recognized them as proper subjects for inquiry. Again and again, academic departments have to be dragged screaming into the twentieth century—especially into the latter half.[24]

The ideal relation between main-campus faculty and extension

[22] Houle, "Community Education Services," p. 12.
[23] Houle, "The American University and Adult Education," cited in Houle, *Major Trends*, p. 34; emphasis added.
[24] Letter from Dean McGhee, July 21, 1958.

administrators would seem to be a dialectical interaction through which both types of virtue could be expressed. Unfortunately, the frequently poor reputation that the extension has in the rest of the university hampers cooperation between the two.

This is an important question, and it is worth citing several, partly conflicting, opinions from a number of authorities. "In most institutions," in Morton's opinion, "the administrative staff members of the extension organization . . . [have] the same status in the university as other university staff members having similar responsibilities,"[25] and Houle believes that the status of general-extension deans has been increasing and is on occasion higher than that of any other dean.[26] According to Neuffer, on the other hand, "evening divisions have not yet reached a position where their status in terms of respect and influence on the campus is equal to that of the day division."[27] One of the major tasks the Center for the Study of Liberal Education for Adults has set itself is "improving relationships between divisions of adult education and their parent institutions."[28] Similarly, according to the executive secretary of the NUEA, this general-extension administrators' association "does not enjoy the eminence . . . it should have . . . among educational circles in Washington and perhaps elsewhere."[29] The difference in opinion may be due to stressing one or another element of that rather vague word "status." In formal terms, as Morton shows, extension staffs usually have equivalent titles, salaries, and personnel working under them; but this does not mean that they have an equal voice in determining over-all university policy, nor that day administrators and faculty necessarily regard them as peers.[30] And the differentiation with respect to faculty is much sharper: in extension they have neither the same prestige nor equivalent salaries and prerogatives.

Most main-campus administrators and faculty, if the question

[25] Morton, *University Extension*, p. 135.

[26] Interview with Professor Houle, June 10, 1958.

[27] Neuffer, *Administrative Policies*, p. 2.

[28] Center for the Study of Liberal Education for Adults, *A Review of 1956*, pp. 12, 44.

[29] McCurdy, "Report of the Executive Secretary," p. 89. See also Gould, "Quality in Adult Education," p. 52.

[30] See, for example, the statement by Donohue quoted earlier (p. 133); Schwertman, "Analysis and Interpretation"; and Miller, "Summary of Workshop III," p. 89.

were put to them in the abstract, would undoubtedly express themselves as in accord with the democratic principle that educational opportunities should be extended to social classes and age groups not able to attend regular college sessions. In practice, however, they ordinarily want as little as possible to do with extension. Even apart from the quality of adult education, deans and department heads prefer to have their faculty do research in their spare time rather than teach additional courses, so that on principle their cooperation with the general-extension division is reluctant and partial. Many of the regular administrators and faculty are thoroughly hostile. "A number of university men," as Houle has put it, think it "highly appropriate" that *adult education* and *adulteration* are coupled as the heading of one page of the *Encyclopedia of the Social Sciences*.[31] The main campus acquiesces, therefore, in the isolation of extension, the low salaries, the commercial standards imposed on it by the university—in short, in conditions that reduce still more extension's standards, and thus also their already low estimate of them.

The tendency is to regard extension work as something inferior to, and generally beneath, residence. Since it is so regarded, the result is that it sometimes is inferior work. All of you are acquainted with the department head who has a feeling that anything goes in extension, and who will approve classes and instructors in extension which he would not in residence.[32]

The reputation that extension has and the one it deserves interact, thus, by what Myrdal has termed "the principle of cumulation."[33] In his classic work on the American Negro, he was able to organize a vast mass of data into an easily assimilable narrative by relating them all to this single theme.

White prejudice and discrimination keep the Negro low in standards of living, health, education, manners and morals. This, in its turn, gives support to white prejudice. White prejudice and Negro standards thus mutually "cause" each other. If things remain about as they are and have been, this means that the two forces happen to

[31] Houle, "Introduction," p. 13.
[32] Bray, "Extension Credit," p. 62.
[33] For another discussion of this theme, see Clark, *The Marginality of Adult Education*, which summarizes one important motif of his *Adult Education*.

balance each other. . . . If either of the factors changes, this will cause a change in the other factor, too, and start a process of interaction where the change in one factor will continuously be supported by the reaction of the other factor.[34]

This pattern is commonly called "the vicious circle," but Myrdal preferred the neutral term because he wanted to stress that the interdependence of factors affecting Negro–white relations can work in either direction. If we apply the principle of cumulation to university adult education, however, it suggests also that great improvement is likely only if it is initiated from the highest university level. If extension attempts by itself to raise its level, this intent is likely to be frustrated by the discriminatory policies reflecting the negative attitude of the main campus. And if, on the other hand, one or another academic department tries to infuse its higher standards into extension's work, it may well find that the danger of adulteration must be taken seriously. Only an executive with control over both sides of this interacting system can negate the dead weight of the past and begin to turn the vicious circle in the opposite direction.

The changes in the organizational structure the president should effect can be stated simply—the elimination of all of extension's differentiating features that do not follow naturally and inevitably from its special educational functions. This means, on the one hand, the abolition of programs in social improvement, individual therapy, recreation, and so on, and the maintenance of equal quality in its educational offerings. It means no less, on the other hand, the removal of discriminatory practices, such as the markedly lower salary of extension instructors or its quasi-commercial status altogether.[35] Such a reform would encounter, of course, entrenched prejudice and opposition from vested authority throughout the university.

It would be necessary, in our opinion, to root such reforms as firmly as possible in new administrative rules. The quality of part-time instruction in extension could undoubtedly be greatly improved if it was made an occasional regular portion of *each* faculty member's teaching load (*not* an addition to it), with extra pay only for travel time and expenses. Apparently this system

---

[34] Myrdal, *An American Dilemma*, pp. 75-76.
[35] See Houle, "The Evening College."

is not followed anywhere. The control that home-campus departments often have over extension courses, usually exercised with listless disinterest, would become more meaningful if all adult courses for "credit" were actually given equivalent credit, and if instructional departments were given a budgetary stake in extension. Full-time instructors, such as are usual in extension centers, would be equally competent if they were hired under the same conditions as their home-campus colleagues and had the same salaries, duties, and prerogatives; and when geography makes it feasible, administrative regulations might also encourage the maximum degree of cooperation and interpenetration between sister departments.

The Financing of Adult Education

In casting the president in the role of adjudicator, we have assumed (for the sake of the argument) that his intent is to foster a significant college-level educational program for adults. While this is certainly true of some university executives, it is hardly the characteristic attitude. The heaviest responsibility for the failings of university adult education, on the contrary, lies with the president. This is true first of all in a formal sense: he is the superior officer to whom the extension dean or director reports. And it is even more true intrinsically. As we pointed out in the last chapter, the main purposes of the adult-education program, as seen by all too many presidents, are to supplement the university's public relations office and its fund-raising efforts. No matter what their other faults, extension personnel must reasonably be adjudged innocent of complicity in the vicious system that keeps their budgets so pinched that they are induced, one might almost say forced, to become peddlers of popular commodities. If there were no such financial discrimination, how much would remain, one wonders, of the felt-needs "approach" and the other sops to adult educators' self-respect? In other words, how much responsibility does the president's office have for the whole range of anti-intellectual "philosophies" and practices that we have examined in this book? Most of these originated, it is true, outside the university, in the broader world of adult education; and those in the college community who profess their faith in groupiness or pledge allegiance to recreation are undoubtedly sometimes sincere. Yet, if the whole perspective were to be changed, one wonders.

The administrator is . . . a victim rather than the villain of the piece. As often as not he is under considerable pressure from a university administration which may well force him to try and increase the size, turnover and income of his department at all costs. In any case he must at least balance his budget and this almost necessarily prevents him from balancing his programme. . . . One's immediate and general impression is one of insecurity, despite the exceptions. The dean appears so often to be, or believe himself to be, caught between the upper millstone of the university administration demanding money and numbers regardless of standards, and the nether one of the day faculty who look down, or appear to look down, on his work, with varying degrees of justification.[36]

It is rather easy, the reader may feel, to hit so large and obvious a target as the commercialization of general extension. We deem our reiterated attacks to be useful, even if they indicate no particularly acute perspicacity on our part, since they serve to emphasize a crucial feature that is all too often played down, or even passed over, when the actors in this sorry drama themselves write of their roles. What should be the financial basis of university adult education?

Since under the present system tuition constitutes so large a proportion of general-extension income, the size of class fees is a matter of unusual importance to the administration. They range from zero to $30 a semester-hour, with most public institutions charging $10 or less.[37] What tuition is just is not a question that can be answered except in terms of a given social philosophy. And what fee is suitable in educational terms depends on data that are mostly not available. While no discussion of the issue

[36] Elsdon, *Reality and Purpose*, pp. 7-8.

[37] Of the 66 NUEA members that were sent a recent inquiry on tuition fees, only 45 replied, and these not to all the questions. According to this source (*1958 NUEA Proceedings*, p. 70), fees per semester-credit ranged from $6 to $18 (median $10) in state institutions, and from $15 to $30 (median $20.50) in private institutions. More detailed information is available from a number of earlier surveys, but whether any of these figures are still wholly correct is doubtful. According to Bell, tuition had almost doubled in the six years since Morton's study was completed; see "Finance," p. 146. Among more than nine-tenths of the institutions surveyed by Morton, tuition fees ranged from $5 to $10 per semester-hour, plus nominal registration or special fees in some cases (*University Extension*, p. 96). Dugan reports median fees of $7 per semester-hour for credit courses, and $7.50 per non-

can pretend to be definitive, it is at least useful to keep the moral question separate from the empirical one.

Let us take the moral issue first. Charging fees, it is sometimes maintained, is undemocratic, because all cannot afford them equally well. Since free public education is available at other levels, it should be made available also for adults.[38] The argument is reinforced by the fact that certain other types of adult education are financed, or at least heavily subsidized, out of public funds: municipal, county, state, and/or federal funds are used to pay for vocational education, various other adult programs in the public schools, and the entire very large Cooperative Extension program. "Should all members, not just farmers and labourers, of a democratic society be given equal adult educational opportunities?"[39]

The argument that democracy implies social equality, however, cannot be accepted in *absolute* terms. Having to attend college in the evening after working all day is in itself discriminatory, and if those who argue from the principle of equality were consistent, they would demand that all who want adult education should be subsidized while they attain it during three mornings a week. If absolute equality is rejected as an irrelevant principle, then the question becomes, what is "reasonable," what is "expedient"; and in that case, it is not at all clear whether university adult education should be free. By our interpretation of democratic principles, tuition should never be so high as to prevent a well prepared, highly motivated person from continuing his education. On the other hand, given the grave and increasing short-

---

credit course ("An Extension Class Program," pp. 95-96). At the *tax-supported* evening colleges surveyed by Neuffer, undergraduate tuition varied from no charge to $10 a credit-hour, with graduate fees sometimes higher; among the *private* evening colleges he surveyed, the fees began at $10 and went as high as $25 per credit-hour (*Administrative Policies*, p. 17).

[38] See, for example, Kempfer, *Adult Education*, pp. 381-383. For a counter argument, see, for example, Grattan, *In Quest of Knowledge*, pp. 309-310.

[39] Woods and Hammarberg, "University Extension," pp. 143-144. The agitation in favor of some sort of federal subsidy to general-extension work has been reflected in several bills, but to date Congress has not acted on any of them. The most recent of these bills, S. 1731, introduced by Senator Hill during the first session of the 85th Congress, would provide a small federal subsidy to the general-extension divisions of land-grant institutions and state universities. An earlier effort to set up a permanent, federally financed Labor Extension Service, analogous to the Cooperative Extension Service, failed—according to Grattan, mainly because of the conflict between the AFL and CIO (*In Quest of Knowledge*, pp. 250-251).

age of funds for all higher education, we must ask whether it
is necessary to cut off entirely the largest present source of extension income. Resolving this dilemma is particularly difficult
because the relevant data are not only scanty but often also ambiguous.

1. The average adult student has considerably more education than the population as a whole, and therefore also an appreciably higher income.[40] One could argue that tuition is therefore
not an unreasonable burden, particularly since most extension
students do not take a full program (and many no more than an
occasional course) and their outlay per semester is thus small. But
would the higher income of adults be meaningfully so if we were
also to compare their financial responsibilities with those of
adolescents? And what is the direction of the presumed cause-
effect relation: to what degree do adults with lower incomes
therefore not continue their education, or enroll in fewer courses?
Educators are in sharp disagreement concerning the effect of
tuition fees on enrollment figures.[41] Apparently no study has ever
been made of this effect in university adult education,[42] but the
several studies of this relation in other types of adult-education
programs, while not entirely relevant to general extension, may
be indicative. One survey of ninety-five cities in a depression
year "showed little difference in the proportion of adults respectively attending free and fee programs,"[43] and a more recent

[40] See, for example, Morton, *University Extension*, pp. 89, 91; Thompson,
University Extension, pp. 56, 68; Chapman, "Some Characteristics," p. 49.

[41] Of the 76 deans who reported on the matter to Neuffer, for example,
exactly half felt that higher fees would reduce enrollments, almost half did
not believe that they would, and three admitted that they did not know
what the effect would be (*Administrative Policies*, p. 19).

[42] A partial exception may be the questionnaire filled in by over 9,000
general-extension students at ten institutions. They had expressed satisfaction
with the services they received, and gave as their reasons for being satisfied
the following: accessibility, 59 per cent; reasonableness of costs, 45 per cent;
quality of department, 17 per cent; other reasons, not specified, 22 per cent
(Thompson, *University Extension*, pp. 87-88). Since we do not know
whether students would not enroll or merely be "less satisfied" if fees were
"unreasonable," nor what they would consider "unreasonable," these figures
do not really indicate the relation of fees to enrollments.

[43] E. E. Clark, *A Study of Fees and Deposits in Adult Education* (1933),
cited in Kempfer, *Adult Education*, p. 382. Surprisingly, in spite of this
study and of the fact that he offers no contrary evidence, Kempfer himself
concludes that "fees reduce the numbers enrolled."

study in six cities confirmed this finding.[44]

2. What effect do fees have on the diligence of students? A number of adult educators, including persons with as wide an experience as Houle, believe that the only argument for tuition is the financial one, that in all educational respects fees are harmful or, at best, irrelevant. However, what little evidence exists suggests the contrary. Lacking data on extension, if we again turn to studies of adult education outside the university, we find that fees do seem to result in better attendance[45]; and this is a reasonable definition of "diligence."

Balancing these several considerations, we make the following proposal as a reasonable compromise:

1. In degree-credit courses, the charge should be precisely the same as for the equivalent courses on the main campus. The democratic impulse that the extension in time and place originally expressed would thus be retained at least for the standard fare of most general-extension divisions.

2. For programs not carrying degree-credit, there should be a charge, ordinarily large enough to cover its cost but with some consideration also to such factors as the ability of the probable participants to pay and the social value of the program. Non-credit programs, though they vary widely, often approximate what we have termed a functional extension; and the very fact that many are designed for specific groups reduces the relevance of moral arguments in favor of free adult education. If such programs pay for themselves, moreover, they permit an imaginative administration really to break new ground.[46]

[44] Olds, "Adult Students"; see also his *Financing Adult Education*, pp. 49-54.

[45] The study by Clark cited earlier found that "free cities maintained an average attendance of 48 per cent of those enrolled, and fee cities maintained an attendance of 61 per cent" (Kempfer, *Adult Education*, p. 382). A study by the U.S. Office of Education, similarly, found that the average attendance in 35 fee schools was 82.5 per cent, as contrasted with 60 per cent in 118 schools with low fees or none (Grace S. Wright, *Persistence of Attendance in Adult Education Classes*, cited in Olds, *Financing Adult Education*, p. 54).

[46] The extension division of the University of California at Berkeley, for instance, during the spring of 1960 presented a four-week advanced course in the cello by Pablo Casals. The tuition fee of $200, though very high by ordinary standards, is reasonable for the unique opportunity offered to a professional group.

This discussion of tuition fees, in any case, hardly touches the central problem. Even if the income from course fees were increased, in many universities this would not in itself solve any problems, for the additional funds would be returned in the form of a profit to the over-all budget of the university. No other division of the university is expected to support itself; and the partial exception to this rule in the case of general extension, merely an accidental effect of its historical development, few administrators even attempt to justify in terms of organizational principles. The crucial reform would be to eliminate this discrimination, as has been done in a number of evening colleges. Rutgers University College, for example, "is not a revenue-producing but an educational unit, with its budget established and operated like the budget of all other colleges. All costs are paid out of funds allotted by the University; all income goes directly to the University."[47] The Division of General Education at New York University, to take a private institution, is similarly "separately budgeted as one of the 14 schools of the University and 'reports' directly to the central administration as do the other schools and colleges." The division administrators, however, believe that "noncredit activities *should* pay their own way, including allowance for institutional overhead."[48] The fact that these two examples are so large and independent as to be more branches than extensions of the main campus is not relevant to the organizational principle. If anything, one might argue that, on the contrary, the smaller and weaker general-extension divisions (or adult-education programs altogether) are less able to stand on their own feet than extension centers.[49]

What effect on quality would substantial new sources of income have? We have argued that its commercialization is an important reason for the frequently low standards of adult education; and it is no paradox to hold that, given the present

[47] Demarest, "Faculty Organization," p. 9.

[48] Letter from Dean McGhee, July 21, 1958.

[49] Among 51 of the universities surveyed by Morton, the annual budget of the general-extension division ranged in 1951-1952 from $10,000 to over $3,000,000, with a median between $200,000 and $500,000 (*University Extension*, Table 55, p. 97). The ratio of 300:1 between the largest and the smallest budget, reflecting mainly differences among the various national regions, had increased from about 100:1 in 1930.

personnel, their "philosophy," and the established routines, additional funds might only furnish a rich breeding ground to anti-intellectual forces. In short, while a reform is urgent in the method by which university adult education is financed, by itself, with no concomitant control over educational policy *per se*, this could do more harm than good.

Summary

Books have been written on higher education, professional and regional organizations established, conferences have met, in which the university's role in adult education was given only a token recognition, or not even that. It is an administrative task of first importance to integrate its adult education with the rest of the university. An institution planning to put its extension activities on a better foundation would do well to recognize the problem and try to cope with it from the very beginning. The optimum organization of university adult education, stated in the broadest terms, is that it should differ from the rest of the university only in those respects that its special function makes necessary. One can compare it with the college education of women. A half century ago, when this was still something of a rarity, the difference between male and female students was very often greatly exaggerated. It was believed that significant adaptations in curriculum and administrative control were necessary, while today relatively slight modifications of standard procedures are seen as appropriate for women's colleges. A similar legend has run the cycle with respect to adults; we have pretty well discarded the myth that there is a substantial physiological basis for the difference between adolescents and mature students, but we have not yet reached the point of recognizing the essential unity of college education irrespective of age. Within this unity there are, indeed, significant differences, but none that warrant the wild aberrations from standard educational aims and methods or, on the other hand, the special and often discriminatory administrative regulations.

In previous chapters, we delineated the main issues in adult education and indicated with respect to each what we deem to be good educational policy. Almost all these questions are relevant to a discussion of the university's role in educating adults. At the most abstract level, as in pronouncements on how "felt needs" should be filled, no distinction is ordinarily made between adult education by a university and that by other agencies. The theme of "democracy" appears in a somewhat altered form: universities, and particularly state universities, must "serve" their community. They must maintain good public relations with the voting public, and they ordinarily use their extension function at least in part for this purpose. In a passage that has become deservedly famous, Dean Nolte asked his audience to imagine the figure of the university, holding aloft the flaming beacon of truth and with its ear to the ground to catch from afar the first rumble of the people's will. He did not think it necessary to specify "what part of the anatomy is most prominent to the beholder."[50] When everything else has been sacrificed to this false image of "democracy," it must not be imagined that the educator's dignity has been saved.

University adult education almost always has to pay its own way in an extraordinary proportion, and in some cases it is almost frankly admitted that its purpose is to return a profit to the other, the educational sectors of the university. A fundamental reform from which all kinds of benefits would flow would be to eliminate the prevalent practice by which extension divisions are encouraged to become quasi-commercial enterprises. In our opinion, the fees for at least credit courses should be identical with those on the day campus; all income collected should go into the general university budget, from which allocations should be made to adult education, as to every activity of the university, solely on the basis of educational requirements. Under such a system, the administrator of the university's adult education would have to compete with other sectors of the institution and demonstrate the intellectual worth of his offerings as compared with those in other colleges; thus, not only would the commercial basis of extension curricula be removed, but an educational one would be substituted for it.

Main-campus faculty, like the university administration, tend

[50] Nolte, "The Role of the State University," p. 65.

to regard extension as second-rate, a source of petty increments to their inadequate salaries but also a threat to the quality of higher education generally. Whether originally true or false, such stereotypes are likely to be self-fulfilling prophecies; for the judgment of main-campus administrators and faculty, who help determine the nature and level of general extension, often prove to be correct in the end. Again, there is no valid educational reason for the differences on and off campus in instructors' salary and status, and such invidious distinctions cannot fail to have their effect on the quality of teaching. When extension courses are taught by regular day faculty, we recommend that they be made a regular rotating portion of each faculty member's teaching load, with no extra pay. When there are full-time extension teachers, we recommend that the same professional qualifications be demanded of them, and that they be paid on the same scale as their main-campus colleagues.

The chief administrative officers of adult education more often receive equivalent salaries and have comparable authority in their own domain, but they generally have little or no voice in broader university councils and thus a reduced prestige among their nominal peers. If they are qualified to administer a division of the university, we feel, their participation in setting over-all policy should be taken for granted. And if they are not really qualified by home-campus standards, then giving them the title of "dean" or "director" or even "vice-president" is not defensible.

The standards in ostensibly equivalent courses taught on campus and in extension often differ considerably, and the lower quality of the latter is sometimes half legitimized by such regulations as, for example, that a certain proportion of the credit toward a degree must be earned in residence. Insofar as it is symptomatic of the lowering of scholastic standards in extension work, this kind of blurring of the distinction between credit and noncredit work is unfortunate. In noncredit programs it is ordinarily even more difficult to establish and maintain quality. The following quotation from the bulletin of a state university's community college contains in succinct form most of the faults to be found in noncredit adult-education programs:

The classes deal with any subject for which there is an expressed interest. Any adult may take these courses regardless of his educational background. Instruction is informal and designed to give each student just what he wants to learn. . . . No listed course will be continued in which the enrollment is less than fifteen.[51]

The courses offered include vocational (acetylene welding, typing, etc.), general (fundamentals of English, etc.), and such miscellaneous items as "self-improvement (charm)," "art of conversation," sewing, gardening, and golf.

In contrast, we believe that the content and teaching methods of a university program should be set by educators in accordance with their professional training. Many adults who attend college programs do so in order to advance in their vocation, and in that case their course demands are ordinarily quite specific. Adults who return to school seeking a liberal education, however, generally have a vague, unfocused, uninformed notion of what they expect to learn. Those who go to the university rather than to a library or museum need guidance, and not merely the so-called "nondirective guidance" that reflects their own "felt needs." If the university is to perform adequately in adult education, there as in every one of its activities it must set its program in accordance with its own policy. That it should be necessary to advance such an argument is in itself indicative. Nothing in adult education is responsible for more shoddiness, for greater hypocrisy, than the notion that in a democracy educators must abrogate their professional responsibilities.

No one organizational structure is called for to implement such educational goals; but certain broad principles are universally valid. On every campus, first of all, it would be useful to establish an accounting system from which university administrators could learn what it is doing in adult education, at what cost, with what changes from past years, and so on. It is necessary, in a word, to recognize the total extension function as a meaningful concept, an entity of which the activities of the general-extension division sometimes make up no more than half. The central agency that computes statistics on all extension activities could also carry out two other useful activities. The first is coordination, to reduce undue waste in the use of personnel and facilities. The second is

[51] University of New Mexico Community College, *Bulletin*, Spring semester 1957-1958.

liaison between the university and the public, in order both to mitigate the exploitation of the faculty that is otherwise common, particularly at a public university, and to maintain good public relations.

Without reforms of the type we have advocated here, it can be safely predicted, academic standards in adult education will suffer more and more from the combined effect of inadequate facilities, poorly paid faculties, sharply increasing enrollments, and a "philosophy" of education that makes it easy to interpret chaos as exhilarating. In self-defense, main-campus administrators and faculty will withdraw still farther from interest in and responsibility for general extension, thus increasing its isolation and aggravating its faults. With the pressure on the main campuses, they will inevitably seek ways of getting rid of their marginal students; and what could be more convenient than to dump them on extension, which already has a tradition of accepting students who have flunked out of regular sessions? The worst that can happen, and also perhaps the most probable, is a "success" of overwhelming proportions, with more students than ever before, more instructors (including more "instructors"), more courses, more groups, more conferences, more money for more community development, more self-congratulatory articles on all the felt needs being met. And the date for this forecast is not 1984 but close to 1964.

7

UNIVERSITY ADULT EDUCATION IN FOREIGN AFFAIRS:
A REVIEW OF THE FIELD

In the last chapter, an attempt was made to bring together the more significant conclusions concerning university adult education and to relate these to problems in making policy. These problems are complex—more so, perhaps, than could be indicated in such an abstract discussion. For while some decisions by an extension administrator are made in a general framework—credit or noncredit courses, how service to the community can be joined with more specific educational goals, how the programs can be financed, who shall be responsible for administering them, and so on—many have a more direct relation to the particular subject matter of one or another program. It may be useful, then, to discuss in some detail one particular application of the general principles of policy in university adult education.

In several respects, education in foreign affairs is a good example of the kind of program that involves special administrative problems. Before undertaking it, a university administrator ought to think through a number of basic questions: (1) When a university sets up a program in citizen education, ought this to be aimed at all citizens, including those not capable of college-level work? (2) A public issue is by definition a subject on which there are varying opinions; how can the university work out its special function without becoming merely one more party to the dispute? (3) What combination of academic disciplines, analysis of current events, and inculcation of basic democratic values is appropriate? (4) If the university is to serve the community in this respect, is an occasional course or off-campus lecture sufficient, or is a more serious organizational effort called for?

Unless such questions are conscientiously thought through, a program in citizen education can do more harm than good—both to the university, which is punished in worsened public relations for walking into a polemical area halfcocked, and to the community, which is sold shoddy wares with an authoritative label. In spite of these difficulties, the university ought to include education in foreign affairs in its extension program, whether or not there is apparent consumer demand for it.

The equipment that the electorate has for coping with the problems of American foreign policy is meager. In all of the many tests of their understanding of the basic issues, or even of information about the rest of the world, Americans have displayed an appalling ignorance, and this is almost as true of college graduates as of the general population. This deficiency is well known, of course, and the statements demanding more education in foreign affairs often sound like a call to arms. Many articles in both scholarly journals and popular magazines have been devoted to the question, as well as entire issues of some journals and numerous conferences. Organizations as different as the NEA and UNESCO have considered it at length. With particular reference to the role of universities, the American Council on Education set up a commission and five subcommittees to deal with various phases of international education.[1] The Association of American Colleges has a Commission on International Understanding,[2] and its Commission on Training for Citizenship is concerned with both domestic and foreign problems.[3] The theme of its 1958 annual meeting was "American Education and World Responsibility."[4] With the financial support of the Carnegie Endowment for International Peace, an eight-year project under Howard E. Wilson has attempted to determine what education in world affairs is available to college students, both through day and extension curricula and outside them.[5]

[1] See *Educational Record*, 37:1 (January, 1956), 36-42.
[2] Hutchins, "Report of the Commission on International Understanding"; its name had been changed from Commission on International Cooperation through Education, as it is listed in the previous year's report.
[3] Bunn, "College Alumni and Citizenship."
[4] See *Association of American Colleges Bulletin*, Vol. 44, No. 1 (March, 1958).
[5] Based on the self-surveys of about 100 institutions of higher education, the following "Studies in Universities and World Affairs" have been or are to be published by the American Council on Education: Wilson, *American College Life as Education in World Outlook*; Du Bois, *Foreign Students and Higher Education in the United States*; Houle and Nelson, *The Uni-*

The vehement consensus that education in foreign affairs is presently inadequate—and that the university can play a decisive role in remedying this deficiency—can be a stimulus to action, but hardly in itself a guide to policy. The very fact that so many millions in foundation funds have had, so far as can be determined, so little effect on American public opinion, suggests that the universities, with their more modest supply of ready cash, ought to expend more intelligence in their effort. This means, among other things, attempting to judge the resources available for college-level education and to adapt these where necessary to new tasks, setting a schedule of priorities among both the sectors of the population and the content areas to be included in the program.

In setting up a program for adults in foreign affairs education, a university administrator ought first to assay the field. What is being taught in this subject, both on the regular campuses and through private organizations? According to one estimate, the United States has more than 3,000 nongovernmental agencies with some interest in foreign affairs, including more than 600 for which this is the primary concern.[6] The relation between these organizations and universities is often close. Faculty and students are frequently members or participants in the agencies' programs; instructors prepare the written materials distributed by the organizations or, vice versa, use in their classes those prepared by agency personnel; joint university–organization programs are common. On their own, universities sponsor a wide variety of courses and less formal offerings, including extracurricular activities, more or less related to foreign affairs. What is the result of all this effort?

As often in university adult education, an important preliminary task is to define the content of the program, since this is not necessarily identical with any academic discipline taught in the day curriculum.

---

versity, the Citizen, and World Affairs; Fuller, *Training of Specialists in International Relations;* Cole, *International Relations in Institutions of Higher Education in the South;* Gange, *University Research on International Affairs;* Swift, *World Affairs and the College Curriculum;* Wilson and Brown, *American Universities in World Affairs: A General Report.* See also Wilson, *Universities and World Affairs.*

[6] Foreign Policy Association, mimeographed report, 1958.

What is it we wish to "extend"? Information? Attitudes? Study habits? What courses? The following labels may have, or should have, some significant differences—"World Affairs," "International Relations," "International Politics," "International Organization," "Understanding Foreign Cultures," "History of U.S. Diplomacy," and so forth. Whatever your stated objective or your response to demands, I doubt whether everything "foreign" is equally useful.[7]

As a first step toward defining an appropriate program, we can differentiate a bit more precisely than in their ordinary usage some of these roughly synonymous designations for this field of study. Which are not suitable at all? Which, though they may be a legitimate element of a liberal arts curriculum, have little or no relevance to adult education in foreign affairs? And what, finally, should be the content of such a program?

Somewhat arbitrarily, *foreign affairs* is here taken as the generic term to define the whole. Within foreign affairs, a wide range of emphases is possible in factual content, in level of presentation, and in ideological message. With respect to the last, thus, at one extreme are organizations that frankly try to propagate a particular credo, such as pacifism. Then there are several types in which the intent to proselytize is not dominant or is not frankly admitted. And at the other extreme are programs whose ostensible purpose it is merely to present the facts about foreign affairs. Let us begin with this last type.

Education in "Current Events"

If the proper role of the university in any polemical area is to remain above the battle, as many educators believe, one apparent method of maintaining objectivity is to restrict any foreign-affairs program to a presentation of "the facts." No one would suggest, indeed, that an adequate program could be divorced from an

---

[7] Heindel, "How 'Worldly' Can We Be?" p. 22. Paul Mantoux has made the same point in defense of setting some limits to the meaning of "international studies." "One can without doubt call international any phenomenon because it belongs to all countries. . . . From this point of view, seasickness is an international fact; not only does one experience it on all oceans; but there are societies against that disease, and one can conceive of an international league whose purpose it is to do research and compare the methods with which to combat the disease. Yet the question remains outside our field of inquiry" (*Coopération Intellectuelle*, Paris, No. 57-58, 1935, p. 490; cited in Morgenthau, *Dilemmas of Politics*, p. 90).

interpretation of current events. But the possibly plausible rationale that these form a sufficient basis for the program, however widely held it may be, is fallacious on several grounds:

1. Adult-education programs with so narrow a purpose are unnecessary. In the 1920's, when universities began to set up courses in foreign affairs and when many of the private agencies were established, it was often difficult to obtain such information from other sources. Today the coverage of foreign events in the mass media, however inadequate, is good enough to make unnecessary adult-education programs that do no more than transmit the news. "World affairs organizations are not extensively relied upon as sources of information even by their formal members."[8]

2. Simply giving the facts with respect to any situation, moreover, often leads not to a clearer understanding but to bewilderment; for the first thing—and sometimes the only thing—one learns from a program in current events is always that the situation is much more complex than one realized. "Anyone who has gone through the experience of trying to analyze a policy is aware of the fact that in the first period of concentrated effort, increased knowledge results in increased confusion and indecision."[9]

3. It is impossible to give *all* the facts, and the selection of the facts chosen ordinarily reflects a bias. One important virtue of a social-science discipline is that it can help students minimize bias: in a graduate seminar, a professor can guide them to a full consideration of every facet of a narrow subject. But one cannot impose this discipline at an undergraduate level on the diversified participants in adult education with respect to so broad a topic as foreign affairs. The facts offered may be true, but they cannot be exhaustive. In such a program, then, it is hardly possible to teach about foreign affairs in a value-free context.

Education in "International Relations"

If it is impossible to avoid at least an implicit endorsement of one system of values at the relatively superficial level of current

---

[8] Cohen, *Citizen Education*, p. 93; see also *ibid.*, pp. 8-11.
[9] Almond, *The American People*, p. 230; cf. Cherrington, *Methods of Education in International Attitudes*, p. 101.

events, can this be done in the professional study of international relations, comprising "such special studies as international politics, international law, international organization, international economics, international education, international ethics, and the psychology and sociology of international relations"?[10] What are the moral premises, if any, typical of such a course? In the abstract, one might expect either that the instructor would attempt to avoid propagating values, in accordance with what many social scientists deem appropriate in the formal training in their disciplines, or that they would instil an American system of values, as part of the professional training of this country's diplomatic staff. Actually, at least some courses in International Relations, whether or not there is a pose of objectivity, propagate for peace and internationalism as absolute values, and this has been true of the discipline from its beginning.

The first courses in the subject in American universities were set up around the time of the First World War, and they generally reflected their instructors' strong partisanship against war and for American participation in the League of Nations.

An emphasis upon what has been variously called "sentimentalism," "idealism," and "Utopianism," dominated the teaching in the new field, and a wholly disproportionate amount of time and energy was given to discussing "international cooperation," while analyses of the forces of conflict in society, and of the institution of war, were subordinated and tainted with the stigma of moral reproach. [This] concentration upon Utopianism . . . cast a shadow of academic disrepute over the new field.[11]

The shift to a more realistic appraisal of power politics in International Relations courses took place, according to Kirk, in the 1930's, when the rise of Nazi Germany seemed to make a mockery of universal cooperation; according to Morgenthau, utopianism remained dominant until the late 1940's.[12] In the 1950's as in the 1920's, the favorite topic for doctoral dissertations in political science was still the subject that is most likely to express a rather high-flown idealism—international organization.[13]

---

[10] Wright, *The Study of International Relations*, p. 7.
[11] Kirk, *The Study of International Relations*, pp. 4-5.
[12] Letter from Professor Morgenthau, July 31, 1958.
[13] Gange, *University Research*, pp. 112-113.

Both tendencies are still evident today, and this exemplifies the point we have made—that even at the level of a professional discipline it is not easy to maintain objectivity in an area as complex, important, and controversial as foreign affairs. It is true that in courses specially designed for majors in the field the trend has continued toward establishing professional standards, with all that these words imply with respect to objectivity. In such a context, for example, war is not condemned as a moral outrage but analyzed as the logical extension under certain circumstances of international relations.[14] The ethical premise of such an approach is not that war is good or even not bad, but that to control we must first understand, and we can understand only by preventing our biases from influencing our perceptions. "Until the basic elements of international affairs and human conduct have been more adequately explored," it is useless to conduct "value-directed research focused on preserving peace."[15]

Such professional courses are, of course, a wholly legitimate element of a general-extension curriculum, useful both as part of a liberal education and as the central component of the college training of students preparing for a diplomatic or similar career. But courses at a professional level could hardly be considered, except in part and then with considerable modifications, appropriate fare for the general public.

Courses for nonmajors are few. Many that exist in name are no more than a shallow review of current events.[16] Almost all are elective, taken by only a small proportion of the students even at those colleges where they are offered.[17] And in them the moral precepts of the 1920's are still common. Their climax often is an appeal to establish a stable, peaceful world order, built now around the United Nations rather than the League of Nations. Writing in 1950, Almond still discerned "an ethical revulsion against 'power politics' and 'national security' among many, perhaps most, school teachers and college instructors."[18]

[14] See, for example, Wright, *The Study of International Relations*, chap. 14 on "The Art of War." See also Hounshell, "A Science of International Politics?"

[15] Gange, *University Research*, p. 128.

[16] Dunn, "Education and Foreign Affairs," p. 142; Furniss, "Theory and Practice," p. 107.

[17] Wilson, *American College Life*, p. 69.

[18] Almond, *The American People*, p. 118.

Education in "World Understanding"

Neither of the two types of ostensibly objective programs in foreign affairs, Current Events and International Relations, is suitable for an educational program for the broader public. And apart from those designed for the training of specialists, there are few programs that even profess not to propagate a point of view. A frequently repeated injunction admonishes program directors to try to reach those not "already convinced" or "converted."[19] This is not the language one uses to describe the imparting of knowledge; there is a faith here that is being proselytized. What faith?

The dogma of this quasi-religion, which we shall designate World Understanding, is difficult to define, for one of its principal characteristics is imprecision. Thus, we are told in a typical essay that educators must get students "away from loaded judgments" and develop in them "world-mindedness and world understanding, [which] are the forerunners of world unity and world brotherhood."[20] Among 150 local agencies engaged in foreign affairs education, 47 per cent described their goal as "increased understanding" in this sense, 25 per cent as "changing attitudes" and 7 per cent as "arousing interest" (which can be taken as other ways of saying the same thing), 18 per cent as "securing action" (which can be taken, again, as a somewhat more vigorous paraphrase of the same goal), and only 3 per cent as "creating critical thinking."[21] Except for the last formulation, the other goals can all be taken as paraphrases of the same one—to increase "understanding."

Several theses in the dogma of World Understanding can be specified:

1. There are no truly significant differences among the world's cultures; there are no really important issues that divide nations. There is only misunderstanding. Wars are made "in the minds of men," and the way to achieve eternal peace is to establish universal understanding.

[19] See, for example, Cohen, "What Voluntary Groups Can Do."
[20] Findings of Group 16, Fifth National Conference on Higher Education, as reported by Whittlesey, "More Effective Education," pp. 120 and 119.
[21] Sillars, "Education for International Understanding," p. 97. His total sample of 250 consisted of the "most active and best developed public affairs programs conducted by their local affiliates," in the judgment of the directors of forty national agencies (pp. 93, 96).

We are here to share our knowledge and by so doing make the most effective use of our combined resources to the end that all peoples will come to understand one another better, and by that understanding realize that the path to peace is one of cooperation—of working together. We are dedicated to this purpose.[22]

Comment: "Understanding" of the political and economic causes of war, thus, consists in ignoring their existence. But international cooperation—a worthy goal in itself—is possible only if the Soviet Union also cooperates.

Only when the Communist ideology has lost its virulence as a world revolutionary movement, and has retreated into the limits of one belief system among many, will it be possible to develop common action between the non-Soviet world and the Soviet bloc in applying the minds-of-men theory to practical affairs.[23]

2.   Cooperation is sought among the "peoples" of the world more than among the nations. The peoples are presumed to be peace-loving, even though their governments may on occasion evince hostility. As a corollary, education in World Understanding can best be furthered by increasing the number of direct, personal contacts across national boundaries.

Real international understanding can be achieved best through personal knowledge of other peoples, their land, their culture, and their customs. . . . The value of this kind of firsthand acquaintanceship is unquestioned. That it is helping to build foundations for a more peaceful world is little doubted.[24]

This interchange of "persons, ideas, information, and culture," moreover, ought to be also with "those nations with which no free exchange now exists." Such an exchange would constitute "a contribution by American liberal education toward the building

---

[22] Johnstone, "Government Programs," p. 83. (Mr. Johnstone was then director, Office of Educational Exchange, U.S. Department of State.)

[23] Dunn, *War and the Minds of Men,* p. 30.

[24] Johnstone, "Government Programs," p. 76. Harold A. Schultz, professor of art education at the University of Illinois, has an addendum to the frequently voiced opinion that through the international dissemination of cultural achievements, "world peace will be achieved." In his paper, "World-Mindedness through Teacher Education in the Arts," he reminds us that, while from this point of view "the most significant ideas are, of course, expressed by the professional artists . . . the art work of children should not be overlooked as a source of international understanding."

of a world in which all nations and peoples can live in peace."[25]

Comment: "Understanding" of the role of the state, thus, is to wish it too out of existence. It is true that in democratic countries some of the people can be reached and that in some cases their will can prevail; but in totalitarian states the people read only the Party press and listen to the Party radio, and they have no avenue short of revolution to impose their will on matters of major concern, such as foreign policy.

If it were true that personal contacts furthered peace, the world would be in a better state—and getting still better—than most persons believe, including World Understanding enthusiasts. For every American citizen, for example, who lived or worked abroad during the past twenty-five years, there will be a hundred or so during the next twenty-five years. These will be not only tourists, students, and government representatives in unprecedented numbers, but engineers of all types, social scientists in all disciplines, experts in trade and finance, shipping and communication—in fact, a fair cross-section of American private enterprise and universities.[26] The cultural interchange that this unparalleled movement exemplifies we freely concede to be a good thing in itself, and we even applaud the Christian ideal of world brotherhood that some of these programs express. The confusion comes from identifying World Understanding with foreign policy.

The artistic product—highly important for civilization and enjoyment—may often be misleading when we try to apply it to the understanding of the political and international realities of a state. Russian music is certainly, for us, much better than the Soviet's foreign policy, and we ought to enjoy that music as often as we wish. But that music is not going to build up much transferable spiritual and intellectual power for dealing with international communism.[27]

3. As many functions of national governments as possible ought to be transferred to the United Nations and other international bodies. Similarly, the identification that people feel with their own governments ought to be merged into a superpatriotism for international bodies. "Quite naturally," the United Nations is

---

[25] Hutchins, "Report of the Commission on International Understanding."
[26] See, for example, Humphrey, *Blueprint and Experience.*
[27] Heindel, "How 'Worldly' Can We Be?" pp. 24-25.

"the central consideration" of programs on world affairs.[28]

Every topic in adult education can be shown to have international significance and can be linked to some part of the work of the United Nations and the Specialized Agencies. . . . The problem is to train leaders to develop a world outlook in themselves and in their group.[29]

Comment: Whether to include the widespread propaganda for the United Nations in a discussion of foreign affairs *education* is a moot point. In both methods and aims, much of it is closer to public relations or even advertising. Tours through the United Nations headquarters in New York, like the Sudan pageant,[30] are intended less to teach than to stimulate an automatic positive response to the brand name, U.N. This dual purpose is reflected in a dual evaluation: the educational effect of the pageant "we have no means of judging accurately," while the public relations campaign was "the most successful case on record." Similarly, making United Nations "flags in thousands of homes and clubs throughout the nation brought some idea of the United Nations to groups which would not ordinarily have been reached by United Nations public information efforts"; but it is not possible to make an objective evaluation of whether such "imaginative programs" as this "really accomplish positive gains in interest and understanding."[31]

Campaigns of this kind may have helped develop the "widespread but vague sense of approval"[32] with which the American public regard the United Nations. There is "clear evidence," the Carnegie Endowment concluded in 1958, "that the United Nations is today accepted as a fact of international life by the overwhelming majority of Americans, but that this acceptance is not firmly rooted in knowledge or understanding."[33] In the programs

[28] Tandler, *Teaching about the United Nations*, p. 33 (U.S. Office of Education).

[29] Spence and Cass, *Guide for Program Service*, p. 5 (Teachers College).

[30] See below, p. 196.

[31] Cory, *Communicating Information*, pp. 60, 62. The flag-making campaign was jointly sponsored by the American Association for the United Nations and the National Citizens Committee for U.N. Day, and carried out by the National Committee on Boys and Girls Club Work.

[32] *Ibid.*, p. 67.

[33] Carnegie Endowment, *The United States Public and the United Nations*, p. 34.

of both universities and a large number of private organizations, these public relations efforts on behalf of internationalism nevertheless continue, with the expenditure of much time and money on still more attempts to break down an open door.[34]

4. Peace is good. Important as it once was to urge pacific solutions to world problems, thermonuclear weapons have made it a thousand times more necessary to do so now.

According to one list of private foreign affairs organizations compiled in 1936, nineteen separate peace societies, plus peace groups within a large number of religious denominations, plus three coordinating pacifist federations, were active in adult education.[35] Since that date, the number of organizations interested in adult education in foreign affairs has grown tremendously; and while the data are not complete enough to warrant a firm statement, it would seem that the principal aim of perhaps half of these is to seek to achieve peace through education and international cooperation.

Comment: No one in the United States advocates war; even the tiny minority in favor of a preventive war are only a partial exception, for they hope thus to avoid a larger, more destructive one. The tremendous effort to proselytize for peace can convert no one, because there is no one to convert.[36] "The real question . . . is not whether we want peace but rather what is tolerable or not tolerable in order to secure peace."[37] Another question, still more to the point, is whether advocacy of peace furthers it. Since such propaganda is not possible in all of the potentially belligerent countries, "working on the minds of one-half the world's population to make them more pacific while the other half is waiting to

[34] Only the minority that has gone beyond support for international organization to propose, or demand, world government, is making a meaningful point. For a survey of organizations and persons that "tell us that world government is possible because it is necessary," see Almond, *The American People,* pp. 217-225.

[35] Ware, *The Study of International Relations,* Chaps. 8 and 9.

[36] Once again, as with the advocates of internationalism, the only proponents of peace who differ from the vast majority of American public opinion are the extremists, the absolute pacifists who would abjure the use of force under any and all conditions. For a postwar survey of pacifist groups interested in foreign-affairs education, see Almond, *The American People,* pp. 209-217.

[37] Educational Policies Commission, *American Education,* p. 30.

dominate them [is] an invidious occupation."[38] One of the important proximate causes of the Second World War, it must be recalled, was the pacifist influences operating on Western statesmen. During the 1930's the Western nations knew from *Mein Kampf* and similar writings what the Nazi program was—a blueprint for the conquest, first of Europe and then of the world; and yet they disarmed themselves before this threat. "Unwillingness to go to war on the part of some nations may operate merely to encourage aggression on the part of others."[39]

In summary, the dogma of World Understanding can be stated in four theses: (1) Wars are made "in the minds of men," not in social, economic, and political relations. (2) We must seek direct contact with all the peoples of the world, short-circuiting the formal intergovernmental channels. (3) Governmental functions should be taken over by international organizations. (4) War should be avoided.

This dogma is transmitted, as one might expect, in a remarkably loose language. Three key terms, "interest," "knowledge," "understanding," differ from each other only in degree, and they invariably lead to a positive policy. A young American becomes "interested" in India, say, by meeting an Indian student visiting his campus. As a consequence, he increases his "knowledge" of India, learning the names of several garments, the significance of caste marks, conditions of village life, perhaps also something about the main social, economic, and political problems facing that country. Thus, he achieves "understanding" in the sense of *tout comprendre, c'est tout pardonner*. From this point on, the American will be better able to judge all issues relating to India: on the matter of foreign aid, he will be in favor of giving more; on the matter of Goa, he will be against Portuguese colonialism (though Kashmir may remain puzzling); concerning India's momentous population increase, he will "understand" that cultures and thus family systems differ; and so on.

Every link in the argument is false:

1. That greater interest leads to a readier acquisition of knowledge is indeed an axiom of educational psychology, provided only that "interest" is defined as an intellectual one. If, as

[38] Dunn, *War and the Minds of Men,* p. 95.
[39] Lazarsfeld and Knupfer, "Communications Research," p. 466.

in this context, the word means an emotional involvement, then a greater interest in the subject can well be a block to knowledge. When a graph is plotted with the degree of interest in a subject along one axis and the amount of knowledge concerning it along the other, the typical relation is not a straight line, as is assumed in the dogma of World Understanding, but a U-shaped (so-called Guttman) curve. If, for example, we test how much American whites know about Negroes, we find that the least knowledgeable (poor southern whites) and the most knowledgeable (northern college graduates) are the two groups most highly interested in the matter.

2. Nor does greater knowledge necessarily lead to greater understanding, if understanding means—as it does in this context —sympathy. The knowledge that the Nazis killed an estimated 4.6 million Jews in their notorious death camps, or that the enforced collectivization of Soviet agriculture and the man-made famine consequent from it killed an estimated 5.5 million Russians,[40] would for most persons result in reducing the sympathy they feel with these regimes.

3. Nor does an understanding (in any other sense than sympathy) necessarily lead to a friendlier policy. "For example, the people of France and Germany have had abundant opportunity to get to know each other well; yet this has not prevented them from engaging in wars of spectacular dimensions."[41]

The imprecision of World Understanding is expressed, finally, in the range of educational and quasi-educational contexts in which such an emphasis is presented on the campuses of American universities. The sloppy thinking and easygoing sentimentality characteristic of this dogma can, as a matter of fact, be applied throughout the curriculum. The teaching of foreign languages can be the occasion for instilling a sympathetic understanding of other cultures.[42] At one junior college, the freshman course in English composition is built around readings on the people, politics, and literature of the Far East, Africa, or Latin America. In courses in literature, art, philosophy, and history, the

---

[40] Reitlinger, *The Final Solution*, p. 501; Lorimer, *The Population of the Soviet Union*, pp. 133-134.

[41] Dunn, *War and the Minds of Men*, p. 6.

[42] This example and most of the following ones are taken from Swift, *World Affairs and the College Curriculum*.

development of West European cultures can be skimped in order to include China, the Arab world, and the other great civilizations. In anthropology, the present mood is to emphasize the essential unity of mankind rather than its cultural diversity. Even mathematics and the physical sciences can be taught so as to stress the ethnic heterogeneity of the persons who have made significant contributions to these fields.

The effect of this sentimental tinge to any subject at all, even when buttressed by a formal course in foreign affairs, may be slight. Some persons believe, as a consequence, that whatever education the college students get in foreign affairs comes in large part through extracurricular activities. It is true that World Understanding is also inculcated outside the classroom—through student clubs, bull sessions, contact with foreign students and professors, pen pals, informal discussion with faculty members, institutes, lectures, debates, films, college newspapers, radio and television programs, library exhibits, travel abroad, visits to the United Nations, dance and music festivals with an "ethnic" emphasis, etc., etc.[43] These activities range from frivolous to potentially significant, from the students' annual exchange of American and Mexican flags on "Pan-American Day" ("a gesture of more than casual importance"![44]) to international professional cooperation of university faculties.

In 1954, as part of the Carnegie Endowment project previously referred to, Wilson surveyed students at fifty colleges in an attempt to determine what gave the students a "world outlook." If their own opinions on what has shaped their views can be taken as at least indicative, this study suggests that campus life outside the classrooms does not have the strong educational role that is usually attributed to it. Of the twenty possible influences on their "world outlook" listed in Wilson's questionnaire, 905 seniors[45] ranked first the courses they had taken; and the next

[43] See Wilson, *American College Life*, Chap. 2.
[44] Findings of Group 16, Fifth National Conference on Higher Education, as reported by Whittlesey, "More Effective Education," p. 121.
[45] Out of a total of 1,500 seniors at the fifty institutions surveyed. The author warns that there is "no assurance that the selected seniors were equally typical or representative in all the institutions concerned" (Wilson, *American College Life*, pp. 94-95).

three influences—newspapers, magazines, newscasts—are not directly related to campus life.[46]

The books by Swift and Wilson do not establish a basis for evaluating the effect of a foreign-affairs emphasis in the general curriculum and extracurricular activities. They do not even provide data to show how widely the programs they describe are distributed among the universities that contributed self-surveys to the study, not to say American higher education in general. The favorable appraisals both books give to most of the programs they describe need not be accepted at face value, since they are merely compilations of self-evaluations. It is hardly probable that the director of a program should denigrate his work in a report to his university's administration, or that the university should pass on that highly unlikely adverse report on a portion of its offerings to a wealthy foundation like the Carnegie Endowment.

Even with better data than now exist, it would be difficult to evaluate most of these programs, for—as has been pointed out—their purpose is not typically defined in precise terms. A display of books in a library corridor—is this a "success" if 10.6 per cent of the students notice it and recall it a week later, or if one student as a consequence *reads* one of the books displayed? A

---

[46] Students were to denote which five of the following twenty factors influenced their "world outlook" most; they are listed here in order, with the one rated most influential first: (1) college courses taken, (2) newspapers, (3) magazines, (4) newscasts, (5) discussions and bull sessions with friends, (6) ideas and opinions of parents, (7) books, (8) lectures, (9) contact with foreign students, (10) travel outside the U.S., (11) faculty members active in world affairs, (12) military service, (13) vocational interests, (14) contact with foreign visitors other than students, (15) high school experience, (16) church, (17) movies, (18) participation in student club activities, (19) concerts, (20) exhibits (*ibid.*, p. 97). From his study Wilson concluded not that extracurricular activities are a weak medium of education in foreign affairs, but almost the opposite: "The main point . . . in the interpretation of these data is the range of influences. . . . Every item on the list of twenty was rated in the top five by some students." In order to reach the maximum number of students, therefore, every kind of activity must be carried on, no matter how few may be influenced by it (*ibid.*, pp. 100-101).

Wilson refers to two other studies on the same subject made in 1954, one of 7,339 students at 19 institutions by World University Service, and the other of 275 students at Pennsylvania State University undertaken as part of the Carnegie Endowment self-survey (*ibid.*, p. 101). Both also showed that formal courses taken and reading are most significant in making the students "aware of international affairs."

student from Afghanistan on campus, one of the 48,486 foreigners studying in the United States in 1960[47]—must he be congenial enough to make a few friends or verbal enough to do some public speaking, or is his mere presence a sufficient symbol that "world outlook" is being fostered? "Almost anything done in the name of international understanding is reasonably safe from criticism. Considerable amounts of money and energy can be expended without any way of determining what has been accomplished."[48] But is it not preposterous to suppose that genuine understanding of a field as difficult as foreign affairs could be furthered by such casual brushes with its subject matter? All that could possibly be developed is a vague, unprincipled acceptance of everything and everyone, and it is just as well that this end is not more often achieved.

The advocacy of internationalism and peace, whatever its effectiveness, can be the expression of any one of three basic political aims. (1) It may be intended as a means of implementing one of the important elements of American national interest, the avoidance of war by cementing friendly relations with other nations. (2) It may be an expression of a belief that world cooperation and peace are paramount values, which take precedence over the national interest of any country, including our own. (3) It may be, finally, a disguised propaganda, intentional or not, for sympathetic tolerance of the Communist enemy. These three political faiths, however different they may be, are very often so intermingled in world affairs programs that they become indistinguishable to the participant. It is important, however, to keep them apart.

Education in Line with Soviet Foreign Policy

If internationalism is the dominant mood in foreign affairs education, this does not mean that the specific policies of various foreign states get no hearing before the American public. As one important function, every embassy and consulate tries to improve the impression of its country held by the American people. Information offices keep a close watch on the mass media and furnish press releases on every relevant topic. Speakers are made

[47] *New York Times*, June 27, 1960.
[48] Dunn, *War and the Minds of Men*, pp. 100-101.

available gratis to any group that will listen to them, particularly to conferences on foreign affairs arranged under the auspices of such a neutral institution as a university. These more or less official efforts are supplemented by a wide array of organizations, each promoting sympathy with one particular country—the English-Speaking Union, the Alliance Française, the various Zionist organizations, and so on; and at a level less directly concerned with foreign affairs, the many fraternal orders, insurance societies, historical and folk associations, and the like, connected with one or another ethnic group.

The spokesman for another country typically argues that its national interests are identical with those of the United States. Someone who reads a number of works on the Near East, for example, will find that American interest "demands" the support of Israel, on the one hand, and the support of the Arab states, on the other; or in the Far East the support of India and that of Pakistan; or in a Latin American country the support of the government in power and of the revolutionary group attempting to overthrow it. Against the background of this constant befuddlement, the American public finds it difficult to define what this country's national interest really is. The confusion is aggravated by the general supposition that in the United States it is unnecessary to propagate American interests. While the United States Government spends millions of dollars each year explaining its foreign policy, and the "American way of life" it is intended to protect, to people in other countries, it does not do nearly so much to inform the public at home on such matters. As we have already shown, the assumption underlying this practice has no basis in fact: whatever differences there may be among commentaries on foreign-affairs education, all agree that the citizens of this country generally are woefully ignorant and that they do not comprehend what it means in concrete political terms to be an American.

The other effects on American public opinion of the spokesmen for other nations are probably not great enough to warrant an extended discussion. The one exception to this statement is the large number of persons and organizations that have been engaged, wittingly or not, in disseminating Soviet propaganda. The necessary background to successful Soviet propaganda is the almost total lack of knowledge concerning Communism and the Soviet Union. This ignorance prevails among all wings of both parties. A Congressman who visited Moscow a year or two ago was pleasantly surprised that he found no barbed-wire barricades in the streets; the anti-Communist exaggerations to which he had listened were as absurd as the statement that there were no such fences in Vorkuta or Karaganda or the other forced-labor camps.[49] In 1946, the year after the war had stimulated the greatest interest in foreign affairs among both the mass media and the reading public, Elmo Roper asked a cross-section of the American people four elementary factual questions about the Soviet Union, and the replies prompted him to comment that the subject is "one of our largest national areas of ignorance."[50]

There is no reason to suppose that this ignorance has been dispelled in the intervening decade. According to one 1957 survey of a stratified nationwide sample, half of the American population did not know who the head of the Russian government was (only one out of four grade-school graduates was willing even to hazard a guess). One out of five college graduates did not know the capital of Russia. Seven out of ten Americans could not name even one Russian author. Half of the respondents believed that there is no free education in Russia. Asked what percentage of the Russian people belong to the Communist Party (the correct answer is about 3 per cent), one quarter of the respondents replied "all," one third "about half," and only 8 per cent more or less correctly.

American men and women who don't know whether Russia produces more or less steel than the United States, who don't know whether Russia is bigger or smaller than the United States, who can't name three countries behind the Iron Curtain, confidently declare that we need not fear war with Russia—or insist that the Russians do not support their own government.[51]

American higher education, unfortunately, has done little to correct this ignorance: college graduates know little more than

---

[49] For a description and analysis of these camps as they existed in the 1930's and 1940's, see Dallin and Nicolaevsky, *Forced Labor in Soviet Russia.*

[50] Quoted in Cottrell and Eberhart, *American Opinion*, p. 49, n. 20.

[51] Salisbury, "What Americans *Don't* Know."

the rest of the population about Communism. The principal effect of their longer education is that they are typically more "liberal" —meaning, paradoxically, more favorably disposed toward the Soviet Union.

Curiously enough, the poorer classes in America, to whom communism is supposed to appeal, were much more distrustful of Russia than the more well-to-do classes, which are supposed to be in mortal fear of a communistic redistribution of their wealth. . . . Who shall say that the graders, on certain broad questions here discussed, were not right? They were most inclined to overrate the destructiveness of the atomic bomb, to show less optimism about the ability of the United Nations to avert a future war, and to reveal deep distrust for the Soviet Union.[52]

Many educators have deplored any expressed hostility toward Communist Russia. Agencies engaged in foreign affairs education, we are told, should try to reduce "attitudes of hostility and fear toward the noncapitalist cultures."[53] We cannot expect Russians to be like Americans, and "no system that lasts over decades is entirely without merits."[54] Some things in the Soviet Union may be objectionable, but its policy toward ethnic minorities, for example, "accords with the best scientific knowledge and the most enlightened moral principles."[55]

Perhaps the most striking example of the sympathetic attitude of some American educators toward the Soviet Union is a Cambridge discussion group in 1947 on "Citizen Participation in World Affairs," reported in a special number of the *Journal of Social Issues*. The discussants were prominent professors at Harvard University and Massachusetts Institute of Technology, plus a few distinguished educators and laymen. That the American public feels too much hostility toward Russia, the participants de-

[52] Bailey, *The Man in the Street*, pp. 137-138. See also, for example, Smith, "The Relation of 'Enlightenment' to Liberal-Conservative Opinions"; Almond, *The American People*, p. 129.

[53] Sillars, "Education in International Understanding," p. 95. (Mr. Sillars is a former editor of *Adult Education*.)

[54] Reid, "The Teacher and World Affairs," p. 2. (Mr. Reid was then executive assistant of the NEA's Committee on International Relations, and in 1960 was with the International Cooperation Administration.)

[55] Wirth, "The Problem of Minority Groups," p. 370. (Mr. Wirth was, until his death, professor of sociology at the University of Chicago.)

cided, constituted the problem they wanted to discuss. Ralph W. Burhoe, executive officer of the American Academy of Arts and Sciences, asked, "Is our attitude toward Russia based on deliberately falsified information, or on misinterpretation?" Erich Lindemann, Harvard University psychiatrist, explained that Americans use Russia as a scapegoat to work off the hostilities they feel toward their own neighbors, and he suggested that a different scapegoat ought to be found for them, such as "vested interests having special reasons for stirring up hostility." (At Ann Arbor, a parallel discussion group agreed with the analysis that Russia is a scapegoat for irrational hostility, and suggested that this be directed against American "isolationists.") Bernard T. Feld, an MIT physicist, urged that newspapers be made to stop emphasizing Russia's lack of cooperation in the United Nations and rather direct public attention to aspects of international affairs where there is little conflict with Russia.[56] It is remarkable that the participants in this conference, who almost certainly were not Communists and probably did not consider themselves pro-Communist, from their initial premise that hostility toward Russia ought to be reduced, followed through to reach conclusions at variance with their own principles. Like the Communists, they thought it desirable to foster antagonism to certain sectors of the American population as scapegoats ("vested interests," certain Congressmen, "isolationists"). Like the Communists, they suggested that news unfavorable to Russia ought to be suppressed. Tolerance of a totalitarian regime is so inimical to liberal principles that it can hardly fail to corrupt them.

Is not such an example from 1947, the reader may ask, digging into the remote past? Have not things changed radically since then? In 1954, a survey of community leaders and a random sample of the public was undertaken under the sponsorship of the Fund for the Republic. The study is interesting in several respects, for it contradicts both the stereotype of an aroused public demanding stern punishment for Communists, and the no less prevalent stereotype of a nationwide witch-hunt threatening civil liberties. Fewer than one per cent of the American population, according to this survey, are seriously "worried" about either Communism or civil liberties. "All categories of community

[56] Maccoby and Willerman, eds., "Citizen Participation," pp. 21-41, 57-58.

leaders, including commanders of the American Legion and regents of the D.A.R., tend on the average to be *more respectful of the civil rights of those of whom they disapprove* than the average person in the general population."[57] One reason for this surprising finding is that a large proportion of community leaders are college-educated. The poorly educated tended to be less tolerant of any deviation, whether atheism, socialism, or Communism; while college taught some who had attended it to be tolerant of all "noncomformists." And within each significant subculture in American society, the more tolerant a person is of nonconformists in general, the less likely is he to perceive a Communist threat to the country's institutions.[58] Neither the more nor the less tolerant were able in any appreciable degree to differentiate between heretics like atheists and conspirators like the American representatives of international Communism.

A heresy is a set of unpopular ideas or opinions on matters of grave concern to the community. The right to profess publicly a heresy of any character, on any theme, is an essential element of a liberal society. . . . A heresy does not shrink from publicity. It welcomes it. Not so a conspiracy. The signs of a conspiracy are secrecy, anonymity, the use of false names and labels, and the calculated lie. It does not offer its wares openly but by systematic infiltration into all organizations of cultural life, it seeks to capture strategic posts to carry out a policy alien to the purposes of the organization.[59]

Working within a community in many respects predisposed to accept a portion of their doctrine, Communists have had a much greater influence in foreign-affairs education than one could suppose from their small number of adherents. They have sought

---

[57] Stouffer, *Communism, Conformity, and Civil Liberties*, p. 27; italics in the original. (Mr. Stouffer is professor of sociology at Harvard University.)

[58] *Ibid.*, p. 208.

[59] Hook, *Heresy, Yes—Conspiracy, No*, pp. 21-22. Even Professor Stouffer did not make this distinction clearly. One purpose of the study, in his words, was to determine the degree of tolerance of "nonconformists, such as Socialists, atheists, or Communists" (*Communism, Conformity, and Civil Liberties*, p. 21), and he constructed a so-called tolerance scale with questions concerning all three groups. He regarded it as a hopeful sign that "ever larger proportions of our population [are being exposed] to the idea that 'people are different from me, with different systems of values, and they can be good people, too' " (p. 220), again with no indication that tolerance of totalitarianism may be undesirable.

and often gained a wide hearing for their point of view through a special type of organization known as a "front."[60] This is an organization created or captured by the Communists, who usually constitute only a minority within it, in order to serve the Party's purposes in one particular field. It has two main features: By creating a kind of associate membership in the Party—fellow-travelers, who adhere to only a certain portion of its program and discipline—its range of power can be increased enormously, both directly and by corrupting liberal institutions that have been successfully infiltrated. And, secondly, since this increase in power is diffused through many supposedly non-Communist organizations, it is less likely to be countered by a comparable rise in anti-Communist sentiment.

The front operating under various names in the field of foreign affairs has been, as one would expect, one of the most important. Founded in 1933 as the American branch of the League against War and Fascism, it was one of a large number of front organizations established in various countries under the guidance of the

[60] Although hundreds of Communist fronts have been operating all over the Western world for several decades, their very existence is still a matter of dispute. As late as 1951, we were told by Ralph Barton Perry, the eminent Harvard professor, that this term is merely an epithet: "The word 'front' . . . has become a verbal weapon used to discredit a mixed group by *naming* it after its most objectionable member. 'Give a dog a bad name and hang him'; or give a man a drop of mixed blood, and be becomes 'colored' to the white supremacists, or 'Jewish' to professional Aryans. Thus, in America today, *Communist front* does not mean an association of different Communist groups and splinters, but an association of Communist and non-Communist groups, named accusingly from its Communist element, however small" (*The Citizen Decides*, p. 47; emphasis in the original). Although Professor Perry warns his readers in the preface that he is compelled in this book "to think about many things of which I have no knowledge," it is doubtful whether a person of his scholarship would write on any other subject with so little regard to fact.

The point of view expressed by Professor Perry, however, is fairly widespread among American academicians, including some of those who know something of the subject on which they write books. Indeed, it is likely that the deepest influence of the late Senator McCarthy, as well as the most damaging, has been on those liberals who accept McCarthy's definition of the situation and automatically oppose his every utterance. If they are too knowledgeable to deny the existence of fronts, they still prefer to pass over this phase of recent American history as too unimportant to be worth mentioning. The mood is somewhat reminiscent of that in West Germany, where there is also a determined effort not to see the possible present relevance of the recent past.

German Communist, Willi Münzenberg.[61] From its inception, it consistently served one purpose—to further the foreign interests of the Soviet Union among as broad a sector of American public opinion as could be reached, changing its line and name whenever this was appropriate:

Name	Period	Reason for Change	Main Propaganda Line
American League against War and Fascism	1933-1937		Fight with Soviet Union against Nazi Germany
American League for Peace and Democracy	1937-1939	Fifth World Congress of the Comintern	Same, but intensified
American Peace Mobilization	1939-1941	Stalin-Hitler Pact	Vociferous isolationism; opposition to lend-lease
American People's Mobilization	1941-1946	Nazi invasion of Russia	All-out war effort; open the second front
National Committee to Win the Peace	1946-1947	End of war	Permit Soviet Union to expand into Europe and Asia
(Dissolved)	1947	To enter Progressive Citizens of America	General pro-Communist line in support of Wallace

Most of the members of this organization and of the scores of fronts like it were *not* Communists; indeed, some of the more credulous may have been unaware that they were cooperating with Communists. Since the turnover in these Communist-dominated organizations is typically large, one can estimate that several million Americans became members of one or more during the Popular Front period and the Soviet-Western alliance. A small percentage of this number were deeply enough involved to

[61] See Fischer, *Stalin and German Communism*, pp. 610 ff.

learn something of Communist Party tactics at first hand, and for them this experience may have constituted a valuable education. For a considerable number, however, the legacy from such a contact is a vague friendliness toward the Soviet government and its parties abroad, an unrecognized predisposition to judge issues in their favor. Such vestigial attitudes may often, of course, have been reinforced by the fear of a new and more terrible war, as well as by the belief that the Soviet Union is basically friendly to the West, or could become so, or whatever.

Perhaps the most significant concept to which the Popular Front substantially contributed was the left–right dichotomy as the perspective in which all political events are generally perceived. While in terms of the cold war Russia is seen as the main enemy, the successor to Nazi Germany as the totalitarian opponent of democracy, in this left–right framework the Soviet Union is the ultimate extension of the social-welfare state that many Americans regard as good.

In arguing against . . . Soviet executives, an American, no matter how well he thinks he knows his own country and his own cause, tends to be drawn into arguing on their grounds. Against their naive and stylized ideas of the capitalist jungle, the temptation is to cite social security, unemployment compensation, the progressive income tax, etc., etc.—in other words to cite the various ways, generally beneficial, in which American capitalism has become to some degree "socialized." But to them, of course, this seems like mere tinkering around the edges of capitalism; they can outsocialize us any day. The tough proposition to argue with them is our reasons for *not* socializing large areas of our life and economy, the virtues we see in private choice, private belief.[62]

Few Westerners have been able to resolve this dilemma completely. The impact of Soviet propaganda, if measured merely by the number who have been convinced, to one degree or another, that Soviet society is good, is not large. If we include the considerably larger number who approve of Communist ideals, or of

[62] Donovan, "Notes on the Russian Tension," p. 222. Mr. Donovan, at the time managing editor of *Fortune*, was one of the American observers of the Soviet elections in the spring of 1958. He traveled around the Soviet Union and talked and argued with about a hundred of the top Party and industrial executives, the equivalents, as he puts it, of $25,000-a-year men in the United States.

the Russian society supposedly in the process of formation, this impact must be reckoned as much greater. And there is a still larger number who automatically, without thinking, analyze all political events with a conceptual tool that places Communist totalitarianism, "the extreme left," at the opposite pole from fascist totalitarianism, "the extreme right."[63]

Summary

In order to lay a basis for discussing policy in university adult education, foreign affairs programs in undergraduate curricula, extracurricular activities, and the offerings of private agencies have been examined.

College graduates have generally received skimpy training in this field. Courses for specialists have improved considerably over the past two decades, but they are taken only by a minute proportion of the student body. Though the situation varies from one campus to another, the vast majority of American college students do not take even one course in foreign affairs. And extracurricular activities, though one may be impressed by their number and imaginative range, are no substitute. Yet however ineffective American colleges have been in educating in foreign affairs, they have succeeded in transmitting a "liberal" orientation to students' opinions, in this as in other subjects. In some areas, such as race relations for instance, this has meant the inculcation of moral values that derive from the core of Western civilization. With respect to foreign affairs, however, "liberalism" has often meant the denial of values, the teaching of a cultural and moral relativism in which all social and political systems are put on a par.

Most foreign-affairs programs of private agencies, similarly, constitute special pleading for peripheral positions. The principal goal of any educational effort in foreign affairs today, one might think, ought to be to clarify the main question: how to deal with

[63] There are other examples of words from another era inadequate to express new political phenomena. For instance, the very word "international" induces a predisposition to regard the Soviet Union as one nation among others, not different in kind from Canada or Thailand or Paraguay. Or compare a political "party" in the West with the Communist "Party" in the Soviet Union—a contrast we have tried to suggest by writing the latter with a capital P.

relations between the democratic West and Communist totalitarianism. A very large portion of the education in this field, on the contrary, either clouds this issue or tends directly to develop sympathy with the Soviet Union. We must "understand" the Russians; we must cooperate with them in international bodies, even if our national interests suffer; we must disarm and maintain peace, again as an absolute; we must oppose hostility to the Soviet Union, even when this is well deserved. Paradoxically, it is the conscious, unambiguous defense of American interests that is underrepresented in agencies' programs in foreign affairs.

These deficiencies in both college courses and the programs of private agencies would seem to invite, as a remedial measure, a strong effort in university adult education. However, the foreign affairs programs offered by universities for adults cannot be said, even by the most charitable estimate, to measure up to this task. Even in terms of quantity, the grossest and least adequate measure of university adult education, the programs in foreign affairs do not make up for known and widely recognized lacks. The most recent data are reported in one volume of the Carnegie Endowment series. From the 57 self-appraisals completed by the time the volume was written, the authors compiled the following summary[64]:

No. of universities		Adult-education programs in foreign affairs—
2		Receive "emphatic attention"
10	12	Are object of conscious positive policy
12		Consist of few or no organized offerings
31	43	Consist of haphazard offerings by individual faculty members
2		Information not available
	57	

"One of the most disturbing conclusions to be drawn from a survey of the field," the authors write, "is that many colleges and universities do little to educate adults in world affairs,"[65] even

[64] Houle and Nelson, *The University*, p. 167. The authors go on to say: "These fifty-seven institutions do not necessarily provide a representative sample of American universities and colleges as a whole."
[65] *Ibid.*, p. 149.

when "education" is defined as loosely as in most adult-education programs. The little that they do, moreover, is very often so haphazard, so totally unrelated to anything else in the extension program, that its effect is probably close to nil. At each of a number of institutions in a recent year, thus, the entire foreign affairs program in extension consisted of *one* of the following: a series of six discussion meetings; an institute on Japan; a discussion series on the United Nations and several on world affairs; "Asia Week"; a conference on UNESCO; informal classes on "Techniques of Travel in Europe"; etc.[66]

[66] See "Report of the Committee on World Affairs," *1955 NUEA Proceedings*, pp. 128-131.

8

UNIVERSITY ADULT EDUCATION IN FOREIGN AFFAIRS:
A GUIDE TO POLICY

From the survey in the previous chapter, it is evident both that Americans generally are ignorant of foreign affairs and that little effective action is being taken to repair this deficiency. Here is an important role for the university, but one that ought not to be lightly undertaken. The hit-or-miss foreign-affairs education ordinarily given in general extension can do little good, and some of it may even do harm. Too large a task to be undertaken by an occasional member of the faculty working in relative isolation, it requires the attention of the institution to organize and consolidate the program.

Content of the Program

"In Defense of the National Interest," the title of a work by Hans Morgenthau, indicates also the appropriate content of a university's adult-education program in foreign affairs.

1. The first characteristic of such a program is the frank avowal of a specific value system. Whether or not social sciences should, and can, avoid a value commitment in graduate training or scholarly research, it is apparent that they cannot at the more superficial level of an undergraduate or adult-education program, and that such an avoidance ought not to be attempted. By their very nature, foreign affairs and international relations imply moral judgments. If other cultures (where, for example, slavery or ritual murder prevail) are presented as in principle equivalent in merit to ours, this in itself represents a value judgment. Or, more to the point, putting the democratic and Communist systems on a level is not objectivity but neutralism.

The admonition that education must not be indoctrination holds for issues involving legitimate alternatives (for example, the

Democratic party vs. the Republican party), but there are some issues that are not "a matter of taste," as Molotov once denoted fascism. The university, in the words of President Gideonse of Brooklyn College, has a clear duty to use its resources in order to emphasize "the philosophical assumptions and commitments that are the intellectual defense in depth of a free society."[1]

Education is not just a mechanical process for communication to the young of certain skills and information. It springs from our most deeply rooted convictions. And if it is to have vitality both teachers and students must be infused with the values which have shaped the system.[2]

2. Perhaps the most difficult step in re-establishing such a moral perspective is, paradoxically, the rejection of what is commonly termed the "utopian" analysis of foreign affairs and the substitution for it of "realism." What constitutes utopianism varies, of course, from one to another exponent of this *Weltanschauung*, but certain characteristics can be denoted as typical. A utopian analysis is often highly simplified, impatient of distinctions: what peoples of the world have in common is significant, and their differences can be passed over. This tends, however, to reduce mankind almost to an animalic level, at which biological needs and the universal modes of satisfying them are relevant,[3]

[1] Gideonse, "Ideals and Goals." See also his "On Re-Thinking Liberal Education," pp. 39-40.

[2] Rockefeller Brothers Fund, *The Pursuit of Excellence*, p. 49. Cf. Raybould, *The English Universities*, p. 14: "What is needed is that as many as possible of the adult population shall understand the nature and implications of democracy, the dangers which threaten it, the problems that beset it, and shall have the will to act on their understanding. This involves more than a knowledge of the structure and functioning of institutions, important as that is. It requires a set of values by which to assess the results of economic and political activity, coupled with the capacity to judge how far proposed policies will further the ends which by those values are deemed to be good. It calls not merely for a factual, but for a philosophic, study of society and its problems. And over and above understanding of any kind, it necessitates the will to act on understanding."

[3] "In a rural school in southern California a group of children cluster around an exhibit of paintings. Their attention is riveted upon a Japanese picture which shows a family harvesting rice. There is much talk about farming—a subject familiar to all the children. 'What do *your* fathers need as they farm *their* land?' asks the teacher. Quickly the children answer, 'Rich soil . . . good seed . . . sun . . . rain . . .' Then, 'Why?' queries the teacher. 'So they will get a big crop.' 'And why do they want a big crop?' 'So as to

while the distinctive features of high civilizations, because they do distinguish, are skimped.

In the utopian advocacy of ultimate principles, one of the factors often brushed aside is the barrier of present, presumably temporary attitudes; and in a totalitarian context, this indifference to the people's wishes has sometimes formed the link between utopianism and terror. For example, in Marxian thought as developed by such early utopians as Marx himself or Rosa Luxemburg, nationalism is a figment fabricated by the exploiting class to facilitate their exploitation; and this vast underestimation of the strength of nationalist sentiment led easily (though not unavoidably) to the ruthless suppression of every national minority by Lenin, Stalin, and their successors.

Perhaps the most pervasive element of utopian analyses is the feeling, sometimes only half expressed, that power is immoral—especially national power, and most especially the power of our own nation. We are told, for example, that world unrest has been the consequence of "the accumulation of power in the United States."

A shift in social values would seem prerequisite to real efforts towards public enlightenment. Our dominant strains which are frankly greed and lust of power will not wither away before a breath of pure benevolence.[4]

The most fundamental postulate of a realist analysis, on the other hand, is that "power as such is amoral. It can be used for good or evil."[5]

This does not mean that for a realist ethical principles are irrelevant to public issues. The point can be aptly made by citing

have something to sell and something to feed their families.' Then, back to the Japanese painting. 'Does this farmer have any of the same needs as he tills *his* field?' Next, the children face the question, 'What kind of a crop does the Japanese farmer hope to have? Why?' And so, through a painting, from the brush of an eleven-year-old Japanese school child, these American pupils discover some of the basic human needs which are universal" (McWhirter, "Service Activities," p. 70; the author is executive secretary of the American Friends Service Committee's Committee on Educational Materials for Children).

[4] Adam, *Education for International Understanding,* pp. 179-180. (Mr. Adam is a professor of political science at New York University.)

[5] Lefever, *Ethics,* p. 6.

Professor Morgenthau, perhaps the best known proponent of realism in America's foreign policy:

The actions of states are subject to universal moral principles. . . . The lighthearted assumption that what one's own nation aims at and does is morally good and that those who oppose that nation's policies are evil is morally indefensible and intellectually untenable and leads in practice to that distortion of judgment, born of the blindness of crusading frenzy, which has been the curse of nations from the beginning of time. . . .
[However,] these universal moral principles cannot be applied to the actions of states in their abstract universal formulation. . . . They must be, as it were, filtered through the concrete circumstances of time and place. . . .
The contest between utopianism and realism is not tantamount to a contest between principle and expediency, morality and immorality, although some spokesmen for the former would like to have it that way. The contest is rather between one type of political morality and another type of political morality, one taking as its standard universal moral principles abstractly formulated, the other weighing these principles against the moral requirements of concrete political action, their relative merits to be decided by a prudent evaluation of the political consequences to which they are likely to lead.[6]

3. The national interest of the United States signifies, at this deepest level, the most effective defense of the values that utopians also insist are paramount. The "fundamental liberties of a free people"[7] rest on a normative system embedded in certain institutions, and to be defended these must first of all be understood. This understanding can be transmitted at several levels: (*a*) by an abstract discussion of basic questions as, for instance, the relation between the state and the individual, church and state, etc.; (*b*) by an analysis of such issues in a historical context, as the acculturation of immigrants, slavery as a cause of the Civil War; (*c*) by a knowledge of the important institutions expressing these values, such as "checks and balances" in the government, the free public school system, and so on; (*d*) by exemplifying this normative, historical, and institutional background with the more important current issues of public life, such

[6] Morgenthau, *Dilemmas of Politics*, pp. 81-86.
[7] This is again the title of a book, by Milton Konvitz .

as desegregation, for instance, or the "socialization" of the market economy.

It is a sad commentary on American education that such basic topics should be appropriate in a program for adults, for graduates, that is, of American high schools and even colleges. Yet it is certain that they are appropriate. Most Americans would designate democracy as "good." A smaller number, though still probably a majority, would be able to define "democracy" meaningfully, say by relating it to certain inalienable civil rights of individuals. But only a small proportion could relate such knowledge to the fact that this "good" "democracy" is associated with the national power of particular countries; and that the exercise of this power, apart from all the stupidities, lacks, and excesses that make up the daily news, is one means by which democracy is maintained.

4. It may be that democratic values have to be defended in a war, and on this subject a university program could usefully add analytical and historical depth to the simplistic negativism that characterizes most adult education in foreign affairs. It aids understanding to distinguish, as Hans Speier has done, between types of war: (*a*) Absolute war, whose purpose is to annihilate the enemy, is conducted without rules. Each belligerent perceives the other not as an opposed force but as animals. (*b*) Instrumental war is waged in order to gain access to values that the enemy controls, with the cost calculated against the possible gain; it is typically regulated by religious or social norms. If what is coveted is considered to be very important, it may verge on the absolute type; or it may approximate the third type, (*c*) agonistic fighting, which is very closely regulated by strict observance of rules.[8] Such a social definition of the purpose of war—annihilation of the enemy, relative advantage (economic or other), or glory—has a much greater effect on mortality than the efficacy of the weapons used. The importance of the differentiation can be illustrated from the history of nineteenth-century Europe, whose leaders maintained an unprecedented era of peace because, by the calculations of realistic statesmen like Bismarck or international financiers, it was seldom worthwhile to go to war.

[8] Speier, *Social Order*, pp. 223-229.

The nineteenth century produced a phenomenon unheard of in the annals of Western civilization, namely, a hundred years' peace—1815-1914. Apart from the Crimean War—a more or less colonial event—England, France, Prussia, Austria, Italy, and Russia were engaged in war among each other for altogether only eighteen months. A computation of comparable figures for the two preceding centuries gives an average of sixty to seventy years of major wars in each.[9]

The military conflicts since 1914 have been more devastating principally because the international structure of the nineteenth century broke down: the balance-of-power system was succeeded by total wars. In the two world wars, regulations of various kinds were successively abrogated—concerning places (e.g., open cities), concerning forms (e.g., declaration of war, treatment of prisoners), concerning weapons (tanks, poison gas, atomic bombs), and concerning values (those, e.g., setting limits to the spoliation of property or of persons). Particularly in the war of 1939-1945, the prior distinction between military and civilians as legitimate targets all but disappeared.

A crucial consideration in judging the probable effects of any future war, thus, is its type. A total war fought with present-day weapons, more destructive than any of the past, would bring about a monstrous depletion of the belligerent countries' populations. But according to a number of analysts, the very fact that both the Soviet Union and the Western powers possess the hydrogen bomb deters either side from using it.

All-out war has . . . ceased to be a meaningful instrument of policy. It cannot be used against the minor powers for fear of the reaction of world opinion and also because its intricate strategy is not appropriate to wars of limited objectives. And it cannot be used against a major power for anything except negative ends: to prevent the opponent's victory. Thus an all-out war which starts as an all-out war is the least likely contingency, although it is the only one for which we have an adequate doctrine.[10]

The sharp contrast between "war" and "peace," made sharper in the minds of Western statesmen by the new weapons, is for-

[9] Polanyi, *The Great Transformation*, p. 5.
[10] Kissinger, *Nuclear Weapons*, p. 128. Cf. Garthoff, *Soviet Strategy*, Chap. 5 and *passim*; Strausz-Hupé et al., *Protracted Conflict*. For an interesting exchange between Sidney Hook and Bertrand Russell on this question, see Hook, *Political Power*, pp. 421-445.

eign to Soviet military–political analysts. For them, the stalemate that mutual deterrence has effected means not peaceful co-existence but the opportunity for the Communist powers to extend their territory and control gradually, indirectly, by force when necessary but not by methods that must lead to a general war.

If the Soviet bloc can present its challenges in less than all-out form it may gain a crucial advantage. Every move on its part will then pose the appalling dilemma of whether we are willing to commit suicide to prevent encroachments, which do not, each in itself, seem to threaten our existence directly but which may be steps on the road to our ultimate destruction.[11]

5. The pedagogic truism that one understands one's own society best comparing it with others certainly applies in foreign-affairs education. In order really to understand Western democracy, we must in particular know something of its present-day antithesis, Soviet totalitarianism.

We must study the Soviet philosophy, we must examine and debate the creed of the Communist party as it has been formulated and defended both here and in foreign lands. Indeed, I would go so far as to say that this is the number one educational need of the present moment. This must clearly involve adult education even more than school and college if an effect is to be produced within the next few years. . . . The twin objectives of discussion groups, radio programs, and evening classes [ought to be] an understanding of the American democratic society and its historic goals, and a dissection of the Soviet philosophy and an exposure of its methods. One of the chief problems of the armed truce is to achieve the second of these objectives in the face of the tendency of certain leaders to confuse a tightening of military security with a witch hunt.[12]

Teaching about Communism, it is still necessary to emphasize, is not the same as teaching Communism; the confusion on this point has run through the political gamut. If "liberals" have often been unable to identify Communists as totalitarian enemies of liberalism, "conservatives" have just as often been unable to distinguish liberals from Communists. In the context of higher

[11] Kissinger, *Nuclear Weapons*, p. 16.

[12] Conant, *Education in a Divided World*, p. 216. For a more specific program along the same lines, see Steibel, "International Understanding."

education, "liberals" have typically held that Communists have a "right" to teach the young people of this country,[13] and some "conservatives" have tried to deny universities, libraries, and even scholars access to Communist books and periodicals. Relatively few have held that it is necessary that Americans learn as much as can be about Communism, whenever possible from original sources, but that for the purpose of defending Western democracy this end could not be achieved by hiring Communist teachers.[14]

6. The centrality of the opposition between democracy and totalitarianism does not mean, of course, that there are no other major problems. What these are depends on how broadly one defines "major," but even the narrowest range would include the following: (*a*) The rapid increase in population in most under-developed countries, and the impediment that this represents to economic and cultural modernization. (*b*) The breakdown of the nineteenth-century empires, and the surge of nationalism in the postcolonial countries. (*c*) Overlapping this to some degree: the influence of racism, including the new version of anti-Caucasianism, on foreign affairs. (*d*) Economic relations among nations, as reflected in trade agreements, tariffs and other barriers, international investment and aid, etc. (*e*) The development of thermonuclear and other new weapons, and their effect on military policy and the nature of war.

While many of these factors are to some degree corollary to the basic division of the world between Communism and the democratic West, the ability to deal with them independently constitutes an important part of the West's *positive* foreign policy. In an educational context, the problem is to avoid both oversimplification and formless clutter, and it can be solved only by concentrating on a few basic issues and relating the rest of the subject matter to them. *All* of the issues are political (or, sometimes, economic-political); and programs that deal only with cultural data, though perhaps worthwhile in themselves, cannot

[13] As recently as the mid-1950's, this stand was reaffirmed and even strengthened by the American Association of University Professors, the largest and most authoritative organization of college teachers. See Hook, *Political Power,* pp. 296-309.

[14] For discussions of this point, see Hook, *Heresy, Yes—Conspiracy, No;* Educational Policies Commission, *American Education,* pp. 37-40.

be the main constituent of foreign-affairs education.

7. The ordinary topics in foreign-affairs programs—like areas of the world (Asia, Africa, Latin America—but also Western Europe, Canada, and other significant even though less exotic places), or the most important of recent events (the Suez crisis, the Hungarian revolution, the war in Algeria, etc. etc.), or quite specific policy decisions (unification of the Armed Forces, reciprocal trade agreements vs. tariffs, another Summit conference or not), or even personalities (the proud Nehru, the touchy Nasser, the bumptious Khrushchev)—these obviously are relevant, but only if they are kept at the level of illustrative examples of the basic issues. An adult-education program on India, for example, should be mainly about neutralism, Asian nationalism, the population explosion, economic aid, and similar general subjects as exemplified by this one country. The recurrent dilemma in pedagogy, how to use the telling detail to convey the whole, is particularly acute in a program designed to educate a group as uninformed as the American public on a subject as complex and controversial as foreign affairs.

Organization of the Program

Good policy includes making the most effective use of any foreign affairs program set up. Some of the administrative problems that have to be met can be illustrated by the "lament of a discouraged adult educator," Dean Horn, then of Johns Hopkins University's evening program.

A review of our results this year at Hopkins . . . is illuminating if disheartening. . . . In the fall of 1948, we had arranged a non-credit course on "The Soviet Union Today," given by Mr. Craig Thompson, then occupying the Russian desk on *Time* magazine, and only recently returned from a two-year stint in Moscow as *Life* and *Time* correspondent. His lectures in this course were significant enough to be published commercially in a book that will come from the press shortly. But even though the tuition fee was only $12.50, the course drew just 41 registrants. The information Mr. Thompson had presented in 1948 seemed so important, however, that we asked him to repeat his course. But this year we enrolled only 15 students and had to cancel the course.[15]

Four other courses—on the Far East, the Near East, and India

[15] Horn, "International Understanding," p. 111.

and Pakistan, plus a general course for teachers—were also cancelled because of the small number of registrants. A particularly ambitious, well publicized program on "The United Nations and World Cooperation," with 32 prominent speakers, had an enrollment of only 89—as compared with 200 in English literature, 300 in economics, 250 in differential calculus, and so on. In Dean Horn's opinion, the reasons for the failure were not specific to the local situation, but were rather that people are "fed up on the international situation" and do not enroll in "courses that by concentrating on the world's problems seem to promise only an aggravation of the individual's sense of confusion and helplessness."[16]

This experience suggests some organizational principles:

1. First of all, so that we do not lose sight of fundamentals, we must emphasize that Dean Horn was correct in two respects. It *was* his function as an educator to decide on what courses are worthwhile, and to offer them irrespective of "demonstrated needs." And he successfully resisted the temptation to reduce the level of the program in the hope of enlisting a larger number of participants.[17]

2. With respect to content, the aim of mitigating the participants' sense of confusion, rather than aggravating it, can be accomplished only by concentrating on a small number of basic issues.

3. The worth and importance of a program cannot be measured wholly by enrollment and cash intake.[18] In a day college, a course in fourth-year Latin, for example, would be given to only

[16] *Ibid.*, pp. 113-114.

[17] The four comments on Horn's article in the same issue of *Adult Education Journal* illustrate some of the recurrent themes that have been discussed in earlier chapters. Two educators berate the dean for thinking that he knew the people's "needs" better than they, or that citizenship "can be learned passively by listening to talk." Two others suggested that the programs ought to talk down, with sure-fire labels like "How Does Our Near-East Policy Affect America's Gasoline Prices?" or "The Sex Life of the Chinese" (pp. 115-118).

[18] "Frequently," moreover, in the opinion of Houle and Nelson, "the financial obstacle is not a cause of failure but a convenient excuse for not trying." When they asked a meeting of extension directors whether they knew of any planned programs in foreign affairs that had to be cancelled because funds could not be obtained, not a single instance could be cited. Several programs, "launched with the slimmest financing," however, "subsequently attracted support sufficient to sustain them" (*The University*, p. 151).

4 or 5 students; is an enrollment of 89, or even 41, small compared with this? Of course, the chronic shortage of funds in general extension cannot simply be wished out of existence. Since it takes so much time, money, and creative energy to launch any extension program, institutions not well equipped ought to restrict themselves to concentrated ventures, deliberately limited in both potential participants and content.

4. Even the best courses, set up one by one, do not add up to an adequate foreign-affairs program with respect to either content or educational method. A busy dean can give the initiative for a foreign-affairs program, and a no less busy member of the faculty can teach a course; but this is not enough. In most cases, it would require a special organizational effort both to establish a good program and to arrange for its financing. How much any institution is willing to do in this respect would depend first of all on the available personnel, academic and administrative, and on their competence and interest in effective foreign-affairs education. A broad and efficient program would require a small permanent secretariat to set it up and maintain it. This would include, in addition to the administrator directing it, persons with three types of skills: subject-matter experts in the various social sciences; teachers, writers, discussion-group leaders, and others able to convert sometimes difficult technical material into generally understandable, but not oversimplified, form; and persons able to organize particular sectors of the population into participating audiences and groups. Such a team of scholars, popularizers, and organizers could conceivably educate a community on foreign affairs.

5. A foreign-affairs program ought to be set up with a specific type of participant in mind, and these participants ought to be specially solicited to take part in it. This is a point important enough to demand amplification.

Who Can Be Educated?

The electorate consists of individuals whose votes are counted one by one. In another sense, it consists of broad groups defined by social characteristics that, particularly in combination, influence both the direction of each person's political opinions and their intensity.[19] An administrator planning a program in public-affairs education wants to reach those with sufficient interest and prior learning to benefit most from it, as well as those whose influence is great enough to warrant a hope that their better understanding of the issues will eventually affect public opinion and policy. It so happens that to a large degree these two groups are made up of the same persons, who can, moreover, be approximately identified. Probably the most important determinant both of interest in public issues and of the ability to understand them is education. And since those with a better education also are congregated in more prestigeful occupations, have higher incomes, live in towns rather than in the country, and so on, one's level of education is also a reasonably good index of one's potential influence on public policy.

A second determinant of political interest is ethnic background (or, what can often be taken as an index of this, religion). Indeed, in the opinion of some analysts, differences among the electorate, particularly on foreign policy, largely reflect the half-hidden ethnic variation of the American population.[20] A third important determinant of political interest is sex. Some decades after 1920, when the nineteenth amendment gave women the vote, they are still—except for a minority exemplified by the League of Women Voters—markedly less interested than men in political questions, including foreign affairs. A fourth important factor is occupation, and a fifth is income. It must be emphasized, however, that the predispositions set by these social characteristics are neither universal among the designated groups nor necessarily fixed, for in this period of rapid social change established patterns of political behavior also tend to break up and re-form.

The combined effect of these various social determinants of political behavior divides the electorate into five roughly delimited, partly overlapping classes:

[19] In one instance, thus, it was possible to calculate from the three factors of socio-economic status, religion, and urban-rural residence, an "index of political predisposition" which some months before an election was a more accurate predictor of how the people would vote than their own forecasts. See Lazarsfeld et al., *The People's Choice*, pp. 25 and 102. For an interesting attempt to reconcile these two concepts of the electorate, see Dahl, *Preface to Democratic Theory*.

[20] See, in particular, Lubell, *The Future of American Politics*.

1. *Opinion molders*, who as public officials or members of other key occupations offer guidance on public policy. Some few of these have a thorough understanding of the issues, but many —clergymen, editors of small newspapers, spokesmen for trade unions or chambers of commerce, etc.—are hardly less ignorant on foreign affairs than the general population. For example, some Protestant ministers, whose whole value system is opposed to totalitarianism, have on occasion been useful dupes of Communism. On the other hand, activists in the large veterans' organizations, whose opposition to Communism cannot be questioned, have sometimes forgotten the meaning of the democratic system they were defending.

If special intensive programs in foreign affairs for such opinion molders were set up, the university's educational impact could be multiplied many times over. The sector might well be defined broadly, to include not only high school history teachers, for example, but all public school teachers; not only editors of local newspapers but all reporters and radio or television commentators; not only educational directors of trade unions but all their officials; etc. Within limits, it would be necessary to adapt the content, the level, and the form of presentation to each particular group. For clergymen, thus, a special seminar on the relation between the Judaeo-Christian ethic and the democratic credo would furnish the meat of a hundred sermons. For newspapermen, a discussion group on the basic issues in American foreign policy might give perspective to a thousand news items. Even with a small number of participants, a foreign-affairs program of this kind would demand a good deal of work to organize. If the resources available limit a university to a relatively small extension program, first priority might well be given to the education of opinion molders.[21]

2. *Policy molders*, who attempt to influence American foreign policy either directly, as by hiring lobbyists, or indirectly, by trying to corral public opinion for or against a given stand.[22] The

[21] For a description of two special programs for what Houle and Nelson term "specialists in adult world affairs education"—the various professionals who direct foreign-affairs programs for adults—see *The University*, pp. 142-143.

[22] This category is similar to what Almond has called "interest elites"; see *The American People*, p. 140.

differentiation between this class and that of opinion molders is obviously not clear in many cases, but in others it may be. Among the nongovernmental agencies that attempt to influence foreign policy, the most successful, it would seem, have been business organizations, trade associations, and the like; and the second most successful have been organized ethnic groups.[23] These two quite different types of groups, business and ethnic associations, are similar in one respect: they ordinarily attempt to influence not American foreign policy as a whole but one small corner of it, highly salient for their members and of relatively little interest to the public at large.

It is at least possible that in an imaginative adult-education program this narrow interest, whether in the tariff on meat, say, or American policy toward Israel, could become the basis for a broader understanding of foreign affairs. Since it has seldom if ever been attempted, it cannot be ruled out a priori. Businessmen, for instance, are obviously most interested in policies directly affecting their particular business; but the contents of such periodicals as the *Wall Street Journal* and *Fortune* suggest that many also see the relevance of America's foreign policy, or are concerned about it as citizens.

3. *Opinion leaders,* who exercise a word-of-mouth influence on public issues over a circle of friends and acquaintances. According to a number of studies, the formal media of communication that the professionals control usually have a significant effect only when they are reinforced by this informal channel.[24] Opinion leaders, however, are distinguished less by their better information on public issues than by their greater interest. The leaders comprise many opinion molders (a clergyman, for example, whose personal advice is sought on any issue), some who know a bit more than their circle (a hardware dealer who subscribes to a news magazine, a gas station attendant who served in the Far East with the

---

[23] Cohen, *The Influence of Non-Governmental Groups,* pp. 6-8. Cohen reports these conclusions from various studies and cites some of the supporting evidence, but he is obviously skeptical on the whole question of whether there actually are private groups that have a direct and effective influence on foreign policy. A lobbyist cannot be deemed successful merely if a certain policy is adopted, but only if it would not have been adopted without his pressure behind it; and the latter point must of course be speculative.

[24] For a competent survey of recent studies, see Hero, *Opinion Leaders.*

Army), and some whose authority is based only on a forceful personality, ethnic identification, or some other characteristic irrelevant to their knowledge of public issues. Merely to identify the opinion leaders of any community would be a sizable and expensive undertaking, and in adult education the rule-of-thumb definition is that self-selected portion of the public that gives some overt evidence of interest in public affairs, such as active support of a political party or participation in a foreign-affairs program. By definition, thus, they constitute part of the public for such a program.

4. The *attentive public*, or those enough interested in public issues to heed the counsel of the opinion molders and leaders. Most adult-education programs in foreign affairs are intended for this sector—if not indeed for the entire population. It must be emphasized, however, that to enlist the participation of a sizable proportion of the attentive public is not easy.[25] Given favorable conditions, it can be done, but unless the institution is willing and able to put forth a sustained effort, allocating a variety of resources over a considerable period, it would be pointless even to make the attempt. How much can be achieved, and by what combination of communication media, are still open questions.

5. The *apathetic public*—which has been variously designated as the "general public," "the inattentive," the "unaware," or the "indifferents."[26] In residual terms, this is the portion of the population that does not fall into any of the other sectors. More specifically, the apathetic are often designated as those persons who do not generally vote. If we accept this line of delimitation, it must be with the understanding that it is only the roughest of definitions. Some who regularly exercise their right to suffrage (a dutiful lower-class wife, for example, who follows her husband to the polls) are apathetic by any other standard. On the other hand, some of those vitally concerned about public issues do not vote,

[25] Perhaps it is becoming feasible, however, because of the increasing awareness that foreign affairs are of crucial importance. In the 1960 election campaign, for instance, both major candidates emphasized America's foreign policy as the primary issue, and according to a number of polls they shared this view with a large majority of the electorate.

[26] These terms are used, respectively, by Almond, *The American People;* Houle and Nelson, *The University;* Kriesberg, "Dark Areas"; and Riesman et al., *The Lonely Crowd,* pp. 193 ff. For an excellent up-to-date survey of voting and nonvoting, see Lipset, *Political Man,* Chap. 6.

and some are disfranchised—Negroes in the South, the fifth of the population that moves to a new residence each year, inhabitants of Washington, D.C. Nonetheless, the regular failure to exercise the most fundamental civil right and duty is probably the best single index of political apathy.[27]

The apathetic public is the object of a guilty preoccupation in adult education, and particularly in public-affairs education. Many adult educators feel that, since in theory all citizens ought to participate in the shaping of all public policy, education in this field should be in the form of mass campaigns, aimed at the entire electorate. Some go even farther and maintain that special exertion is warranted in order that one may reach the apathetic.

These widely held opinions, however, can be challenged on a number of grounds:

a. The first objection is pragmatic: efforts to reach the apathetic, however strenuous, are not generally successful. It is known that nonvoters are generally at a lower level of intelligence, education, and income,[28] and are therefore inherently much more difficult to interest in public affairs. In the few instances when the effect of mass education campaigns was tested, the clear conclusion generally has been that it was close to nil. For example, the intensive six-month campaign in Cincinnati that we have already described[29] reduced the proportion of the city's population "totally unacquainted with the main purpose of the United Nations" from 30 to 28 per cent.

b. The exceptions to the generalization that mass education campaigns in public affairs do not succeed are likely to be only seeming exceptions, based on a confusion of mass participation with education. If "starting with people where they are" is adopted too wholeheartedly, the "educator" may also end with the people where they were, with the only criterion of "success" being that large numbers enthusiastically marked time. The

---

[27] But see Riesman and Glazer, "Criteria for Political Apathy." In recent presidential elections, almost four out of every ten Americans with the right to vote did not exercise it. The proportion of nonvoters varied enormously from region to region, from about one-fifth in Utah to more than three-quarters in Alabama and Mississippi. As these extremes suggest, not only race relations but also such factors as religion can be important determinants of the voting record.

[28] See, for example, Connelly and Field, "The Non-Voter," pp. 179-180.

[29] See above, p. 47.

United Nations pageants in Sudan, Texas, for example, have been described as "the most successful case on record of citizen participation in the cause of the United Nations," since 1,000 of Sudan's 1,400 inhabitants took part in it. But—

> Only a few of the leaders really participated in a way which required them to have knowledge of the United Nations. Most of the citizens participated in roles such as band members, choristers, purveyors of refreshments, or as designers of floats for the parade. . . . [Moreover] a big festival meant good business. . . . Just what was the effect of the Sudan Festival in creating understanding of the role of the United Nations in world politics, we have no means of judging accurately.[30]

That is to say, the often repeated dictum that public-affairs education must be scaled down to the level of the students, that it must be tied to their everyday interests and concerns, is valid only within a certain narrow range. Foreign affairs in particular are not simple, and oversimplifying the issues is equivalent to falsifying them, or even to not raising them at all.

c. As has been pointed out, the general population often responds more to informal communications on public issues than to mass media. If over half of the people cannot be reached directly with college-level materials, those who insist on principle that they *must* be reached might well concentrate on doing so indirectly, by improving the education of the other half, and particularly the sizable number among this latter group whom we have defined as opinion molders and leaders.

d. If the apathetic continue not to vote, this is in many instances all to the good, in spite of the fetish to the contrary.[31] The nonvoter is much less well informed on public issues,[32] and in his ignorance he is more likely to be manipulated by special-interest groups or to follow a demagogue.[33] "Instead of urging people to

---

[30] Cory, *Communicating Information*, pp. 2, 3.

[31] The nonvoter, in the words of one practicing politician, must "face the combined scorn of both political parties, the schoolteachers, boy scouts, war veterans, chambers of commerce, . . . leagues of women voters, . . . bar associations, girl scouts, tavern keepers, President Eisenhower, radio and TV stations, and junior chambers of commerce" (Coulson, "Let's Not Get Out the Vote," p. 52).

[32] Connelly and Field, "The Non-Voter," pp. 182, 185.

[33] Riesman et al., *The Lonely Crowd*, p. 200.

vote, we ought to be urging them to study and form opinions."[34] "Not all people in a democracy need concern themselves continuously with public affairs (or with the union, or with the PTA, or what not), but . . . all should have a 'right of veto' of which to make sparing, residual exercise" on issues of sufficient moment to engage their spontaneous interest.[35]

The general rule that universities should restrict themselves to persons of college level, then, applies to education in foreign affairs no less than to that in other fields. In fact, the very importance of this subject strengthens the dictum, makes it more essential that the scarce resources available for college-level education of adults should not be used frivolously. The rule is reinforced in a practical sense, moreover, by the fact that even college graduates are often distressingly ignorant of the issues in foreign affairs. No community in the United States lacks potential participants capable of learning from a college-level program in this field.

Conclusions

It is usual in discussions of adult education in foreign affairs to end with an exaggerated appraisal of the recommended program's potential effects. We have cited a number of authors who believe, or at least say, that the highway to eternal peace and prosperity lies through the office of the adult-education administrator. We do not believe this. The effect of adult education, even of the best and largest conceivable programs, on the future of international relations will not be decisive. Even so, with proportions guarded, a university program in adult education along the lines described in this chapter would in our opinion be of great importance.

There is no reason, first of all, to suppose that the eventual effect of such a program would be limited to the actual participants. So uncommon an initiative would undoubtedly appeal to other university administrators, so that it might well be followed in other extension programs. More—the "extension" in this case might very well be to the regular campus, with the novel consequence that graduates of American universities would be at least

[34] Coulson, "Let's Not Get Out the Vote," p. 53. See also Dunn, *War and the Minds of Men*, p. 96; Almond, *The American People*, p. 70.
[35] Riesman, *Individualism Reconsidered*, p. 37.

modestly equipped to think about American foreign policy in-telligently. This "extension" would follow in any case if, as we have suggested, the first and main effort is to teach the opinion molders, whose improved knowledge and understanding would reverberate through the community.

Whatever its specific content—and the possible range is very wide—one main feature of the program we advocate would be to alter basic ideas about power and nationalism. Power as such is not evil; on the contrary, in a world where evil forces have great power, only counterpower can prevent the victory of evil. The nation is not an abstraction but the embodiment of values and institutions that may be worth defending. To the degree that the nation is conquered, or is submerged in a homogeneous inter-national organization, the values specific to it will tend to dis-appear. In short, such a university program in adult education would help to re-establish among the participants the legitimacy of patriotism, not in the sense of the adolescent jingoism to which it is now more or less restricted, but in the sense of support for the moral, social, and military bulwark of the democratic tradi-tion and, indeed, of the ordinary day-to-day decencies that in the West are taken for granted.

The possible range in organizational patterns, also, is great. The main point we have tried to make is that some special organiza-tional effort is called for, and that the importance of the subject demands that this be a serious effort. The random programs of-fered *ad hoc* whenever someone's casual interest is aroused cannot be adequate. It is not a matter of size; on the contrary, perhaps the worst programs of all are the mammoth campaigns to "edu-cate" the masses with flying banners and blaring brasses. If a uni-versity can afford—in terms of money, time, and personnel—only a small program, this can still be eminently worthwhile if it is intelligently planned and executed.

University adult education makes up no more than about 4 per cent of all adult education in this country. It is impossible for universities to cover the entire field of education in foreign affairs and unreasonable of them to make the attempt. Offering college-level programs to an unselected mass audience, moreover, is bound to fail. Either the content of the program becomes diluted down to sloganizing, or the interest of about half the population cannot be engaged. The legitimate function of the university, to teach those adults capable of absorbing them facts and ideas about foreign affairs at the level of college work, is an imperative task. No contrast in public life is more striking than that between the great and growing importance of foreign affairs in shaping American society and, on the other hand, the ignorance of even well educated persons about the most elementary facts and the most basic issues.

Public affairs generally tend more and more to be dominated by the relations of the United States to the rest of the world, so that today few domestic issues can be really understood or intelligently resolved without relating them to foreign affairs. Isolationism, in spite of such postwar manifestations as the Bricker amendment, is moribund. The main problem is wise foreign policy, and this is a problem of global significance. As Barbara Ward put it, with no more than literary hyperbole, "America's foreign policy is everybody's destiny."[36] And the interdependence works both ways; one could say with no greater exaggeration that everybody's destiny is America's fate. As a businessman George Humphrey was a hard-money conservative with isolationist tendencies; after he became Secretary of the Treasury, he confessed that he had had "no idea of the extent to which our own security was involved in whatever happens in the world."[37]

[36] Quoted in Lefever, *Ethics*, p. 1.
[37] Quoted in Lubell, *Revolt of the Moderates*, p. 143.

Appendix 1

COOPERATIVE EXTENSION
AND THE LAND-GRANT SYSTEM
IN UNIVERSITY ADULT EDUCATION

by Warren Rovetch

In the main body of this book, university adult education was discussed as the product of the two institutions of which it forms a part, the university and adult education. Cooperative Extension was deliberately passed over, excluded even from what the authors term the total extension function. The rationale for this limitation of the subject has a substantial basis in fact: Cooperative Extension is indeed a world apart, with different purposes, adequate financing, an elaborate staff and service structure, personnel more or less isolated from both the main campus and its extension. What Cooperative Extension does is relevant, of course, to a discussion of general extension, but mainly in the sense that anything happening in American education has some effect, or may have, on university adult education.

This was the pattern, at any rate, of the past, but it will certainly be less so in the future. Both university adult education and Cooperative Extension are changing rapidly, and some type of convergence is generally considered to be both likely and desirable. "Everybody feels that general and Cooperative extension must somehow be made to work more closely together but nobody knows how that result can be brought about."[1] The process of bringing these two "extension services" together, however, will prove to be considerably more complex than most persons imagine. They are animals of different species.

Nonetheless, it is true that a new cooperative pattern relating the two institutions will serve the best interests of both. The land-

[1] Houle, *Major Trends*, p. 25.

grant system with its Cooperative Extension has a well financed administrative structure and trained personnel; the university has academic resources. To analyze fully the means by which these can be integrated, wholly or in part, toward common ends would demand another book, rather than a supplement to this one. This discussion has neither the scope nor the depth of a guide to policy; it is intended to suggest rather than to define. But in view of the magnitude of the land-grant system, its significance for American higher education and particularly for adult education, and the new potential of the Cooperative Extension service, even such a preliminary presentation may be useful to the reader.[2]

The Land-Grant System in Higher Education

In 1862, when President Lincoln signed the Morrill Act, the land-grant system came into existence. Colleges were established "to insure the development of institutions adapted to the educational needs of agricultural and industrial classes."[3] Service to society is as much part of the institutions' responsibility as resident instruction. Through Cooperative Extension, engineering extension, agricultural experiment stations, engineering experiment stations, and other organized research, they perform a public service that is peculiar to American education. Conceived as "democracy's colleges," the system grew together with modern America. Though federal in origin, each institution is historically local, administered and primarily supported by the people it serves.[4]

Today there are 69 land-grant institutions, out of the total 1,355 four-year colleges and universities in the United States.

[2] The generalizations of this discussion cover states as diverse in population, geography, and economy as New York, Montana, New Mexico, and California; Cooperative Extension services ranging in size of state staffs from over 800 to under 50, and in annual budgets from over $6 million to under $500,000; land-grant institutions with budgets of over $30 million and under $5 million; universities where large and well staffed general-extension divisions already exist side by side with Cooperative Extension and those where general extension is not even acknowledged in a table of organization or the budget. For these many differences the reader must make his own adjustments.

[3] U.S. Office of Education, *Statistics*, p. 10.

[4] For one history of land-grant institutions, see Eddy, *Colleges for Our Land and Time.*

They range in size and importance from some of the great American universities (California, Illinois, M.I.T., Michigan State, Minnesota, Cornell, etc.) to smaller and more specialized institutions, including 17 attended primarily by Negroes. Their combined budgets total over one billion dollars annually, or almost a third of the total for all four-year institutions. More than a fifth of all degree-credit students in the country are enrolled in members of the system. About a quarter of the college graduates, including a third of all engineering graduates, get their degrees from land-grant institutions.[5]

Land-grant institutions have an annual budget of $114 million for extension and public service. This is 83.6 per cent of such expenditures in all four-year institutions combined.[6] In over half the land-grant institutions, the outlay for extension and public service comprises approximately one-fifth of the total budget. On the average, one-fourth of all staff positions are classified as extension.[7]

Of the $270 million that land-grant institutions spend annually on research, nearly half is used to support the agricultural experiment stations. While the largest portion of their budget goes to production research, it also includes research in economics, rural sociology, marketing, etc. The total comprises over half of all organized research financed by four-year institutions in the United States.

Both the concept and the operations of land-grant institutions are inseparable from the society they serve. Thus, the social, economic, and political forces remaking America are, simultaneously, pressures on the land-grant system. Moreover, "the whole course

[5] U.S. Office of Education, *Statistics*, pp. 43, 3-5. Trends since 1956-1957 do not substantially change the picture given here.

[6] *Ibid.*, p. 43. Includes expenditures for correspondence courses, radio courses, adult-study courses, non-degree-credit courses, institutes, public lectures, some Cooperative Extension, radio and television stations; but does not include college-credit courses even when offered under an extension department. Also, does not cover the total Cooperative Extension budget which includes additional county and federal funds and does include functions outside the Cooperative Extension budget (p. 24).

[7] *Ibid.*, p. 32. Of the 102,034 positions in the 69 land-grant institutions, over 15,000, mainly full-time, are in Cooperative Extension; 6,145 positions, many part-time, are allocated to degree and non-degree extension courses, and 3,164 to correspondence and short courses.

of higher adult education, in all its aspects, will be influenced by the events which take place on land-grant college campuses in the next few years."[8] The future of the land-grant institutions with respect to resident teaching and departmental research is comparatively easy to estimate. At least its scope is clear. State colleges are becoming state universities, with a concomitant expansion of the A & M college's once traditional vocational curriculum. Small institutions are becoming large, large ones are growing beyond the bounds of yesterday's imagination.

What will happen to extension is more difficult to forecast. If the argument of this book is correct, college-level adult education is a most important university function, now seriously hampered by lack of funds, lack of personnel, lack of organization and clear purpose. Cooperative Extension, on the other hand, is in transition from its prior well-nigh exclusive concern with agriculture, home economics, and rural welfare. The number of farm families has been steadily cut by urbanization and rising agricultural production. And with the transition of rural America, Cooperative Extension has been forced to go beyond the narrow interests of its constituency and examine some of the complex and diverse forces remaking America. This search for a new purpose and a new constituency has been well endowed: Extension's annual budget has been substantially increased over the last decade. It is this contrast—the penurious general extension with an important job to do, and the comparatively affluent Cooperative Extension looking for employment[9]—that suggests some pattern of cooperation between them. If this suggestion is to be realized, it will have to be in terms of the two very different traditions.

Cooperative Extension—Part of and Apart from the Institution

The Federal Cooperative Extension Service was established in 1914 by the Smith-Lever Act. This was designed to facilitate education "relating to agriculture and home economics" for persons "not attending" college, with special stress on "practical demon-

---

[8] Houle, *Major Trends*, p. 20.

[9] As in many marginal or even rapidly changing endeavors, "employment" should not be confused with the amount of work done on the existent job. It could be said of many of the state and county Cooperative Extension staff that they are overworked and underemployed.

strations." So fearful was Congress of an intellectual ivory tower that the act restricted state expenditures on "printing and distribution of publications" to no more than 5 per cent of each federal appropriation. "No portion of said monies shall be applied, directly or indirectly, to . . . buildings, or . . . land, or in college-course teaching, lectures in colleges, . . . or any other purpose not specified in this act."[10] Under the act, each state is required to match funds appropriated by the federal government. The Cooperative Extension thus established is administered as a separate division of the land-grant institution. Its projects are based on a plan developed in each state and approved by the Secretary of Agriculture.

The historical roots of the Smith-Lever Act go deep. Most of the founding fathers, men as diverse otherwise as Benjamin Franklin and Thomas Jefferson, believed that the small independent farmer was the firmest foundation of a democratic society; and this ideology is related to the long record of federal support to agriculture. In 1887, an organized lobby of the Land-Grant College Association helped get the Hatch Act through Congress. Under this law, federal funds were provided for agricultural experiment stations operated by state colleges, and thus for a base from which scientific and technical information could be disseminated. The country was seeking "any effective system for getting accumulated knowledge in practice among the farmers generally."[11] For with the growing interdependence of the nation's economy, banking, transportation, and marketing interests favored a rapid commercialization of agriculture no less than many farmers themselves. The colleges, however, "were mainly confining their efforts to more or less formal teaching . . . and comparatively little study to the problems of reaching the farmer in such a way to induce him to adopt better farming practices."[12] By this time, the "demonstration method" was a tested means of communication to the sectors of the population that could not be reached through books. In the early 1900's, it had been widely

---

[10] "Legislation Authorizing Cooperative Extension Work: Act of 1914 Providing for Cooperative Extension Work, Smith-Lever Act," in U.S. Department of Agriculture, *Federal Legislation*, pp. 7-9. For recent revisions in the law, see below, pp. 220-221.

[11] True, *Report*, part 2, p. 15.

[12] *Ibid.*

used by federal agricultural agents in their campaign against the
Mexican boll weevil. Then the United States Department of Agriculture was provided with some $860,000 in Rockefeller funds to
teach farmers in the South, in the hope that with the demonstration method Southern agriculture could be greatly improved and
an economic base would be established for better public schools.
The department increased the number of its agents from 25 in
1906 to 583 in 1914.[13] In 1911, Clemson College signed an agreement with the department to carry on all its extension work in
South Carolina; and that same year a department county agent
was appointed for Broome County, New York, with the New
York State College of Agriculture, the Binghamton Chamber of
Commerce, and the Delaware, Lackawanna, and Western Railroad as cooperating parties. This "seemed to be a pattern which
appealed to businessmen wherever it was presented."[14] The Chicago Board of Trade offered $1,000 to each of the first hundred
counties that organized in support of the work of county agents.
The Soil Fertility League—with President Taft, James J. Hill of
the Great Northern Railroad, William Jennings Bryan, and Samuel Gompers as prominent members—engaged in a countrywide
campaign for better agriculture. To emphasize its concern with
the "practical," the league argued that three-quarters of the federal funds allocated for extension should go to actual demonstration work. Over the whole country, private and county support to
cooperative demonstration work increased from $2,800 in 1907 to
more than $730,000 in 1915.

Why should this "practical" program, with all its anti-intellectual overtones, have been linked to the country's colleges? Public
sentiment was strong for a demonstration system not associated
with higher education, and the Association of Agricultural Colleges and Experiment Stations' Committee on Extension Work
urged the "prime necessity of getting into the public mind" that
existing forms of college extension were not just a "scheme to
advertise the college" or even get boys and girls interested in agricultural schools and colleges.[15] The main reason for the formal
association was the colleges' struggle for financial support from

[13] *Ibid.*, pp. 16-17.
[14] *Ibid.*, p. 153.
[15] True, *A History of Agricultural Extension Work*, p. 53.

rural-dominated states legislatures.[16] Moreover, the Association feared that federally financed county demonstration agents would undercut the colleges' local influence.[17]

The Congressional bill that developed out of this national debate, the Smith-Lever Act, reflected the background in all its main features. The Cooperative Extension Service was set up with a legal and financial link to Washington, and in each state administrative responsibility for it was vested in the land-grant college. Actually, however, college headquarters had little control over "its" agents in the field, who were denied even the symbolic bond of academic status. The fine American tradition of mud on the boots would not be sullied by a firm link to an ineffective faculty with their heads in the clouds. Domination by Washington was averted; still today authority in the system flows from the states to the federal office, rather than the other way. Federal services are made available to states on request. The federal office is headed by an administrator rather than by a director.

In the four years following the enactment of the Smith-Lever bill, the number of county agents went up from 928 to 2,435, and appropriations increased by five times to $17 million.[18] This rapid growth, based primarily on federal funds, was an important part of the national effort to increase agricultural production during the First World War, which got the Service off to a running start. Federal farm programs sustained Extension during the depression years of the 1930's.

Today the Cooperative Extension Service consists of 3,151 county offices, manned by nearly 12,000 county plus over 3,000 state professionals. A breakdown of personnel and of funds for work in the states is given in Tables A-1 and A-2. In each of the 50 states and one territory, Cooperative Extension has the same

---

[16] In a statement reminiscent of Galbraith's concept of Dependence Effect (see above, p. 4), Dean W. Robert Parks of Iowa State University has argued that the land-grant college was not the culmination of a broad mass movement, "for supply frequently is the creator of demand. It was not until the land-grant college had begun producing an educational program which fitted popular needs that the common man began to demand its product" ("History, Philosophy, and Tradition," p. 3). However, the college could never ignore the necessity of obtaining a broad base of political support.

[17] See Bailey, *Seaman A. Knapp*, Chap. 12.

[18] Iowa State University, *Extension Worker's Training Handbook*, p. 4.

administrative and legal relations to a land-grant institution and to the United States Department of Agriculture. While there are some local differences in purpose and operation, broad similarities are maintained in the Service by its national committees, such as the Extension Committee on Organization and Policy; by the common procedures for statistical reporting; by regional organizations of Extension directors and associations of county agents; by joint financing from county, state, and federal funds.[19] The statistics recording the activities of this organization are somewhat overpowering. During one recent year, agents held 23,157,292 personal consultations; held or organized 2,744,381 meetings with a total attendance of 77,021,640 persons; held 185,536 "result demonstrations"; issued 781,509 news stories, 288,408 radio broadcasts, and 18,584 television programs; distributed free 32,873,401 copies of education bulletins, leaflets, and circulars.[20]

The Circumstances Have Changed

The educational functions of Cooperative Extension were narrowly defined by its tradition—agriculture for men, home economics for women, and 4-H for youth. This was not the extension of college-level disciplines but, on the contrary, the translation for a single occupational group—farm people—of written generalizations into specific "demonstrations," directives that could have been assimilated even by an illiterate peasantry. This task, superbly performed in its day, has all but disappeared, in part because of the very success of the Cooperative Extension Service in improving rural living and American agricultural production.[21]

This point can be made first of all negatively—by noting the few peripheral areas of American society that are still "rural" in the same sense as in 1914: relative isolation, frequent poverty, slight access to "urban" amenities, and so on. In the Northeast and Middle West, the farmer is in these respects almost a subur-

[19] The average *state* budget of Cooperative Extension for the year ending June 1960, was divided as follows: 22 per cent county, 39 per cent state, and 39 per cent federal (calculated from Table A-3, on page 216, omitting starred items).

[20] Gordy, *Extension Activities*, pp. 6-9.

[21] As one indication of this success, the number of result demonstrations, "conducted by a farmer, homemaker or other person under the direct supervision of an extension worker, to prove the value of a recommended practice," fell off from around 240,000 in 1940 to 185,536 in 1958 (*ibid.*, p. 6).

Table A-1. Number of Cooperative Extension Agents, July 1, 1959

State or Territory	Number of Agricultural Counties	Directors and Assistant Directors	Management Personnel	Specialists	County Agricultural Work		County Home Economics Work		4-H Club Leaders and Supervisors	Total
					Supervisors	County Agents[1]	Supervisors	County Home Demonstration Agents[2]		
Alabama	67	2	4	40	7	238	7	176	4	478
Arizona	14	2	—	17	1	36	1	16	2	75
Arkansas	75	2	3	50	6	176	7	113	3	360
California	58	7	2	74	—	305	4	80	8	480
Colorado	63	3	—	22	6	86	2	37	3	159
Connecticut	8	2	—	31	1	25	1	20	2	82
Delaware	3	1	—	17	—	7	1	5	—	31
Florida	67	2	3	49	4	144	6	93	5	306
Georgia	159	2	2	72	10	270	8	199	14	577
Idaho	44	2	2	24	3	66	2	31	3	133
Illinois	102	4	3	64	5	173	5	144	12	410
Indiana	92	3	2	95	6	174	4	88	12	384
Iowa	99	4	1	85	6	195	6	96	10	403
Kansas	105	3	1	73	5	173	8	94	8	365
Kentucky	120	2	3	61	7	211	6	135	7	432
Louisiana	64	3	3	49	10	183	5	148	7	408
Maine	16	2	1	19	1	32	1	28	2	86
Maryland	23	1	1	59	4	71	4	58	4	202
Massachusetts	12	1	1	46	2	50	2	44	5	151
Michigan	83	6	3	97	8	181	3	87	7	392
Minnesota	87	2	—	55	5	162	5	101	7	337
Mississippi	82	2	4	52	5	277	7	198	9	554
Missouri	115	1	2	61	8	267	6	114	8	467
Montana	56	2	1	32	4	67	3	34	4	147
Nebraska	93	2	1	54	9	131	5	44	7	253
Nevada	17	2	1	7	—	19	—	10	1	40
New Hampshire	10	1	1	15	1	22	2	18	3	63
New Jersey	21	1	—	42	2	59	2	38	3	147
New Mexico	32	3	1	21	2	58	2	34	3	124
New York	62	2	—	111	6	231	6	172	6	534

Table A-1—*Continued*

State or Territory	Number of Agricultural Counties	Directors and Assistant Directors	Management Personnel	Specialists	County Agricultural Work		County Home Economics Work		4-H Club Leaders and Supervisors	Total
					Supervisors	County Agents[1]	Supervisors	County Home Demonstration Agents[2]		
North Carolina ..	100	3	—	113	10	390	11	285	9	821
North Dakota ...	53	1	3	32	5	72	2	22	6	143
Ohio	88	3	1	78	6	174	5	85	6	358
Oklahoma	77	3	1	58	8	182	9	126	3	390
Oregon	36	5	2	50	5	118	5	48	3	236
Pennsylvania	67	7	5	96	—	184	5	100	9	406
Rhode Island	5	1	—	12	—	6	1	6	1	27
South Carolina ..	46	2	2	50	4	173	6	117	8	362
South Dakota ...	67	1	2	36	2	86	2	45	9	183
Tennessee	95	3	2	54	8	225	6	161	4	463
Texas	254	4	2	73	18	409	16	273	5	800
Utah	29	2	3	21	2	37	2	24	3	94
Vermont	14	1	—	18	—	27	1	19	2	68
Virginia	100	5	2	81	9	212	8	152	7	476
Washington	39	2	1	31	4	108	3	49	3	201
West Virginia ...	55	2	1	28	4	82	3	71	5	196
Wisconsin	71	4	2	77	6	184	5	84	8	370
Wyoming	23	2	1	20	1	29	1	21	3	78
Alaska	4	1	1	3	—	4	—	4	1	14
Hawaii	12	1	—	16	1	30	1	21	3	73
Puerto Rico	67	4	6	55	11	172	10	105	2	365
Total	3,151	129	83	2,496	238	6,993	223	4,273	269	14,704

[1] Includes County Extension Directors, Assistant County Agents and 4-H Club Agents.
[2] Includes Assistant Home Demonstration Agents and 4-H Club Agents.
Source: U.S. Department of Agriculture, Federal Extension Service, FES-120, July 1, 1959.

Table A-2. Sources of Funds Allotted for Cooperative Extension Work
in the States and Puerto Rico, Fiscal Year Ending June 30, 1960

States	Grand Total	Total Federal Funds	Total Within States
Alabama	$ 3,737,241	$ 1,896,106	$ 1,841,135
Alaska	230,640	107,993	122,647
Arizona	930,575	348,662	581,913
Arkansas	3,239,847	1,591,603	1,648,244
California	6,853,109	1,376,895	5,476,214
Colorado	1,629,706	557,564	1,072,142
Connecticut	918,840	275,098	643,742
Delaware	350,929	160,181	190,748
Florida	2,694,661	630,957	2,063,704
Georgia	4,709,096	2,058,289	2,650,807
Hawaii	927,119	262,359	664,760
Idaho	1,389,942	400,409	989,533
Illinois	3,938,479	1,608,083	2,330,396
Indiana	3,766,927	1,371,702	2,395,225
Iowa	4,364,177	1,458,934	2,905,243
Kansas	3,862,416	1,024,561	2,837,855
Kentucky	3,516,685	1,942,286	1,574,399
Louisiana	3,961,156	1,307,599	2,653,557
Maine	840,117	374,290	465,827
Maryland	2,197,708	538,274	1,659,434
Massachusetts	1,629,589	423,637	1,205,952
Michigan	4,792,575	1,611,898	3,180,677
Minnesota	2,868,137	1,418,031	1,450,106
Mississippi	4,083,591	2,005,247	2,078,344
Missouri	3,895,521	1,773,232	2,122,289
Montana	1,457,765	451,855	1,005,910
Nebraska	2,134,068	856,114	1,277,954
Nevada	495,380	176,799	318,581
New Hampshire	590,734	189,112	401,622
New Jersey	1,848,178	390,190	1,457,988
New Mexico	1,273,533	449,060	824,473
New York	6,684,761	1,393,108	5,291,653
North Carolina	6,808,089	2,628,560	4,179,529
North Dakota	1,353,458	617,633	735,825
Ohio	3,807,616	1,844,410	1,963,206
Oklahoma	3,710,372	1,395,842	2,314,530
Oregon	2,963,953	613,442	2,350,511
Pennsylvania	3,827,047	1,812,974	2,014,073
Puerto Rico	2,581,715	1,592,715	989,000
Rhode Island	270,086	102,854	167,232
South Carolina	2,534,998	1,391,688	1,143,310
South Dakota	1,516,200	581,993	934,207
Tennessee	3,444,501	1,932,553	1,511,948

Table A-2—*Continued*

States	Grand Total	Federal Funds Total	Within States Total
Texas	6,837,895	3,114,910	3,722,985
Utah	935,731	327,912	607,819
Vermont	714,992	249,227	465,765
Virginia	4,112,618	1,549,669	2,562,949
Washington	2,310,367	729,157	1,581,210
West Virginia	1,739,678	975,371	764,307
Wisconsin	3,823,536	1,419,881	2,403,655
Wyoming	845,358	284,095	561,263
Unallotted	19,986	19,986	—
AMA Contracts	100,000	100,000	—
Grand Total	$ 140,071,398*	$ 53,715,000	$ 86,356,398

* Does not include items starred in Table A-3, on page 216.
Source: U.S. Department of Agriculture, Federal Extension Service, MO-246, September, 1959.

banite, traveling a shorter distance to his market town than many commuters go each day to their place of work. "Outside the Great Plains, the Mountain states, and some areas of the South, there are few farm families that are not within ten miles of a physician and twenty miles of a hospital."[22] In these hyper-rural regions, however, a dominant influence on social life is still low population density,[23] often coupled with a debilitating poverty. The relation between the size of a community and the services that can reasonably be provided for it has been summarized in these general terms:

Seventy thousand . . . corresponds roughly to that size of community which, perhaps, represents a minimum population necessary to support certain essential public services such as full-time public health units; a strong public library program; strong high school, grade school, and religious service opportunities; and a hospital and medical

[22] Nelson, *American Farm Life*, p. 172.
[23] Most of Nevada and portions of eastern Oregon, Idaho, Montana, Wyoming, Utah, western Colorado, northern Arizona, New Mexico, and western Texas have a population density of under two persons per square mile; and most of the rest of these states are not much more populous. See Taeuber and Taeuber, *The Changing Population*, Figure 8, p. 22.

care service program of adequate volume and specialization to bring economy and quality to the community.[24]

This is a list, in short, of services that are largely unavailable to the population of these sparsely settled or very poor regions.

This generalization can be specified in terms of university adult education. Institutions of higher education in rural states have always had to subsidize their adult programs much more than elsewhere if they wanted to provide educational opportunities for citizens throughout the state.[25] General extension has, therefore, usually been a limited service in sparsely populated regions; the oldest and most diversified university adult-education programs are in such populous states as Pennsylvania, Ohio, Michigan, Wisconsin. Indeed, apart from Cooperative Extension and the programs of various farm associations, adult education of all kinds has been largely concentrated in cities and towns. The percentage of public schools engaged in adult education in 1950-1951, for example, ranged from 97 in cities of over 100,000 down to 42 in towns between 2,500 and 5,000.[26] Partly because of the relative lack of programs, partly for other reasons, rural participation in adult education has also been lower,[27] with a relatively large part of it made up of correspondence students.[28]

In these regions—portions of the rural South, the Mountain West, and the Great Plains—Myrdal's "principle of cumulation"[29] is still at work. They are poor in large part because they

[24] Kraenzel and Engstrom, *Montana's Population Changes*, p. 59.

[25] See, for example, Dugan, "An Extension Class Program," pp. 86, 142-143. According to this source, about 40 per cent of the cost of the University of Wyoming's extension class program is paid for by a legislative appropriation. This percentage is "not comparable to the proportion for the country as a whole because the sparsity of population and the great distances of travel make such a program more expensive than in more densely populated states."

[26] Study by the National Education Association, cited in Thaden, "Adult Education," p. 47.

[27] See, for example, Leonard and Lowry, "Continuation Education," p. 234. Among the 5,000 persons using general-extension services who answered Morton's questionnaire, only about a quarter lived in rural areas, as compared with one-third of the country's population (*University Extension*, p. 90).

[28] According to one survey, 27.3 per cent of correspondence students, as compared to 18.1 per cent of class students, lived in rural areas (Thompson, *University Extension*, Table A2, p. 289).

[29] See above, p. 139.

have been poor; without wealth they are unable to lay the economic, social, and educational foundations for improvement. In the past, Cooperative Extension has done comparatively little to break this vicious circle. The dominant measure of accomplishment by the county agent has always been "change of practice" by an individual or family. Thus, Extension has tended to provide its services to those comparatively well educated and well off, who were better able to carry out proposed changes. Breaking of the vicious circle of poverty requires both individual and family education (literacy, speech, dress, nutrition, hygiene) and services by society (schools, vocational training, electricity, roads). Clearly, administering this task is within the traditional responsibility of Cooperative Extension, though it may demand an approach far different from any it has used in the past.

More generally, however, the traditional functions of Cooperative Extension have been obliterated by the momentous changes that rural America has undergone. Most persons are aware that agricultural production has risen, that surpluses have built up, that more persons have left the farm; but few realize the dimensions of this postwar revolution.[30]

It took a full century, from 1820 to 1920, for farm productivity to double. In the following twenty years it increased by another 13 per cent. Then, in only 16 years, from 1940 to 1956, productivity per worker doubled again. It has continued to increase at a faster rate in agriculture than in any other sector of the economy.

In 1820 one farm worker produced enough for himself and 3.1 other people, in 1940 for himself and 9.7 people, in 1956 for himself and 19.8 people.

The American farm produces more food and fiber than the American people want or need. From 1948 to 1956, the value of support crops held in government stocks rose from under $3 million to over $8 billion, or by 2,700 times.

Between 1940 and 1956 over 3 million workers, or 38 per cent of the agricultural labor force, left the farm. With their families, this meant an exodus of 8.5 million from farm life.

The proportion of the labor force in agriculture, around 12 per cent

[30] The following data were assembled from *Challenge to Iowa*, 1958; Committee for Economic Development, *Toward a Realistic Farm Program*; and reports of the U.S. Bureau of the Census and Department of Agriculture.

in 1950, is nearer 8 per cent today; and some U.S. Department of Agriculture estimates predict a drop to 4 per cent by 1975.

The traditional clientele of Cooperative Extension services have been melting away also in another sense. Though the rural population is still less well educated than the national average,[31] many who live in the country are now high school or college graduates. Almost all now have access, through television and radio, newspapers and magazines, to some urban culture. With the breakdown of the isolation typical of the farm of several decades ago, the cultural difference between rural and urban has become less significant, and this trend is bound to continue. The upper-income, better educated sector of the rural population is now fully comparable to its urban equivalent.

These factors have moved many persons in the land-grant system to question the nature of their responsibility to agriculture. From one-tenth to one-half of the budget of land-grant institutions is directed toward rural and agricultural services. Colleges of agriculture, experiment stations, and Cooperative Extension had a clear mandate under the Morrill, Hatch, and Smith-Lever Acts to continue and even improve their specialist services to the farmer. Better agricultural technology and farm management, however, will compound the problem of the marginal farm, will further reduce the size of the farm population, and will contribute still more to the already monstrous farm surpluses. Ought the land-grant institution, which has helped agriculture become more and more efficient, to assume some responsibility for the consequences of this greater efficiency? If so, what sort of responsibility? And if not, what is the future of these services to be?

Political Sensitivity vs. Tradition and Rigidity

Three possible reactions to these transformations in rural America are conceivable. The first is to close down Cooperative Extension with a suitable commendation for a job well done and now virtually completed. While such a solution is possible in the

[31] Of whites aged 25 years and over, in 1950 the median schooling completed ranged from 10.9 years in middle-sized cities down to 8.5 years on farms. If both the poorest regions and the oldest and thus least educated group are omitted, the difference still remains: in the West, thus, for males aged 14 to 24 years, the comparable figures were 11.4 and 9.9 years (Duncan and Reiss, *Social Characteristics*, pp. 88-91).

abstract, one would hardly call it likely. Between 1946 and 1957 —that is, concomitant with the decline in farm population and the rise in agricultural surpluses that we have noted—the county and state staffs of Cooperative Extension increased from 9,000 to well over 14,000, its budget from $45 millon to $119 million. The year ending June 1960 showed a budget of over $140 million, an increase of more that $20 million, and further growth in staff. This is a vital organization, with undiminished political power.

Table A-3. Appropriations by Source for Cooperative Extension Work
1948, 1954, and 1960

	1948	1954	1960
	(thousands of dollars)		
Cooperative Extension Work:			
Federal Funds:			
Payments to States	27,641	32,256	53,715
Retirement costs for			
extension agents			5,674*
Penalty mail		1,685	2,491*
Federal Extension Service[1] ...	1,198	1,349	2,243*
Total, Federal Funds	28,839	35,290	64,123
Within State Funds:			
State	17,174	33,875	53,583
County	12,268	21,166	31,231
Non-Tax	1,564	2,327	1,542
Total funds within State	31,006	57,368	86,356
Total, Cooperative Extension Work	59,845	92,658	150,479

[1] Adjusted for comparability with the current appropriation structure.
* These items not included in Tables A-1 and A-2, on pp. 209-212.
Source: U.S. Department of Agriculture, Federal Extension Service, MO-272, September, 1959.

A second "solution" is to ignore, to the extent that it is still feasible, the changes that have taken place and to continue along the old road. In 1958, it was estimated that nearly 12.5 million families all over the country were "assisted in adopting improved farming or home-making practices, . . . 14 percent more than in 1957 and 29 percent more than in 1955. Of this total number, 32 percent were farm families, 22 percent were rural nonfarm, and 46 percent were urban families."[32] In the main, these services have followed Extension's tradition, shifting mainly in the sense of

[32] Gordy, *Extension Activities*, p. 1.

doing the old things for new people. Even in agricultural work, 40 per cent of the assisted families were urban; they were given advice on how to grow better lawns and rose bushes.

The third alternative is to adapt more basically to the changed circumstances, following the population both to greater literacy and to the cities. Bluntly put, this would seem to be the best solution, but it will not be a simple matter for Cooperative Extension to change as fundamentally and rapidly as has rural America.

In 1958, after an infinity of committee discussions, Cooperative Extension issued "A Statement of Scope and Responsibility," an attempt to map its route into the complicated future. With the "increasingly complex interdependence of agriculture and other segments of our economy," the report asserted, "programs and procedures appropriate and adequate yesterday are likely to be inappropriate today—and obsolete tomorrow." When this generalization was spelled out, however, the program sounded very much like a defense of the "inappropriate" and soon to be "obsolete."

> Extension's function . . . is . . . education for action. . . . Extension's responsibilities are to farm families first, but not to them alone. . . . Care must be exercised by Extension and the people it serves that problems of major importance at any given time are given priority.[33]

The final determination of program priorities, the report concluded, is the job of each state and each county. And in subsequent reviews written by a number of state offices, the unresolved conflict between glorification of the past and challenges posed by necessary changes has too frequently resulted in a justification of what is now being done and the way it is now being done. Cooperative Extension is not comfortable in its view of what the future seems to demand. The experience in helping individuals make personal decisions through simple "problem solving" techniques is a far cry from the social action now called for.

In spite of its political sensitivity, Cooperative Extension has shown a remarkable rigidity in its response to new demands. This inflexibility is related to the highly structured staff organization of the Service and to its ideology. In both respects, there is a marked parallel with the public school system: local control, with

[33] Miller et al., *The Cooperative Extension Service Today*, pp. 12, 7, 3, 13.

the very weak state and national direction that this connotes, is considered to be the proper organizational pattern of a democracy.

Only one-fifth of the total Extension staff is at the state level. Of this portion, one out of four are administrators: the director, assistant director(s), supervisors of county work, and state leaders of the 4-H and home-economics programs. Three out of four are technicians: specialists in animal and plant industry, social sciences, home economics, and staff services such as information. In some states certain of Extension's subject-matter specialists may also teach at the university or, if full-time Extension specialists, may nevertheless be members of such a university department as agronomy or economics. This dual attachment, Extension and a department of the university, gives the specialist a high degree of autonomy. Moreover, the largest group of specialists, those in agricultural sciences, typically have close personal and professional relations with one or another commodity or similar organization, which encourages a definition of Extension's service as narrow as its own interest. To shift the emphasis of a specialist, thus, is not merely a matter of Extension policy, but a decision involving political forces at several levels.

In administrative terms, the consequence of the specialist's power is a segmented approach to the problems with which Cooperative Extension copes. In the past, his specialized knowledge was his great strength. The boll weevil destroyed cotton, smut reduced oat and wheat yields, sour soils reduced clover crops; and in each case the county agent depended on the specialist's scientific knowledge in his effort to help the farmer. Today, the major problems in agriculture for the farmer, farm families, and rural communities are less likely to be technical in this sense than managerial: new relations between agriculture and business, farm and home development, ten-year projections of county plans by volunteer county committees, new forms of vertically integrated farm market relations—but this change has not basically disturbed the categorized approach of state specialists to county problems.[34] Extension has no administrative post that effectively cuts across the various disciplines: it is difficult and frequently impossible for

[34] Edwards, "Balanced Farming." However, this may be changing somewhat. Extension plans as submitted for federal appropriation have each item of work listed separately—agronomy, economics, dairy groups, etc. Organiza-

the director himself to influence the state staff even on narrowly agricultural issues.

However little control the director has at the state level, he has even less over the counties, where 80 per cent of the total Extension staff are employed. It is told of two directors who tried to fire a county agent that one had a heart attack and the other lost all his hair; and while the stories are apocryphal, the point they make reflects the actual power relations. Cooperative Extension, it is often said, has not one national program or even 50 state programs, but 3,000 county programs. "Extension educational programs are developed by the people in each county with the help of the local extension staff who in turn are supported by state and federal extension personnel."[35]

The dominance of the county organization is ordinarily based in part upon legally elected or voluntary county councils, which oversee all aspects of county Extension activity; separate program committees for 4-H activities, dairy, home economics, plant industry and every other phase of county Extension work; and the county commissioners, who have been given the power to control the county budget and any changes in it because the county Extension office and activities depend in part on county taxes. This structure is given strong ideological support by the fact that it is the county agent who is close to the people Extension serves; and, according to Extension's vision of itself, the people it serves actually govern the agency. Similarly, Extension's rural constituency frequently think of its activities as "our" program. This myth[36] of the grass roots is a formidable obstacle to change. Agents will not move without the sanction of their county, and in response to any new idea they can always say, "My people won't buy it." The language is consciously homespun, but the doctrine is the same as that denoted by the phrase "felt needs." And as in university adult education, so also in Cooperative Extension, the

tion by project rather than specialist area is now being considered—thus, agricultural production, management, and natural resource development, together would be considered one of eight project areas.

[35] Ferguson, *Adjusting to the Changing Scene*, p. 3.

[36] The word "myth" is not used in the pejorative sense, but in the way Richard Hofstadter uses it in his study, *The Age of Reform:* "I do not mean an idea that is simply false, but rather one that so effectively embodies men's values that it profoundly influences their way of perceiving reality and hence their behavior. In this sense myths may have varying degrees of fiction or reality" (p. 24, n. 1).

myth that the people are sovereign and the trained specialists are merely their servants, though it has an element of ultimate validity, is essentially false.

Even in a democratic state, where the people are really sovereign in a meaningful sense, they expect to be led. They demand to be consulted, to retain the power to protest or reject; but they expect their leaders to formulate the substance of public debate, policy, and action. And when the leaders are not merely the people's representatives but trained specialists, "democracy" is not the appropriate relation. In the history of Cooperative Extension, thus, the farmer refused to learn from books and forced the agents to adopt the demonstration method. In the crucial area, however, the expert retained control. Land-grant institutions and Cooperative Extension won the confidence of the people they serve not by acquiescing in their limitations and prejudices, but by proving to them the value of research, technology, and education. A similar kind of adaptability and educational leadership, one might say, is called for today.

In summary, Cooperative Extension is a network of locally based and largely independent county offices, served by a collection of state resources. The county office, the key point of Extension services and programs, is the principal measure of the effectiveness of the whole system. A social and educational agency ruled by its field representatives has certain typical virtues and faults. Within the limits of traditional practices, it is likely to be highly flexible, adapting readily to local variation. But the control by parochial men, who tend to see their county as the limit of the universe, also creates an insensitivity to demands for global change, for changes in, rather than within, the tradition. The nub of the question is how to preserve the values of an educational service in intimate and continuing contact with its constituency while helping it rise to a new level of performance, involving efforts broader than the interests of a single county.

Adjustments in the Land-Grant System

The rigidity in the land-grant system is in part a consequence of the laws that established it. In the Smith-Lever Act, for instance, Cooperative Extension work was defined as "the giving of instruction and practical demonstrations in agriculture and home economics." In 1953, Congress added the phrase, "and subjects relating thereto," and thus opened up a new world. The new law also permits "the necessary printing and distribution of information" in connection with *all* the work that Cooperative Extension undertakes. Significantly, the new act, "as introduced and . . . passed without amendment," had been approved by the Association of Land-Grant Colleges and Universities, a committee of Extension directors, the House Committee on Agriculture, and the Secretary of Agriculture. There is now legal authority for work as "flexible and dynamic as the needs of the Agricultural Extension Service may require."[37] Two years later, in 1955, a special appropriation was made to Cooperative Extension, to enable it to give "assistance and counseling to local groups in appraising resources for capability of improvement in agriculture or introduction of industry designed to supplement farm income," and to do this "in cooperation with other agencies and groups."[38]

The Extension Service, in spite of its past limitation primarily to agricultural production, is able to take advantage of these broader opportunities if it so chooses. It has the capacity, even if mostly unrealized, to serve all families and communities on matters relating to broad economic and social change. The county office is an intimate vantage point from which to view changes in family life and community welfare. The network of county offices provides a system for statewide approaches to problems and programs. The state specialists, it is true, see the same world in a more limited focus, and this is as it should be: the function of a specialist is to be competent in a narrowly defined field. His professional concern with agricultural problems, however, will in most cases inhibit the development of a broader perspective.

How can Extension continue to serve the agricultural sector with its specialized skills and at the same time develop the capacity for service on broader problems? In a number of states the administrative response to this question has been to add new specialists, either directly or to "borrow" the specialist capability from the university faculty. Neither course is satisfactory. No matter how many specialists it adds to its staff, Extension can never acquire the range and diversity of all university disciplines.

[37] "Extension Legislation Modernized."
[38] Rural-Development Act, Public Law 360, 84th Congress, 1955.

And if its expansion is in terms of "borrowing" faculty, or more faculty time, Extension will often be able to influence unduly the direction and composition of a broad range of the university's total extension activity. It would be no solution to the dilemma of Cooperative Extension if it were permitted to direct the land-grant institutions as a whole toward a greater concern with rural reconstruction.

The quest for a solution may be aided by dividing the system's functions into two parts, the traditional aid to agriculture and rural society, and increments to this that are now called for.

Mission to Agriculture.   There is still a mopping up to be done in traditional agriculture. A substantial portion of the poverty remaining in the United States is among subsistence farmers. In 1954, 27.4 per cent of all farm families had cash incomes of less than $1,000, as compared with 4.9 per cent of urban families.[39] It is doubtful if aid in adopting improved seeds, fertilizers, and so on could mean the beginning of a new life; at this level the only rational solution may be the abandonment of the marginal farm and a transfer to another occupation. At some level above this an increment of land, capital, or managerial skill may provide the margin essential for an economically viable family farm. In either case, the services of Cooperative Extension are relevant.

More generally, the future of Extension's service to farmers and agriculture will depend on whether it can shift its emphasis to guidance in management. This is the one area where many farmers will continue to need assistance and the one, moreover, where farm journals, implement and fertilizer salesmen, and other "competitors" of Extension cannot offer comparable service. With more and more technological change, and fewer and larger farms, the need will increase for management guidance, with stress on *why* rather than *how*. The competent manager will wish to make his own decisions: he needs facts, education, and consultation to refine his judgment. The resources required to implement this new role now exist in the present system of land-grant institu-

[39] It is true that the cash incomes of farms are supplemented by shelter and home-grown food; but "there is probably more danger," as Galbraith remarks, "of exaggerating than of minimizing the contribution of the unpainted shacks, the reluctant animals, and the barren garden patches by which the rural poor eke out their living" (*The Affluent Society*, p. 324).

tions, colleges of agriculture, research units, and the Cooperative Extension Service.[40]

To perform these two kinds of function for agriculture, it will be necessary to define more or less precisely the level at which a farm is socially and economically viable. Farm units above the line will be helped with guidance in management. Those below will be helped out of agriculture. This dual function is part of a more complex perception of "agricultural adjustment," which is now seen as including much more than the pure farm problem. Some of its elements are wholly technical, relating to efficiency and the economics of farm management. Others are legislative, stemming from state and national laws that need revision. Still others are economic and political in the broadest sense, concerning national and world markets and possibilities of expanding food and fiber consumption, or of using farm surpluses as instruments of United States foreign policy.

Mission to Society. What is the distinctive obligation of the land-grant institution, that projection of rural America's needs and aspirations, now that the whole fabric of the society has changed? Some administrators feel that the best avenue to the heart of the people, and the handouts of the legislature, is to obliterate the past as rapidly as possible and show that their institutions, at least in formal terms, are on a par with higher education generally. One can challenge this mood on several points. Is not diversity in itself a virtue in so large and complex an institution as America's higher education? Is not the shift from state colleges to state universities, with the accretion of new departments and graduate programs, sometimes too rapid to be sound? How often is the change-over based, as general extension often is, on the hope of thus promoting good public relations? Yet this transformation is essentially a healthy reaction to the new circumstances—the drastic shortage of college facilities generally, and the increasing demand for trained professionals of all kinds.

The future of land-grant institutions, however, is complicated by its relation, even if not always fully acknowledged, to the future of Cooperative Extension. In the past, Extension's service

[40] In this regard the land-grant institution may have come full circle, with no more than it was able to offer farmers before Cooperative Extension was created.

consisted in the distribution of some of the institution's scientific findings to the rural population, and this ability to adapt academic materials to a more popular level is a useful one. Its intimate involvement in local political processes, its sensitivity to local pressures, make it a likely candidate for a general service agency at the county level, one that could administer not only new developments in agriculture but also social and economic innovations of various types.

In the future, Cooperative Extension could function at three levels, with three administrative patterns involving three degrees of relative independence from the land-grant institution and of change in the Service's tradition. These three levels are:

1. To continue, with such adaptations as are called for by new developments, its traditional service to agriculture. This function demands changes within rather than in Extension's tradition; and it can be carried on, as in the past, in virtual isolation from the rest of the institution, with personnel primarily from the Division or College of Agriculture.

2. To assist in bringing about social and economic changes, and the adjustment to such changes. This function would involve, for instance, vocational guidance, particularly for displaced farmers; education on public affairs, and guidance toward appropriate action on such matters of public policy as education; or the planning of industrial development, including specific features such as sewage disposal and recreational facilities. In order to undertake such tasks, Extension would have both to enlarge its definition of its purpose and to learn to work with other elements of the institution's total extension function. The land-grant institutions, created in the era of rural America, developed a complex of research and educational capabilities designed to serve the economic and social interests of a farm economy, with service focused on the individual farm and farm family rather than agriculture as an industry. Today's urban-industrial society cannot be effectively assisted, even within the meaning of the land-grant institution's legal obligation to serve the public, merely by minor adaptations in this past emphasis. Cooperative Extension is an appropriate instrument for new functions, particularly if the institution becomes involved in such broad areas as controlling economic growth, suburbanization, the planning of land use, school re-

districting, and general reform of public education. At a less ambitious level, academic disciplines other than agriculture would find Cooperative Extension an able and available administrative unit for extending their specific knowledge throughout the state. More generally, Cooperative Extension could organize resources from various sectors of the university on broad issues, demanding the contribution of several disciplines, whose findings Extension could translate into a suitable form and administer for community service.

3. To participate in adult education, which in a limited sense has been a traditional function of Cooperative Extension. However, the rising level of education among the general public will force its attention to university-level offerings. Which would many young mothers choose—a discussion group on family life or a course in child psychology? Which should they be encouraged to choose? In the area of university adult education, it goes without saying, the university must retain full control of offerings and standards. Cooperative Extension would provide the institution with an administrative structure at the county level. Having established this pattern within the land-grant institution, Extension could provide a similar administrative service in extending the adult-education programs of other colleges in the state, and of non-university agencies.

These three levels of Extension's future potential are summarized schematically in Table A-4.

"The Two Extension Services"

In 1954, the Association of Land-Grant Colleges and Universities initiated an inquiry "to explore the problems and practices of extension in the Land-Grant Colleges and Universities, and to recommend areas of development and coordination, including methods of finance."[41] There was little experience, the study concluded, to guide any institution attempting to enter the maze of unexplored relations. Even when the two types of extension function side by side on the same campus, they do not communicate. In the land-grant institutions with which Cooperative Extension is formally associated, probably no more than one top administrative officer out of five could offer a reasonably accurate interpre-

[41]Association of Land-Grant Colleges, *A Study of Problems*, p. 1.

Table A-4. The Three Levels of Extension's Future Potential

	Subject Matter	Method	Relation to Other Agencies*	Relation to Cooperative Extension Tradition
1.	Agriculture	Technological services designed for individual farm units, with increasing emphasis on management consultation and written rather than "demonstration" communication	Virtually independent	Minor adaptations called for within tradition
2.	Broad social-economic adjustment and development	Education and service to assist the political process and management of change in society as distinct from change of practice in the individual farm unit	Coordinate resources and administer in close cooperation with other agencies on equal basis	Sharp departure in several respects from tradition
3.	Adult education	Increasing emphasis on education and teaching methods appropriate to content at a college level	Administrative subsidiary of substantive agencies	Total departure from tradition

* Includes all divisions and departments of the land grant institution, other state institutions of higher education, and all other appropriate agencies and institutions.

tation of Extension's traditions, structure, and functions, not to mention its prospects for the future. Needless to say, Cooperative Extension is equally ignorant of the campus. Such facts indicate the dimensions of the problem in establishing a new pattern of interaction and the administrative system to guide it.

A number of organizational devices have been tried on various campuses where the extension divisions and Cooperative Extension function side by side: joint staff meetings, liaison officers, joint declarations of policy, a vice-president for Cooperative and general extension, the requirement that the general-extension administrator report to the director of Cooperative Extension, and so on. These may be useful steps, but "these are all patchwork devices; perhaps a new roof is needed."[42] Where should this new roof be found?

> It is probably pointless to try to begin on the university campus itself. Instead, one should begin in the field to work out a pattern of service to the people in which elements from both extension services may be blended. . . . The process [of merging their efforts] will take from ten to twenty-five years.[43]

The difficulty with this view, as with most discussions of how to define the new administrative rules and relationships, is that it passes too lightly over the chasm that separates Cooperative from general extension.[44] The adjustments required for fruitful interaction are too fundamental to be made in the field. Indeed, such a phrase as "the two extension services," it must be remembered, is a convenient shorthand, not a designation of two members of the same genus.

Cooperative Extension has its complex origins in rural America. To term it an "extension" of the university is not appropriate even as a metaphor. It began with the agent, for whom a lodging was found in the land-grant institution. But the same economic and political factors created legal and operational ties outside the college, and these multiple links give Cooperative Extension its unique independence. It is a self-contained system, whose

[42] Houle, *Major Trends*, p. 25, citing Julius M. Nolte and Robert Bell Browne, "Extension and Field Services in the State-controlled Colleges and Universities," p. 4.
[43] Houle, *Major Trends*, pp. 25, 20.
[44] See Miller, "Extension Education," p. 9.

essential isolation is reinforced by the range of its own activities. A farmer's son can be recruited into 4-H work as a boy of twelve, go on to get a B.S. in some agricultural pursuit at a land-grant college, become a county agent, and eventually get his Ph.D.— all without ever leaving the system. Such a lifelong association fosters a sense of common origin, concurrence on basic purposes, a code of professional ethics and standards, and agreement on the need to insure next year's tax support for increased activity.

The obverse of this isolation, thus, is the Service's adeptness in its relations with government, business, the university, and people. Indeed, Cooperative Extension is fundamentally a political organization, dependent on funds from federal, state, and county budgets; dependent in a different sense on its corps of volunteer leaders, and thus on its link to the "grass roots" and to commodity groups and farm organizations, which are themselves unabashedly political. This very fact that Cooperative Extension is political provides its basic strength. In terms of comparative power, it would almost be appropriate on some campuses to call the university the "extension" and Cooperative Extension with other agricultural services the center.[45]

General extension, in marked contrast, has no roots outside the university; and in the university it is a marginal activity, lacking both the prestige and the funds afforded to nominally equivalent divisions. Among university adult educators, one can find little or no agreement on basic mission, educational practices, or organization and administrative pattern.

These are not, in short, two equal services which, left to themselves, will, in time, find a way to come together. Cooperative Extension can offer a powerful army of administrative staffs, agents and specialists, a strong constituency and annual appropriations; what it lacks is a broadly meaningful function. General extension has nothing more than access to the academic world; and even though by campus standards this access is pitifully meager, any degree of literacy is a potent force when measured against "the demonstration method." Indeed, one of the important blocks to cooperation is the legitimate concern whether the

---

[45] The diminishing truth of this statement is one of the many pressures on Extension for change. One land-grant president in a major farm state has said that once the division of agriculture carried the college; now the college carries agriculture.

academic standards in general extension, already frequently some-what precarious, may not be overwhelmed by association with the anti-intellectual tradition of Cooperative Extension.

The initiative for adjustments will have to come from the land-grant institution, from enlightened leaders within Cooperative Extension, and, sooner or later, from the office of the university president. Experimentation is possible in the field, but not definition of policy. Unless the president accepts the responsibility of defining the institution's extension function and, within this, the role of Cooperative Extension, policy of the university that he nominally heads will be set, more and more, by one adjunct of which he may have been hardly aware. In spreading beyond its traditional service to agriculture, Cooperative Extension is seeking new resources in the university; and in view of its access to funds and political power, this new relation can establish an unhealthy dominance.

Should the land-grant system be able to devise a pattern combining the academic expertise of general extension with the operational resources of Cooperative Extension, it could have a profound impact on adult education throughout the United States. One cooperative effort in Iowa indicates the possibilities: a six-week discussion program of the major issues facing the state and the nation involved over twenty thousand adults.

This is not the place to offer a blueprint. Details would vary according to local conditions, but the basic structure of the interaction could be the same throughout the land-grant system. In many rural and suburban areas, the county office of Cooperative Extension is the best, sometimes the only, center for adult education. On the other hand, the university must determine the content of any program offered in its name and maintain its academic standards. A relation between the university and Cooperative Extension need not be a total one on either side, even within adult education. Once the county office took on the function of administering programs, it could also do so for other institutions than the university. It could act, for example, as a booking agent for itinerant cultural activities or, say, for a vocational guidance expert from the Bureau of Employment Security. The state network of county offices allows for statewide patterns of such services.

To what degree is "a radical revision in the traditional mission of the Cooperative Extension Service," as Hannah has phrased it,[46] a likely development? Where will the balance between flexibility and the rigidity in the system be drawn? A most relevant factor is the extraordinarily high proportion of new blood among the state directors of Cooperative Extension. As of 1958, 26 had been in office five years or less, and 15 others were to retire within the next five years. Thus, within the decade 1953-1963, 41 new state directors out of the 50 will have been appointed.[47] This turnover may be the single most potent force for change.

Because Extension is so many things, pulling in so many different directions, the director frequently finds the best, or at least safest, policy is for him to stand still. But it may be that new leadership in Extension will develop that sense of tangible purpose which, when combined with the forces of changing society, will loosen the rigidities of a system now still serving the past. Cooperative Extension does possess a fundamental and sincere desire to serve society. What it lacks is an articulation with the public and educational requirements of today, in place of the point of departure provided by what Extension did yesterday. The intuitive sense of this lack has uprooted the county agent and lowered the guard of the specialist. The uncertainty among local personnel gives Extension's new leadership the opportunity it needs to effect a new turn. Were this not so fluid a period, it would be useless to talk of new roles for Cooperative Extension, and especially in relation to university adult education.

Past attempts to establish a new relation between the two services have not been encouraging, but principally because the efforts were based on the premise that these are two parallel systems that could work together on selected matters of common interest. To be meaningful, the cooperation must be founded also on a general recognition of the profound differences between Cooperative Extension, solidly based in a significant tradition, amply supported out of tax funds, oriented toward a politically powerful constituency—and the much weaker, relatively amorphous general extension.

[46] Hannah, "Higher Education and Agriculture," p. 54.
[47] Data assembled by Joseph P. Flannery, director of the Division of Management Operations, Federal Cooperative Extension Service, Washington, D.C.

If something significant is to be accomplished, it will be based on different definitions of role, staff structures, and administrative patterns from those that now prevail within and between Cooperative and general extension. It is in fact possible for a land-grant institution to do a great deal in university adult education without ever creating a general-extension division. As has been argued in this book, the significant concept is the total extension function; and specific administrative organizational patterns are less important than such a guiding principle.

Author's concluding note to Cooperative Extension Appendix

Many of the ideas I advance in this Appendix have been shaped by work as a consultant to land-grant institutions and their Cooperative Extension Services. Much of this work has been done in close collaboration with my friend and associate, Philip Van Slyck. I would like to acknowledge my deep debt of gratitude to him for the ideas he has stimulated me to reach for and those I have simply borrowed from his profuse and intelligent collection.

Appendix 2

1959 Member Institutions of the
National University Extension
Association and the
Association of University Evening Colleges

	NUEA	AUEC
Adelphi College		x
Akron, University of		x
Alabama, University of	x	
American International College		x
American University		x
Arizona, University of	x	
Arkansas, University of	x	
Aurora College		x
Baldwin-Wallace College		x
Baylor University		x
Bellarmine College		x
Beloit College		x
Boston College		x
Boston University	x	x
Bradley University		x
Bridgeport, University of		x
Brigham Young University	x	
British Columbia, University of		x
Brooklyn College		x
Buffalo, University of		x
Butler University		x
California, University of	x	x
Canisius College		x
Carnegie Institute of Technology		x
Case Institute of Technology		x
Centenary College		x
Chattanooga, University of		x
Chicago, University of	x	x

	NUEA	AUEC
Cincinnati, University of	x	x
City College of New York		x
School of General Studies		x
Clark University		x
Coe College		x
Colorado, University of	x	
Columbia University		x
Connecticut, University of	x	
Dayton, University of		x
Delaware, University of	x	x
Denver, University of		x
DePaul University		x
Detroit, University of		x
Drake University		x
Drexel Institute of Technology		x
Drury College		x
Eastern New Mexico University	x	
Elmira College		x
Evansville College		x
Fairleigh Dickinson College		x
Fenn College		x
Florida, General Extension Division of	x	
Fordham University		x
Georgia Institute of Technology	x	
Georgia State College of Business Administration		x
Georgia, University System of	x	
Hartford, University of		x
Harvard University	x	x
Hawaii, University of	x	
Hofstra College		x
Howard Payne College		x
Hunter College		x
Idaho, University of	x	
Illinois Institute of Technology		x
Illinois, University of	x	
Indiana University	x	x
Iona College		x
Iowa State University	x	
Iowa, State University of	x	
John Carroll University		x
Johns Hopkins University	x	x

	NUEA	AUEC
Kansas City, University of		x
Kansas State College	x	
Kansas, University of	x	
Kentucky, University of	x	
La Salle College		x
Long Island University		x
Louisiana State University	x	x
Louisville, University of		x
Loyola College (Baltimore)		x
Loyola University (Chicago)	x	x
Loyola University (New Orleans)		x
McNeese State College		x
Manitoba, University of		x
Marquette University		x
Maryland, University of	x	x
Massachusetts Department of Education	x	
Miami University (Ohio)	x	
Miami, University of		x
Michigan College of Mining and Technology	x	
Michigan State University	x	x
Michigan, University of	x	
Minnesota, University of	x	x
Mississippi Southern College		x
Mississippi State College	x	
Mississippi, University of	x	
Missouri, University of	x	
Montana State University	x	
Nebraska, University of	x	x
Nevada, University of	x	
New Hampshire, University of	x	
New Mexico, University of	x	
New York State School of Industrial and Labor Relations (Cornell University)	x	
New York University	x	x
Newark College of Engineering		x
Niagara University		x
North Carolina, University of	x	
North Dakota Agricultural College	x	
North Dakota, University of	x	
Northeastern University		x
Northern Illinois University		x

	NUEA	AUEC
Northern Michigan College	x	
Northwestern University		x
Ohio State University		x
Ohio University	x	
Oklahoma State University	x	
Oklahoma, University of	x	x
Omaha, Municipal University of	x	x
Oregon System of Higher Education	x	x
Pace College		x
Pennsylvania Military College		x
Pennsylvania State University	x	x
Pennsylvania, University of	x	x
Pittsburgh, University of	x	x
Polytechnic Institute of Brooklyn		x
Pratt Institute		x
Providence College		x
Puerto Rico, University of	x	
Purdue University	x	x
Queens College (New York)		x
Queens College (North Carolina)		x
Regis College (Colorado)		x
Rhode Island, University of	x	x
Richmond, University of		x
Rochester Institute of Technology	x	x
Rochester, University of		x
Rockhurst College		x
Roosevelt University		x
Russell Sage College		x
Rutgers University	x	x
St. John's University (New York)		x
St. Joseph's College (Indiana)		x
St. Joseph's College (Pennsylvania)		x
St. Peter's College		x
San Francisco, University of		x
Scranton, University of		x
Seton Hall University		x
Sir George Williams College		x
South Carolina, University of	x	
South Dakota, University of	x	
Southern California, University of	x	x
Southern Illinois University	x	x

	NUEA	AUEC
Southern Methodist University	x	x
Spring Hill College		x
Suffolk University		x
Syracuse University	x	x
Utica College		x
Temple University		x
Tennessee, University of	x	x
Texas Christian University		x
Texas Technological College	x	
Texas, University of	x	
Thomas More Institute		x
Toledo, University of		x
Tulane University		x
Tulsa, University of		x
Utah State University	x	
Utah, University of	x	
Villanova University		x
Virginia State College		x
Virginia, University of	x	
Washburn University of Topeka		x
Washington, State College of	x	
Washington University	x	x
Washington, University of	x	x
Wayne State University		x
West Virginia University	x	
Western Reserve University	x	x
Wichita, University of		x
William and Mary, College of		x
Wisconsin, University of	x	x
Wyoming, University of	x	
Xavier University (Ohio)		x

BIBLIOGRAPHY

This is a list of the books and articles that have directly contributed to the ideas expressed in this work, including all that have been cited. No attempt was made to compile a complete bibliography, or even to refer to all the sources that we read.

ADAM, THOMAS R. *Education for International Understanding.* New York, Institute of Adult Education, Teachers College, Columbia University, 1948.

ADLER, MORTIMER J., and MILTON MAYER. *The Revolution in Education.* Chicago, University of Chicago Press, 1958.

ADOLFSON, L. H. "The University's Role in Adult Education." *Adult Education,* V:4 (Summer, 1955), pp. 231-232.

Adult Education—issued quarterly by the Adult Education Association of the U.S.A.; formed by the union of the *Adult Education Bulletin* and the *Adult Education Journal,* beginning October, 1950.

"Adult Education." *Review of Educational Research,* Vol. XXIII, No. 3, June, 1953.

Adult Education Association of the U.S.A. *How To Teach Adults.* Leadership Pamphlet No. 5. Chicago, The Association, 1955.

——. "Report of the Committee on Social Philosophy and Direction Finding." *Adult Education,* I:6 (August, 1951), pp. 208-210.

——. *Taking Action in the Community: How Can You Plan—and Carry Out—A Constructive Program of Social Change?* Leadership Pamphlet No. 3. Chicago, The Association, 1956.

——. *Understanding How Groups Work: Help from Applied Group Dynamics.* Leadership Pamphlet No. 4. Chicago, The Association, 1956.

Adult Education Bulletin—published from June, 1936, through August, 1950, by the Department of Adult Education of the National Education Association.

Adult Education Journal—published from January, 1942, through

July, 1950, by the American Association for Adult Education; supersedes the *Journal of Adult Education.*

Adult Leadership—issued monthly by the Adult Education Association of the U.S.A., beginning May, 1952.

ALMOND, GABRIEL A. *The American People and Foreign Policy.* Yale Institute of International Studies. New York, Harcourt, Brace & Co., 1950.

——, et al. *The Appeals of Communism.* Princeton, Princeton University Press, 1954.

ALTER, HENRY C. "A House Divided." *Adult Education,* IX:2 (Winter, 1959), pp. 100-107.

American Association for Adult Education, Committee on Community Organization. *Community Education in Action: A Report on Community Organization and Adult Education.* Cleveland, The Association, 1948.

American Council on Education. *Credit Courses by Television.* Washington, The Council, 1955.

——. *Teaching by Closed-Circuit Television.* Washington, The Council, 1956.

"American Education and World Responsibility." Proceedings of the 44th Annual Meeting, 1958. *Association of American Colleges Bulletin,* Vol. XLIV, No. 1, March, 1958.

American Heart Association, "Educational Materials," Nos. 119, 119A, 119B, revised. May 9, 1957. Mimeographed.

——. *Publications and Teaching Aids for Physicians.* New York, The Association, 1957.

American Political Science Association, Committee for the Advancement of Teaching. *Goals for Political Science.* New York, William Sloane Associates, Inc., 1951.

ANDERSEN, MARTIN PERRY. "A Study of Discussion in Selected Wisconsin Adult Organizations and Public Agencies." Unpublished Ph.D. dissertation, University of Wisconsin, 1947.

ANDERSON, HOWARD R. (ed.) *Approaches to an Understanding of World Affairs.* Twenty-fifth Yearbook, National Council for the Social Studies, National Education Association. Washington, The Council, 1954.

Association of Land-Grant Colleges and Universities, Senate Committee on Problems of Urban Educational Extension. *A Study of Problems and Practices of Cooperative and General Extension Services in Land-Grant Colleges and Universities and non-Land-Grant State Universities.* November, 1954. Offset.

Association of University Evening Colleges, *Proceedings of Annual Meetings*, various years.

BAILEY, JOSEPH CANNON. *Seaman A. Knapp, Schoolmaster of American Agriculture.* New York, Columbia University Press, 1945.

BAILEY, THOMAS A. *The Man in the Street: The Impact of American Public Opinion on Foreign Policy.* New York, The Macmillan Co., 1948.

BAKER, GLADYS LUCILLE. *The County Agent.* Chicago, University of Chicago Press, 1939.

BANTA, C. O. "Sources of Data for Program Evaluation." *Adult Education*, V:4 (Summer, 1955), pp. 227-230.

BARBASH, JACK. *Universities and Unions in Workers' Education.* Fund for Adult Education. New York, Harper & Brothers, 1955.

BEALE, LATHROP VICKERY—see JAMES A. DAVIS.

BEALS, RALPH A., and LEON BRODY. *The Literature of Adult Education.* New York, American Association for Adult Education, 1941.

BELL, WILMER V. "Finance, Legislation, and Public Policy in Adult Education." MALCOLM S. KNOWLES (ed.). *Handbook of Adult Education in the United States.* Chicago, Adult Education Association of the U.S.A., 1960. Pp. 138-155.

BENJAMIN, HAROLD. "The University's Responsibility in Adult Education." *Educational Method*, XVII:6 (March, 1939), pp. 300-302.

BENNE, KENNETH D. "Adult Education in the University." *Journal of Higher Education.* "A 'Primitive' Look at the University System," XXVII:8 (November, 1956), pp. 413-418; "Rôle of Adult Education in University Affairs," XXVII:9 (December, 1956), pp. 467-470.

——. "The Future of the Work-Survey Conferences," in *Evaluation of Adult Education. Baltimore Bulletin of Education*, XXV:4-6 (January-March, 1948), pp. 172-175.

——. "Some Philosophic Issues in Adult Education." *Adult Education*, VII:2 (Winter, 1957), pp. 67-82.

——. "Why I Ran for President of AEA." *Adult Leadership*, 4:7 (January, 1956), pp. 6-8.

BERELSON, BERNARD. "Democratic Theory and Public Opinion." *Public Opinion Quarterly*, 16:31 (Fall, 1952), pp. 313-330.

BESTOR, ARTHUR E. *Educational Wastelands: The Retreat from Learning in Our Public Schools.* Urbana, University of Illinois Press, 1953.

BIRNBAUM, MAX. "Mind and Emotion in Adult Education." *Adult Education*, VII:3 (Spring, 1957), pp. 144-151.

BITTNER, WALTON S., and HERVEY F. MALLORY. *University Teach-*

ing by Mail: A Survey of Correspondence Instruction Conducted by American Universities. New York, The Macmillan Co., 1933.

BLAKELY, ROBERT J. "Adult Education Needs a Philosophy and a Goal." Adult Education, III:1 (November, 1952), pp. 2-10.

——. "The Path and the Goal." Adult Education, VII:2 (Winter, 1957), pp. 93-98.

BLISS, RALPH K. (ed.). The Spirit and Philosophy of Extension Work. Washington, Graduate School, U.S. Department of Agriculture, and Epsilon Sigma Phi, 1952.

BOWERS, JOHN Z.—see ROBERT S. WARNER.

BRADFORD, LELAND P. "Introduction." "The Dynamics of the Discussion Group." Journal of Social Issues, IV:2 (Spring, 1948), pp. 2-7.

——. "Report of the Division of Adult Education Service of the National Education Association." Adult Education Bulletin, XI:6 (August, 1947), pp. 164-178.

——. "Toward a Philosophy of Adult Education." Adult Education, VII:2 (Winter, 1957), pp. 83-93.

BRAY, RICHARD. "Extension Credit in Degree Programs." Proceedings of the 37th Annual Meeting of the National University Extension Association, 35 (1952), pp. 60-62.

BROADY, KNUTE O., BETTY B. DIMMITT, and RUSSELL GRUMANN. Three Arts Go on Tour. National University Extension Association Studies in University Extension Education, No. 6. Bloomington, Ind., The Association, 1951.

BRODERICK, GERTRUDE G. "List of Educational AM and FM Radio and Television Stations by State and City." Washington, U.S. Office of Education, November, 1956. Offset.

BRODY, LEON—see RALPH A. BEALS.

BROWN, FRANCIS J. (ed.). University and World Understanding: A Report of a Conference of Fulbright Scholars on Education. Reports of Committees and Conferences, Series I, No. 58, Vol. XVIII. Washington, American Council on Education, 1954.

BROWN, GILES T. "Two Minutes Are Not Enough!" Junior College Journal, XXV:2 (October, 1954), pp. 75-82.

BROWN, MURIEL W. With Focus on Family Living: The Story of Four Experiments in Community Organization for Family Life Education. Vocational Division Bulletin 249, Home Economics Education Series 28. Washington, U.S. Office of Education, 1953.

BROWN, SPENCER. "Have Our Schools Failed? The Record and the Potential." Commentary, June, 1958, pp. 461-471.

BROWNE, ROBERT B. "Winds of Doctrine." *Adult Education,* VIII:2 (Winter, 1958), pp. 106-109.

BROWNELL, BAKER. *The College and the Community: A Critical Study of Higher Education.* New York, Harper & Brothers, 1952.

——. "The College and the Community: A Disintegrative Influence on the Small Communities of the Country." *Journal of Higher Education,* XVII:6 (June, 1946), pp. 294-300.

——. "The Montana Project." *Recreation,* 40:3 (June, 1946), pp. 146-148.

——. "The Montana Study." MARY L. ELY (ed.) *Handbook of Adult Education in the United States.* New York, Institute of Adult Education, Teachers College, Columbia University, 1948. Pp. 113-117.

——. "The Value of the Humanities: The Interpretation Being Used in the Montana Study." *Journal of Higher Education,* XVI:8 (November, 1945), pp. 405-412.

BRUNNER, EDMUND DES., and E. HSIN PAO YANG. *Rural America and the Extension Service: A History and Critique of the Cooperative Agricultural and Home Economics Extension Service.* New York, Teachers College, Columbia University, 1949.

——, IRWIN T. SANDERS, and· DOUGLAS ENSMINGER (eds.). *Farmers of the World: The Development of Agricultural Extension.* New York, Columbia University Press, 1945.

——, DAVID E. WILDER, CORINNE KIRCHNER, and JOHN S. NEWBERRY, JR. *An Overview of Adult Education Research: A Report to the Fund for Adult Education from the Bureau of Applied Social Research, Columbia University.* White Plains, N.Y., Fund for Adult Education, 1958. Mimeographed.

BUNN, EDWARD B. "College Alumni and Citizenship." *Journal of Higher Education,* XVII:2 (February, 1946), pp. 91-96.

BURCH, GLEN. "Community Organization for Adult Education." MARY L. ELY (ed.). *Handbook of Adult Education in the United States.* New York, Institute of Adult Education, Teachers College, Columbia University, 1948. Pp. 281-288.

——. "Evaluating Adult Education: Some Principles of a Community-Centered Program." *Adult Education Journal,* 6:2 (April, 1947), pp. 70-75.

BURKETT, JESSE E. *Comprehensive Programming for Life Long Learning: A Preliminary Report.* Norman, Okla., Extension Division, University of Oklahoma, 1957. Mimeographed.

BURNS, NORMAN. "Self-Evaluation in the Evening College." *Proceedings of the Association of University Evening Colleges, Seven-*

teenth Annual Meeting, 1955, pp. 23-30.

——, and CYRIL O. HOULE (eds.). *The Community Responsibilities of Institutions of Higher Learning.* Proceedings of the Institute for Administrative Officers of Higher Institutions, Vol. XX. Chicago, University of Chicago Press, 1948.

BURRELL, JOHN ANGUS. *A History of Adult Education at Columbia University: University Extension and the School of General Studies.* New York, Columbia University Press, 1954.

BUSWELL, G. T. "Conditions for Effective Adult Learning." NORMAN BURNS and CYRIL O. HOULE (eds.). *The Community Responsibilities of Institutions of Higher Learning.* Proceedings of the Institute for Administrative Officers of Higher Institutions, Vol. XX. Chicago, University of Chicago Press, 1948. Pp. 14-23.

CALIVER, AMBROSE. "Continuous Learning for a Changing World: How Education Helps Young Adults Adjust to the Demands of Today." *Adult Leadership*, September, 1957 (reprint).

——. "For a More Literate Nation." *School Life*, 40:3 (December, 1957), pp. 13-14.

CAMPBELL, ANGUS, GERALD GURIN, and WARREN E. MILLER. *The Voter Decides.* Evanston, Ill., Row, Peterson & Company, [1954].

CANTRIL, HADLEY. *Gauging Public Opinion.* Princeton, Princeton University Press, 1944.

CAREY, JAMES T. *Why Students Drop Out: A Study of Evening College Student Motivations.* Chicago, Center for the Study of Liberal Education for Adults, 1953.

Carnegie Endowment for International Peace. *The United States Public and the United Nations: Report on a Study of American Attitudes on the U.N. and the Communication of Information to the U.S. Public.* New York, The Endowment, 1958.

CASS, ANGELICA W.—see RALPH B. SPENCE.

Center for the Study of Liberal Education for Adults. *Conference Report: New Dimensions of University Responsibility for the Liberal Education of Adults.* Chicago, The Center, 1956. Mimeographed.

——. "Eighth Interim Report Submitted to the Fund for Adult Education Covering the Period from October 1, 1955 to December 31, 1956." Chicago, The Center, 1957. Mimeographed.

Challenge to Iowa. Pamphlets 246-A through F. Ames, Iowa, Cooperative Extension Service in Agriculture and Home Economics, Iowa State College, 1958.

CHAMBERLAIN, LEO M. "Should Our Colleges and Universities Rethink the Objectives in Adult Education?" *Current Issues in Higher Education*, 1954, pp. 242-243.

CHAPMAN, CHARLES E. "Some Characteristics of the Adult Part-Time Students Enrolled in the Public Schools of Contra Costa County, California, During the Fall Term, 1957." Unpublished Ed.D. dissertation, University of California, 1959.

CHARTERS, ALEXANDER N. "Quality during Expansion." *Proceedings of the Association of University Evening Colleges, Twentieth Annual Meeting, 1958*, pp. 43-48.

———. "A Role of Adult Educators in a University." *Adult Education*, VIII:2 (Winter, 1958), pp. 81-86.

CHERRINGTON, BEN M. *Methods of Education in International Attitudes.* Teachers College Contributions to Education, No. 595. New York, Teachers College, Columbia University, 1934.

CHRISTENSEN, WILLIAM R., and ROBERT S. WARNER. "The A-V Lecture Kit." *Radiology*, 68:3 (March, 1957), pp. 415-417.

CLAGUE, EWAN. "Opportunities for the Professionally Trained from the Standpoint of Society." JOHN GUY FOWLKES (ed.). *Higher Education for American Society.* National Educational Conference, 1948. Madison, University of Wisconsin Press, 1949. Pp. 64-71.

CLARK, BURTON R. *Adult Education in Transition: A Study of Institutional Insecurity.* Berkeley, University of California Press, 1956.

———. *The Marginality of Adult Education.* Notes and Essays on Education for Adults, No. 20. Chicago, Center for the Study of Liberal Education for Adults, 1958.

COHEN, BERNARD C. *Citizen Education in World Affairs.* Princeton, Center of International Studies, Princeton University, 1953. Offset.

———. *The Influence of Non-Governmental Groups on Foreign Policy-Making.* Studies in Citizen Participation in International Relations, Vol. II. Boston, World Peace Foundation, 1959.

———. "What Voluntary Groups Can Do." *Adult Leadership*, 2:3 (July-August, 1953), pp. 10-12.

COLE, FRED. *International Relations in Institutions of Higher Education in the South.* Washington, American Council on Education, 1958.

Committee for Economic Development. *Paying for Better Public Schools.* New York, 1959.

———. *Toward a Realistic Farm Program*, New York, 1957.

Community Development Review—published by the Community Development Division, Office of Public Services, International Cooperation Administration, Washington. Various issues.

CONANT, JAMES BRYANT. *Education in a Divided World: The Function of the Public Schools in Our Unique Society.* Cambridge, Harvard University Press, 1948.

CONLEY, WILLIAM H. "The Mission of Evening College Leadership." *Proceedings of the Association of University Evening Colleges, Nineteenth Annual Meeting,* 1957, pp. 20-26.
——. "The University's Role in Adult Education." *Journal of Higher Education,* XXVI:1 (January, 1955), pp. 14-17.
CONNELLY, GORDON M., and HARRY H. FIELD. "The Non-Voter—Who He Is, What He Thinks." *Public Opinion Quarterly,* 8:2 (Summer, 1944), pp. 175-187.
COOMBS, PHILIP H. "How Will Institutions of Higher Education Secure and Maintain an Adequate Supply of Qualified Teachers?" *Current Issues in Higher Education,* 1957, pp. 170-174.
COREY, HERBERT—see JOSEPH B. GUCKY.
CORY, ROBERT H., JR. *Communicating Information and Ideas about the United Nations to the American People.* New York, Carnegie Endowment for International Peace, 1955. Offset.
COTTRELL, LEONARD S., JR., and SYLVIA EBERHART. *American Opinion on World Affairs in the Atomic Age.* Princeton, Princeton University Press, 1948.
COULSON, ROBERT E. "Let's Not Get Out the Vote." *Harper's Magazine,* November, 1955, pp. 52-53.
Council for Financial Aid to Education, Inc. *Backing Up Brains: Modest Proposals on Behalf of College Teachers.* New York, The Council, 1957.
Council of State Governments. *Higher Education in the Forty-Eight States: A Report to the Governors' Conference.* Chicago, The Council, 1952.
CRABTREE, ARTHUR P. "Comment on Richard W. Poston, 'The Relation of Community Development to Adult Education.'" *Adult Education,* IV:6 (September, 1954), pp. 198-199.
CRIMI, JAMES E. *Adult Education in the Liberal Arts Colleges.* Notes and Essays on Education for Adults, No. 17. Chicago, Center for the Study of Liberal Education for Adults, 1957.
Current Issues in Higher Education. Proceedings of the Annual National Conference on Higher Education. Washington, Association for Higher Education, National Education Association. Various issues.
DAHL, ROBERT A. *A Preface to Democratic Theory.* Chicago, University of Chicago Press, 1956.
DALGLIESH, W. HAROLD. *Community Education in Foreign Affairs: A Report on Activities in Nineteen American Cities.* New York, Council on Foreign Relations, 1946.
DALLIN, DAVID J., and BORIS I. NICOLAEVSKY. *Forced Labor in Soviet*

Russia. New Haven, Yale University Press, 1947.

DAVID, HENRY. "Higher Education and the American Economy." *Current Issues in Higher Education,* 1955, pp. 11-18.

DAVIS, JAMES A., LATHROP VICKERY BEALE, and RUTH URSULA GEBHARD. *The Great Books Program: A National Survey.* Chicago, National Opinion Research Center, University of Chicago, 1959. Mimeographed.

DEANE, STEPHEN R. "Who Seeks Adult Education and Why." *Adult Education,* I:1 (October, 1950), pp. 18-25.

DEMAREST, G. STUART. "Faculty Organization at Rutgers." *New Directions for University Adult Education: Institution-Centered.* Notes and Essays on Education for Adults, No. 11. Chicago, Center for the Study of Liberal Education for Adults, 1955.

DENNEY, REUEL—see DAVID RIESMAN.

DEWHURST, J. FREDERIC, and ASSOCIATES. *America's Needs and Resources: A New Survey.* New York, Twentieth Century Fund, 1955.

DIEKHOFF, JOHN S. "From the Cradle to the Grave." *Journal of Higher Education,* XXVI:1 (January, 1955), pp. 10-12.

———. *Schooling for Maturity.* Notes and Essays on Education for Adults, No. 13. Chicago, Center for the Study of Liberal Education for Adults, 1955.

DIMMITT, BETTY B.—see KNUTE O. BROADY.

DONOVAN, HEDLEY. "Notes on the Russian Tension." *Fortune,* June, 1958, pp. 114-115, 220-225.

DRUCKER, PETER F. *America's Next Twenty Years.* New York, Harper & Brothers, 1957.

DU BOIS, CORA. *Foreign Students and Higher Education in the United States.* Washington, American Council on Education, 1956.

DUGAN, ARTHUR H. "An Extension Class Program with Special Reference to Wyoming." Unpublished doctoral dissertation, University of Wyoming, 1952.

DUNCAN, OTIS DUDLEY, and ALBERT J. REISS, JR. *Social Characteristics of Urban and Rural Communities, 1950.* New York, John Wiley & Sons, Inc., 1956.

DUNHAM, FRANKLIN. "List of Closed Circuit Educational Television in Schools, Colleges, Universities, and Defense Installations." Washington, U.S. Office of Education, 1957. Dittoed.

———, and RONALD R. LOWDERMILK. *Television in Our Schools.* Bulletin 1952, No. 16, rev. ed. Washington, U.S. Office of Education, 1956.

———, ———, and GERTRUDE G. BRODERICK. *Television in Education.* Bulletin 1957, No. 21. Washington, U.S. Office of Education, 1957.

DUNN, FREDERICK S. "Education and Foreign Affairs: A Challenge for the Universities." JOSEPH E. McLEAN (ed.). *The Public Service and University Education.* Princeton, Princeton University Press, 1949. Pp. 121-143.

------. *War and the Minds of Men.* Council on Foreign Relations. New York, Harper & Brothers, 1950.

DYER, JOHN P. *Ivory Towers in the Market Place: The Evening College in American Education.* Indianapolis, The Bobbs-Merrill Company, 1955.

------. "Possibilities for AUEC-NUEA Cooperation." *Proceedings of the Fortieth Annual Meeting of the National University Extension Association,* 38 (1955), pp. 38-42.

EBERHART, SYLVIA—see LEONARD S. COTTRELL, JR.

EDDY, EDWARD DANFORTH, JR. *Colleges for Our Land and Time: The Land-Grant Idea in American Education.* New York, Harper & Brothers, 1957.

Educational Policies Commission. *American Education and International Tensions.* Washington, National Education Association and American Association of School Administrators, 1949.

EDWARDS, A. "Balanced Farming in Missouri Meets the Needs of Farm People." *Extension Service Review,* 29:4 (April, 1958), pp. 80-81, 87.

ELSDON, K. T. *Reality and Purpose: A Visitor's Reflections on Some Aspects of American Adult Education.* Notes and Essays on Education for Adults, No. 16. Chicago, Center for the Study of Liberal Education for Adults, 1957.

ELY, MARY L. (ed.). *Handbook of Adult Education in the United States.* New York, Institute of Adult Education, Teachers College, Columbia University, 1948.

ENSMINGER, DOUGLAS—see EDMUND DeS. BRUNNER.

ESSERT, PAUL L. "Adult Education in the United States: A Report on General and Institutional Trends Based on an Extended Tour of the Nation in 1947-1948." New York, 1948. Mimeographed.

------. *Creative Leadership of Adult Education.* New York, Prentice-Hall, Inc., 1951.

EURICH, ALVIN C. "Better Instruction with Fewer Teachers." *Current Issues in Higher Education,* 1956, pp. 10-16.

"Evaluating Program and Performance." *Adult Leadership,* Vol. 1, No. 11, April, 1953.

"Evaluation of Adult Education." *Baltimore Bulletin of Education,* Vol. XXV, Nos. 4-6, January-March, 1948.

EVERETT, SAMUEL (ed.). "Teaching and World Affairs." Middle

States Council for the Social Studies. *Annual Proceedings*, Vol. 51, 1954.

"Extension Legislation Modernized." *Extension Service Review*, 24:8 (August, 1953), pp. 149, 159.

FAUST, CLARENCE H. "Educational Philosophy and Television." *Educational Record*, January, 1958 (reprint).

FERGUSON, C. M. *Adjusting to the Changing Scene*. Report of Cooperative Extension Work in Agriculture and Home Economics, 1957. Washington, Federal Cooperative Extension Service, February 3, 1958. Offset.

FERNBACH, ALFRED P. *University Extension and Workers' Education*. National University Extension Association Studies in University Extension Education, No. 3. Bloomington, Ind., The Association, 1945.

FIELD, HARRY H.—see GORDON M. CONNELLY.

FISCHER, RUTH. *Stalin and German Communism: A Study in the Origins of the State Party*. Cambridge, Harvard University Press, 1948.

FISHER, CHARLES A., KNUTE O. BROADY, and CYRIL O. HOULE. *Adult Education in the Modern University: A Preliminary Report by a Special Committee of the National University Extension Association*. Ann Arbor, University of Michigan Press, 1949.

FLETCHER, C. SCOTT. *The Battle of the Curriculum*. White Plains, N.Y., Fund for Adult Education, 1958.

FORTUNE, EDITORS OF. *America in the Sixties: The Economy and the Society*. New York, Harper & Brothers, 1960.

FOSDICK, DOROTHY. "Higher Education and World Affairs." *Current Issues in Higher Education*, 1955, pp. 18-25.

FULLER, C. DALE. *Training of Specialists in International Relations*. Washington, American Council on Education, 1957.

Fund for Adult Education. *Annual Reports*, 1953-1954, 1954-1955, 1955-1957.

——. *Liberal Adult Education*. White Plains, The Fund [1956]. Offset.

FURNISS, EDGAR S., JR. "Theory and Practice in the Teaching of International Relations in the United States." GEOFFREY L. GOODWIN (ed.). *The University Teaching of International Relations*. International Studies Conference. Oxford, Blackwell, 1951.

GALBRAITH, JOHN KENNETH. *The Affluent Society*. Boston, Houghton Mifflin Co., 1958.

GALLAGHER, BUELL G. "The Meaning and Mission of Higher Education." *Current Issues in Higher Education*, 1955, pp. 1-11.

GANGE, JOHN. *University Research on International Affairs*. Washington, American Council on Education, 1958.

GARRETT, MYRTLE E. "The Influence of Extension Organization on Community Development." Unpublished M.S. thesis, Prairie View A. & M. College, 1955.

GARTHOFF, RAYMOND L. *Soviet Strategy in the Nuclear Age*. New York, Frederick A. Praeger, Inc., 1958.

GAUDET, HAZEL—see PAUL F. LAZARSFELD.

GEBHARD, RUTH URSULA—see JAMES A. DAVIS.

GIBB, JACK R.—see CLARENCE D. JAYNE.

GIDEONSE, HARRY D. "Ideals and Goals of Citizenship Education." Middle States Council for the Social Studies. *Annual Proceedings*, 1953, 50, pp. 25-33.

———. "On Re-Thinking Liberal Education." ARTHUR E. TRAXLER (ed.). *Strengthening Education at All Levels*. Eighteenth Educational Conference, Educational Records Bureau and American Council on Education, 1953. Washington, The Council, 1954. Pp. 30-52.

CILLEN, WILFRED D. "The Institute of Humanistic Studies for Executives: An Experiment in Adult Education." Fund for Adult Education. *Liberal Adult Education*. White Plains, N.Y., The Fund [1956]. Pp. 15-27.

GLAZER, NATHAN—see DAVID RIESMAN.

GLEAZER, EDMUND J., JR. (ed.). *Junior College Directory, 1959. Data for June 1, 1957 to May 31, 1958*. Washington, American Association of Junior Colleges, 1959.

GLICK, PAUL C., and HERMAN P. MILLER. "Educational Level and Potential Income." *American Sociological Review*, 21:3 (June, 1956), pp. 307-312.

GODARD, J. M. "Relation of Academic Standards to Off-Campus Programs." *Proceedings of the Thirty-eighth Annual Meeting of the National University Extension Association*, 36 (1953), pp. 58-60.

GOODWIN, GEOFFREY L. (ed.). *The University Teaching of International Relations*. International Studies Conference. Oxford, Blackwell, 1951.

GORDON, MORTON. "The Meaning of University Level." *Adult Education*, X:1 (Autumn, 1959), pp. 22-26.

GORDY, AMELIA S. *Extension Activities and Accomplishments, 1958*. Extension Service Circular No. 522. Washington, U.S. Government Printing Office, 1959. Offset.

GOULD, SAMUEL B. "Quality in Adult Education." *Proceedings of* the *Association of University Evening Colleges, Twentieth Annual Meeting,* 1958, pp. 49-61.

"Government by the People: Community Clinics and Development Councils Promote Many Local Improvements in Arkansas." *American City,* LXVII:1 (January, 1952), pp. 106-107, 179.

GRANEY, MAURICE. "General Extension Courses: Their Place in Publicly Supported Institutions of Higher Education." *Journal of Higher Education,* XXVIII:1 (January, 1957), pp. 10-14, 57-58.

GRATTAN, C. HARTLEY. *In Quest of Knowledge: A Historical Perspective on Adult Education.* New York, Association Press, 1955.

GRUEN, WILLIAM. "A Pragmatic Criticism of Community-Centered Adult Education." *Adult Education,* VI:2 (Winter, 1956), pp. 81-90.

GRUMANN, RUSSELL M.—see KNUTE O. BROADY.

GUCKY, JOSEPH B., and HERBERT COREY. "A Community Organizes to Help Itself." *Educational Leadership,* VII:6 (March, 1950), pp. 388-392.

GURIN, GERALD—see ANGUS CAMPBELL.

HADLOCK, ALTON P. "A Study of the Development of Critical Thinking through Adult Discussion Groups." Unpublished Ed.D. dissertation, University of California at Los Angeles, June, 1958.

HAMILTON, THOMAS H. "The Recruitment and Retention of College Faculty." *Current Issues in Higher Education,* 1955, pp. 210-215.

HAMMARBERG, HELEN V. *Informal Adult Education Programs at the Pennsylvania State College, the University of Chicago, the University of California.* National University Extension Association Studies in University Extension Education, No. 9. Bloomington, Ind., The Association, 1953.

HANNAH, JOHN A. "Higher Education and Agriculture." RAYMOND F. HOWES (ed.). *Higher Education and the Society It Serves.* Washington, American Council on Education, 1957. Pp. 49-55.

HANSEN, BERT B. "Darby, Montana, Looks at Itself." *Adult Education Bulletin,* X:4 (April, 1946), pp. 99-106.

——. "An Evaluation of the Montana Study: An Adult-Education Program in Community Activities in the Humanities." *Journal of Higher Education,* XX:1 (January, 1949), pp. 18-27.

——. "A Project in Community Education." *Journal of General Education,* I (January, 1947), pp. 114-119.

HARDIN, CHARLES M. *Freedom in Agricultural Education.* Chicago, University of Chicago Press, 1955.

——. *The Politics of Agriculture: Soil Conservation and the Struggle for Power in Rural America.* Glencoe, Ill., Free Press, 1952.

HARLESS, WILLIAM H.—see B. LAMAR JOHNSON.

HARRIS, SEYMOUR E. *How Shall We Pay for Education? Approaches to the Economics of Education.* New York, Harper & Brothers, 1948.

HARRISON, JAMES W. "Analyzing Adult Education in Universities and Colleges." Chicago, Center for the Study of Liberal Education for Adults, 1955. Mimeographed.

———. "Designing Educational Programs for Adults: A Comparison of Non-Credit and Credit Courses in University Evening Colleges." Unpublished Ph.D. dissertation, University of Chicago, August, 1957. Mimeographed abstract.

HAVIGHURST, ROBERT J., and BETTY ORR. *Adult Education and Adult Needs.* Chicago, Center for the Study of Liberal Education for Adults, 1956.

HEARNE, CANNON CHILES—see LINCOLN DAVID KELSEY.

HEINDEL, RICHARD H. "How 'Worldly' Can We Be?" *Proceedings of the Forty-second Annual Meeting of the National University Extension Association,* 40 (1957), pp. 21-28.

HERO, ALFRED O. *Americans in World Affairs.* Studies in Citizen Participation in International Relations, Vol. I. Boston, World Peace Foundation, 1959.

———. *Mass Media and World Affairs.* Studies in Citizen Participation in International Relations, Vol. IV. Boston, World Peace Foundation, 1959.

———. *Opinion Leaders in American Communities.* Studies in Citizen Participation in International Relations, Vol. VI. Boston, World Peace Foundation, 1959.

———. *Voluntary Organizations in World Affairs Communication.* Studies in Citizen Participation in International Relations, Vol. V. Boston, World Peace Foundation, 1959.

HIETT, NORRIS A. "Community Organization." *Proceedings of the Fortieth Annual Meeting of the National University Extension Association,* 38 (1955), pp. 56-58.

HILL, RICHARD J. *The Ways of Mankind Study: A Comparative Evaluation of Lecture and Discussion Group Methods in Liberal Adult Education.* White Plains, N.Y., Fund for Adult Education, 1959. Mimeographed.

HOFSTADTER, RICHARD. *The Age of Reform: From Bryan to FDR.* New York, Alfred A. Knopf, Inc., 1956.

HOIBERG, OTTO G. *Exploring the Small Community.* Lincoln, University of Nebraska Press, 1955.

———, et al. *Resources for Community Development Programs.* Committee on Community Organization, National University Extension Association, 1953. Mimeographed.

HOLLANDER, LOUIS. "Higher Education and Labor." RAYMOND F. HOWES (ed.). *Higher Education and the Society It Serves.* Washington, American Council on Education, 1957. Pp. 38-43.

HOLT, ANDREW D. "Extension's Role in Public Relations." *Proceedings of the Thirty-ninth Annual Meeting of the National University Extension Association,* 37 (1954), pp. 48-57.

HOOK, SIDNEY. *Education for Modern Man.* New York, The Dial Press, Inc., 1946.

———. *Heresy, Yes—Conspiracy, No.* New York, The John Day Co., 1953.

———. *Political Power and Personal Freedom: Critical Studies in Democracy, Communism, and Civil Rights.* New York, Criterion Books, Inc., 1959.

HORN, FRANCIS H. "International Understanding: The Lament of a Discouraged Adult Educator." *Adult Education Journal,* 9:3 (July, 1950), pp. 109-118.

HORTON, MILDRED McAFEE. "Notions and Nations." ARTHUR E. TRAXLER (ed.). *Modern Educational Problems.* Seventeenth Educational Conference, Educational Records Bureau and American Council on Education, 1952. Washington, The Council, 1953. Pp. 100-110.

HOULE, CYRIL O. "Community Education Services as an Emerging Function of Higher Education." NORMAN BURNS and CYRIL O. HOULE. (eds.). *The Community Responsibilities of Institutions of Higher Learning.* Proceedings of the Institute for Administrative Officers of Higher Institutions, Vol. XX. Chicago, University of Chicago Press, 1948. Pp. 5-13.

———. "The Development of Leadership." Fund for Adult Education. *Liberal Adult Education.* White Plains, N.Y., The Fund [1956]. Pp. 53-67.

———. "The Energy of Local Liberty." *Adult Leadership,* 4:7 (January, 1956), pp. 8-10.

———. "The Evening College: Its Purposes and Its Relationships within the University." *Journal of Higher Education,* XXV:7 (October, 1954), pp. 362-372, 398-399.

———. "Introduction." *Universities in Adult Education.* Paris, UNESCO, 1952. Pp. 9-26.

———. *Libraries in Adult and Fundamental Education: The Report of the Malmö Seminar.* Public Library Manuals, No. 4. Paris, UNESCO, 1951.

——. *Major Trends in Higher Adult Education*. Notes and Essays on Education for Adults, No. 24. Chicago, Center for the Study of Liberal Education for Adults, 1959.

——. "University Adult Education in the United States." *Universities Quarterly*, 6:3 (May, 1952), pp. 277-286.

——. "The Use of Print in Adult Educational Agencies." National Society for the Study of Education. *Fifty-fifth Yearbook*. Chicago, The Society, 1956. Part II, pp. 157-187.

——, and CHARLES A. NELSON. *The University, the Citizen, and World Affairs*. Washington, American Council on Education, 1956.

HOUNSHELL, CHARLES D. "A Science of International Politics?" *Journal of Higher Education*, XXVII:6 (June, 1956), pp. 291-296.

HOWES, RAYMOND F. (ed.). *Higher Education and the Society It Serves*. Washington, American Council on Education, 1957.

HSIN PAO YANG, E.—see EDMUND DES. BRUNNER.

HUDSON, ROBERT B. *Radburn: A Plan of Living*. New York, American Association for Adult Education, 1934.

HUGHES, HELEN MACGILL—see SHIRLEY A. STAR.

HUMPHREY, RICHARD A. (ed.). *Blueprint and Experience: Addresses and Summary of Proceedings of the Conference on University Contracts Abroad, 1957*. Washington, American Council and Education, 1958.

HUNSAKER, HERBERT C. "What Are the Responsibilities of Higher Education for the Continuing Education of Adults?" *Current Issues in Higher Education*, 1955, pp. 85-90.

HUTCHINS, FRANCIS S. "Report of the Commission on International Cooperation through Education." *Association of American Colleges Bulletin*, XLIII:1 (March, 1957), pp. 163-164.

——. "Report of the Commission on International Understanding." *Association of American Colleges Bulletin*, XLIV:1 (March, 1958), pp. 148-149.

Iowa State University. Center for Agricultural and Economic Adjustment. *Problems and Policies of American Agriculture*. Ames, Iowa State University Press, 1959.

——. ——. *Extension Worker's Training Handbook: Farm Policy*. Ames, Iowa State University, 1959. Offset.

JACOB, PHILIP E. *Changing Values in College: An Exploratory Study of the Impact of College Teaching*. New York, Harper & Brothers, 1957.

JAMES, BERNARD J. "Can 'Needs' Define Education Goals?" *Adult Education*, VII:1 (Autumn, 1956), pp. 19-26.

JAYNE, CLARENCE D., and JACK R. GIBB. "The Mountain-Plains

Project." *Adult Education,* V:4 (Summer, 1955), pp. 195-209.

JOHNSON, B. LAMAR., and WILLIAM H. HARLESS. "Implications of the Citizenship Education Project for the Junior College." *Junior College Journal,* XXV:7 (March, 1955), pp. 369-375.

JOHNSON, EUGENE I. *The Community Education Project: A Four-Year Report.* Pioneering with Mass Media in Community Development. San Bernardino, San Bernardino Valley College, 1957.

JOHNSTONE, WILLIAM C., JR. "Government Programs that Call for Cooperation with Higher Education." HOWARD LEE NOSTRAND and FRANCIS J. BROWN (eds.). *The Role of Colleges and Universities in International Understanding.* American Council on Education Studies, Series I, No. 38, Vol. XIII. Washington, The Council, 1949. Pp. 75-83.

Joint Council on Educational Television. *Educational Television Directory, January, 1960.* Washington, The Council, 1960. Offset.

——. *Educational Television Factsheet.* Various issues.

JONES, BERTIS L. "Neighborhood Council in the City: Community Development Procedures Can Be Modified to Meet the Needs in Urban Areas." *Adult Leadership,* 8:2 (June, 1959), pp. 44-46.

Journal of Adult Education—published bimonthly by the American Association for Adult Education, from February, 1929, through October, 1941; it superseded the *Journal of the American Association for Adult Education* (December, 1926-June, 1928) and was replaced by the *Adult Education Journal.*

KAPLAN, A. ABBOTT. "Labor-Management Programs." MARY L. ELY (ed.). *Handbook of Adult Education in the United States.* New York, Institute of Adult Education, Teachers College, Columbia University, 1948. Pp. 37-41.

——. *Socio-Economic Circumstances and Adult Participation in Certain Cultural and Educational Activities.* Teachers College Contributions to Education, No. 889. New York, Teachers College, Columbia University, 1943.

KELLER, E. L. "What Should We Expect of University Extension?" *Proceedings of the Thirty-fifth Annual Meeting of the National University Extension Association,* 33 (1950), pp. 25-29.

KELSEY, LINCOLN DAVID, and CANNON CHILES HEARNE. *Cooperative Extension Work.* 2nd ed. Ithaca, N.Y., Comstock Publishing Associates, 1955.

KELSO, LOUIS O., and MORTIMER J. ADLER. *The Capitalist Manifesto.* New York, Random House, 1958.

KEMPFER, HOMER. *Adult Education.* New York, McGraw-Hill Book Co., 1955.

——. "Identifying Educational Needs and Interests of Adults: A Summary of an Evaluative Study." *Adult Education,* II:1 (October, 1951), pp. 32-36.

——, and STEPHEN R. DEANE. *Springfield, Massachusetts, Looks at Adult Education.* Springfield, Adult Education Council, 1951.

——, et al. *Program Evaluation in Adult Education.* Chicago, Committee on Evaluation, Adult Education Association, 1952.

KIDD, J. ROBY. *Adult Education in the Canadian University.* Toronto, Canadian Association for Adult Education, 1956. Offset.

——. "The Observer's Report." PETER E. SIEGLE (ed.). *The University's Responsibility for the General Education of Adults.* Chicago, Center for the Study of Liberal Education for Adults, 1955. Pp. 1-17.

KIRCHNER, CORINNE—see EDMUND DeS. BRUNNER.

KIRK, GRAYSON. *The Study of International Relations in American Colleges and Universities.* New York, Council on Foreign Relations, 1947.

KISSINGER, HENRY A. *Nuclear Weapons and Foreign Policy.* Council on Foreign Relations. New York, Harper & Brothers, 1957.

KNOWLES, MALCOLM S. "Adult Education in the United States." *Adult Education,* V:2 (Winter, 1955), pp. 67-76.

——. *Informal Adult Education: A Guide for Administrators, Leaders, and Teachers.* New York, Association Press, 1950.

——. "An Overview and History of the Field." *Adult Education,* VII:4 (Summer, 1957), pp. 219-230.

——. "Philosophical Issues that Confront Adult Education." *Adult Education,* VII:4 (Summer, 1957), pp. 234-240.

—— (ed.). *Handbook of Adult Education in the United States.* Chicago, Adult Education Association of the U.S.A., 1960.

KNOX, ALAN B. "Adult College Students: An Analysis of Certain Factors Related to the Characteristics of Students Attending a University Adult College." Unpublished Ed.D. dissertation, Syracuse University, 1958.

KONVITZ, MILTON R. *Fundamental Liberties of a Free People: Religion, Speech, Press, Assembly.* Ithaca, N.Y., Cornell University Press, 1957.

KRAENZEL, CARL FREDERICK. *The Great Plains in Transition.* Norman, University of Oklahoma Press, 1955.

——, and GEORGE ENGSTROM. *Montana's Population Changes, 1920 to 1950, Especially as to Numbers and Composition.* Bulletin 520. Bozeman, Montana State College Agricultural Experiment Station, June, 1956.

KRIESBERG, MARTIN. "Dark Areas of Ignorance." LESTER MARKEL et al. *Public Opinion and Foreign Policy*. Council on Foreign Relations. New York, Harper & Brothers, 1949. Pp. 49-64.

KROPP, RUSSELL P., and COOLIE VERNER. "An Attitude Scale Technique for Evaluating Meetings." *Adult Education*, VII:4 (Summer, 1957), pp. 212-215.

KUZNETS, SIMON. *Shares of Upper Income Groups in Income and Savings*. New York, National Bureau of Economic Research, 1953.

LACKEY, KATHARINE. "Eight Communities in Action." *Adult Leadership*, 7:6 (December, 1958), pp. 173-174.

LAVES, WALTER H. C. "International Understanding and Our Schools." American Association of Colleges for Teacher Education. *Ninth Yearbook*. Chicago, The Association, 1956. Pp. 91-103.

LAZARSFELD, PAUL F., and GENEVIEVE KNUPFER. "Communications Research and International Coöperation." RALPH LINTON (ed.). *The Science of Man in the World Crisis*. New York, Columbia University Press, 1945. Pp. 465-495.

——, BERNARD BERELSON, and HAZEL GAUDET. *The People's Choice: How the Voter Makes Up His Mind in a Presidential Campaign*. New York, Columbia University Press, 1948.

LEFEVER, ERNEST W. *Ethics and United States Foreign Policy*. Living Age Book 19. New York, Meridian Books, Inc., 1957.

LEONARD, OLEN E., and SHELDON G. LOWRY. "Continuation Education in Colleges and Universities." CHARLES P. LOOMIS et al. *Rural Social Systems and Adult Education*. East Lansing, Michigan State College Press, 1953. Pp. 230-244.

LEYS, WAYNE A. R. "The Two Rôles of the University in Adult Education." *Journal of Higher Education*, XXVI:1 (January, 1955), pp. 12-14.

LINDEMAN, EDUARD C. "Adults Evaluate Themselves." Adult Education Association of the U.S.A. *How To Teach Adults*. Leadership Pamphlet No. 5. Chicago, The Association, 1955. Pp. 45-48.

LIPPITT, RONALD. "Group Self-Analysis of Productivity in the Work Conference." *Adult Education Bulletin*, XII:3 (February, 1948), pp. 74-79.

LIPSET, SEYMOUR MARTIN. *Political Man: The Social Bases of Politics*. Garden City, N.Y., Doubleday & Company, Inc., 1960.

LIPSETT, LAURENCE—see BURTON E. STRATTON.

LIVERIGHT, A. A., et al. *A Review of 1956: A Report of Center Activities during the Past Year, and a Look Ahead*. Chicago, Center for the Study of Liberal Education for Adults, 1957.

LONDON, JACK. "Program Development in Adult Education." MAL-

COLM S. KNOWLES (ed.). *Handbook of Adult Education in the United States.* Chicago, Adult Education Association of the U.S.A., 1960. Pp. 65-81.

LOOMIS, CHARLES P., et al. *Rural Social Systems and Adult Education.* East Lansing, Michigan State College Press, 1953.

LORIMER, FRANK. *The Making of Adult Minds in a Metropolitan Area.* Brooklyn Conference on Adult Education. New York, The Macmillan Co., 1931.

——. *The Population of the Soviet Union: History and Prospects.* Geneva, League of Nations, 1946.

LOWDERMILK, RONALD R.—see FRANKLIN DUNHAM.

LOWRY, SHELDON G.—see OLEN E. LEONARD.

LUBELL, SAMUEL. *The Future of American Politics.* Rev. ed. New York, Doubleday-Anchor, 1956.

——. *Revolt of the Moderates.* New York, Harper & Brothers, 1956.

LUKE, ROBERT A., et al. *Community Education in Action: A Report on Community Organization and Adult Education.* Committee on Community Organization, American Association for Adult Education. New York, Teachers College, Columbia University, 1948.

McCARTY, H. B. "Radio and Understanding." MARY L. ELY (ed.). *Handbook of Adult Education in the United States.* New York, Institute of Adult Education, Teachers College, Columbia University, 1948. Pp. 259-262.

McCLUSKY, HOWARD Y. "Community Development." MALCOLM S. KNOWLES (ed.). *Handbook of Adult Education in the United States.* Chicago, Adult Education Association of the U.S.A., 1960. Pp. 416-427.

——. "Community Self Help in Michigan." *University Extension Experiments in Community Self Help Education.* National University Extension Association Studies in University Extension Education, No. 4. Bloomington, Ind., The Association, 1946. Pp. 7-12.

McCONNELL, GRANT. *The Decline of Agrarian Democracy.* Berkeley, University of California Press, 1953.

McCURDY, CHARLES P., JR. "Report of the Executive Secretary." *Proceedings of the Fortieth Annual Meeting of the National University Extension Association,* 38 (1955), pp. 88-91.

McGEOCH, JOHN A. *The Psychology of Human Learning: An Introduction.* New York, Longmans, Green & Co., 1942.

McGHEE, PAUL A. "Adult Education and Community Action." *Adult Education,* VI:2 (Winter, 1956), pp. 67-81.

——. "Higher Education and Adult Education: Four Questions."

Current Issues in Higher Education, 1953, pp. 196-206.

——. *A School for Optimists.* Notes and Essays on Education for Adults, No. 6. Chicago, Center for the Study of Liberal Education for Adults, 1953.

——. "Three Dimensions of Adult Education." *Educational Record,* 35:2 (April, 1954), pp. 119-130.

McGinnis, Robert, and Raymond W. Mack. "A Study of Belief in the Bill of Rights." Summary of paper delivered at the meeting of the American Sociological Society, 1957.

McLain, Charles W. "The Present Status of the Junior College in the United States." Unpublished Ed.D. dissertation, Colorado State College of Education, August, 1953.

McMahon, Ernest E. "Concentric Ripples from a Pebble." *Adult Leadership,* 7:1 (May, 1958), pp. 11-12.

McMichael, Morris H. "A Comparison of Student Achievement, as Measured by Marks Received, in Residence and Extension Courses at the University of New Mexico." Unpublished M.A. thesis, University of New Mexico, 1950.

McWhirter, Mary Esther. "Service Activities." Ralph C. Preston (ed.). *Teaching World Understanding.* New York, Prentice-Hall, Inc., 1955. Pp. 67-90.

Maccoby, Eleanor E., and Ben Willerman (eds.). "Citizen Participation in World Affairs: Problems and Possibilities." *Journal of Social Issues,* Vol. IV, No. 1, Winter, 1948.

Mack, Raymond W.—see Robert McGinnis.

Mallory, Hervey F.—see W. S. Bittner.

Malone, Carl C., and Lucille Holaday Malone. *Decision Making and Management for Farm and Home.* Ames, Iowa State College Press, 1958.

Manny, Elsie S. *Rural Community Organization: Selected Annotated References.* Miscellaneous Publication No. 729. Washington, U.S. Department of Agriculture, 1956. Mimeographed.

Matthews, Joseph L. "The Cooperative Extension Service of the United States." Charles P. Loomis et al. *Rural Social Systems and Adult Education.* East Lansing, Michigan State College Press, 1953. Pp. 51-80.

Mayer, Milton—see Mortimer J. Adler.

Meder, Albert E., Jr. "The University Providing Service to the People in an Industrial State." *Proceedings of the Thirty-third Annual Meeting of the National University Extension Association,* 31 (1948), pp. 82-93.

Mial, H. Curtis. "Community Development: A Democratic Social

Process." *Adult Leadership,* 6:10 (April, 1958), pp. 277-282.

Michigan State University. *Telecourses for Credit.* Vol. 4. East Lansing, Continuing Education Service, University of the Air, September 1, 1957. Mimeographed.

MILLER, HARRY L. "Comments on this Workshop." *Adult Leadership,* 5:10 (April, 1957), pp. 316-317.

———. *Evaluating Courses, Not Students: An Evening College Experiment with Objective Devices.* Notes and Essays on Education for Adults, No. 3. Chicago, Center for the Study of Liberal Education for Adults, 1953.

———. "Group Discussion—Specific or Panacea?" *Etc.,* XI:1 (Autumn, 1953), pp. 49-58.

———. "Summary of Workshop No. III." *Proceedings of the Association of University Evening Colleges, Seventeenth Annual Meeting,* 1955, pp. 88-90.

MILLER, HERMAN P.—see PAUL C. GLICK.

MILLER, K. M. "Evaluation in Adult Education." *International Social Science Bulletin,* VII:3 (1955), pp. 430-442.

MILLER, PAUL A. "Extension Education in the Land-Grant Universities." *Farm Policy Forum,* 11:4 (1958-1959), pp. 8-14.

———, et al. *The Cooperative Extension Service Today: A Statement of Scope and Responsibility.* Extension Committee on Organization and Policy, Subcommittee on Scope and Responsibility [1958].

MILLER, WARREN E.—see ANGUS CAMPBELL.

MINNIS, ROY B. *The Adult Education Council of Denver: An Evaluative Report Based upon Case Studies in Two Cities.* Denver, 1955.

MIRE, JOSEPH. *Labor Education: A Study Report on Needs, Programs, and Approaches.* Fund for Adult Education. Inter-University Labor Education Committee, 1956.

———. "The University and the Union in Workers' Education." *Adult Education,* V:4 (Summer, 1955), pp. 232-236.

MOORE, ASHER. "The Philosophy of General Education." *Journal of Higher Education,* XXVIII:2 (February, 1957), pp. 65-69, 115-116.

MORGENTHAU, HANS J. *Dilemmas of Politics.* Chicago, University of Chicago Press, 1958.

———. *In Defense of the National Interest: A Critical Examination of American Foreign Policy.* New York, Alfred A. Knopf, Inc., 1951.

MORTON, JOHN R. *University Extension in the United States: A Study by the National University Extension Association, Made with the Assistance of a Grant from the Fund for Adult Education.* Birmingham, University of Alabama Press, 1953.

MUNRO, W. B. "Is the Slacker Vote a Menace?" *National Municipal Review*, 17 (1928), pp. 80-86.

Myrdal, Gunnar. *An American Dilemma: The Negro Problem and Modern Democracy*. New York, Harper & Brothers, 1944.

National Education Association, Research Division. *Status and Trends: Vital Statistics, Education, and Public Finance*. Research Report 1959-R13. Washington, The Association, August, 1959.

National Educational Television and Radio Center. "Educational Television Stations Affiliated with the National Educational Television and Radio Center." No date.

National Manpower Council. *A Policy for Scientific and Professional Manpower: A Statement by the Council with Facts and Issues Prepared by the Research Staff*. New York, Columbia University Press, 1953.

National University Extension Association. *Proceedings of Annual Meetings*, various years.

——. *University Extension Experiments in Community Self Help Education*. National University Extension Association Studies in University Extension Education, No. 4. Bloomington, Ind., The Association, 1946.

NELSON, CHARLES A.—see CYRIL O. HOULE.

NELSON, LOWRY. *American Farm Life*. Cambridge, Harvard University Press, 1954.

NEUFFER, FRANK R. *Administrative Policies and Practices of Evening Colleges, 1953*. Chicago, Center for the Study of Liberal Education for Adults, 1953.

——. "The Evening College Movement." *Proceedings of the Association of University Evening Colleges, Twentieth Annual Meeting*, 1958, pp. 84-87.

NEWBERRY, JOHN S., JR.—see EDMUND DeS. BRUNNER.

NEWBURN, HARRY K. "The Role of State Universities in Educational Television." *Transactions and Proceedings of the National Association of State Universities in the U.S.A.*, LII (1954), pp. 61-73.

NICHOLLS, WILLIAM M., II, and EDMUND DeS. BRUNNER. "Composition of AEA's Membership." *Adult Education*, IX:4 (Summer, 1959), pp. 211-221.

NICOLAEVSKY, BORIS I.—see DAVID J. DALLIN.

NOLTE, J. M. "The Role of the State University in Adult Education." *Transactions and Proceedings of the National Association of State Universities in the U.S.A.*, L (1952), pp. 57-70.

NORMAN, ARTHUR, and LEWIS SAWIN. "What Johnny Don't Know." *New Republic*, August 12, 1957, pp. 14-17.

NOSTRAND, HOWARD LEE, and FRANCIS J. BROWN (eds.). *The Role of Colleges and Universities in International Understanding.* American Council on Education Studies, Series I, No. 38, Vol. XIII. Washington, The Council, October, 1949.

NYQUIST, EWALD B. "The Soft Pedagogy of Evening Programs." *Proceedings of the Association of University Evening Colleges, Fourteenth Annual Meeting,* 1952, pp. 57-65.

OGDEN, JEAN and JESS. *Small Communities in Action: Stories of Citizen Programs at Work.* New York, Harper & Brothers, 1946.

——. "Special Projects in Adult Education: An Experiment in Community Development." MARY L. ELY (ed.). *Handbook of Adult Education in the United States.* New York, Institute of Adult Education, Teachers College, Columbia University, 1948. Pp. 118-125.

OLDS, EDWARD B. "Adult Students and Their Teachers: A Study Based on Six Communities." *Adult Education,* V:4 (Summer, 1955), pp. 210-219.

——. *Financing Adult Education in America's Public Schools and Community Councils.* National Commission on Adult Education Finance. Washington, Adult Education Association, n.d. Offset.

——. "How Adult Education Can Help in Meeting the Higher Education Needs of the Rising College-Age Population." *Educational Record,* 36:3 (July, 1955), pp. 229-239.

ORCUTT, ALBERT W. "The Role of the College or University Consultant in Community Development." Unpublished Ed.D. project, Teachers College, Columbia University, 1955.

ORR, BETTY—see ROBERT J. HAVIGHURST.

OZANNE, JACQUES. *Regional Surveys of Adult Education.* New York, American Association for Adult Education, 1934.

PALMER, ROBERT E., and COOLIE VERNER. "A Comparison of Three Instruction Techniques." *Adult Education,* IX:4 (Summer, 1959), pp. 232-238.

PARKS, W. ROBERT. "History, Philosophy, and Traditions of the Land-Grant College." Unpublished paper, 1955.

PASCHAL, ELIZABETH. "What New Developments and Techniques, Other than TV, Indicate that the Quality of Instruction Need Not Be Sacrificed, nor the Teaching Load Increased, While Increasing the Number of Students Taught?" *Current Issues in Higher Education,* 1958, pp. 240-246.

PELL, ORLIE A. H. "Social Philosophy at the Grass Roots: The Work of the AEA's Committee on Social Philosophy." *Adult Education,* II:4 (April, 1952), pp. 123-134.

PERRY, RALPH BARTON. *The Citizen Decides: A Guide to Responsible Thinking in Time of Crisis.* Bloomington, Indiana University Press, 1951.

PITKIN, ROYCE S. *The Residential School in American Adult Education.* New Directions for University Adult Education: Looking Forward. Notes and Essays on Education for Adults, No. 14. Chicago, Center for the Study of Liberal Education for Adults, 1956.

POLANYI, KARL. *The Great Transformation.* New York, Rinehart & Co., Inc., 1944.

POSTON, RICHARD WAVERLY. "The American Community in Trouble." Mimeographed excerpt from "A Report of the Plans and Operations of the Department of Community Development." Carbondale, Southern Illinois University, March 15, 1957.

———. *Democracy Is You: A Guide to Citizen Action.* New York, Harper & Brothers, 1953.

———. "The Relation of Community Development to Adult Education." *Adult Education,* IV:6 (September, 1954), pp. 191-196.

———. "Report of the Chairman, Division of Community Development." *Proceedings of the Forty-third Annual Meeting of the National University Extension Association,* 41 (1958), pp. 23-29.

———. *Small Town Renaissance: A Story of the Montana Study.* New York, Harper & Brothers, 1950.

POWELL, JOHN WALKER. *Learning Comes of Age.* Adult Education Association of the U.S.A. New York, Association Press, 1956.

———. " 'Where Did You Go?' 'Out to Change the World.' 'What Did You Do?' 'I Dunno.' " *Adult Leadership,* 6:10 (April, 1958), pp. 261-263.

———, and KENNETH D. BENNE. "Philosophies of Adult Education." MALCOLM S. KNOWLES (ed.). *Handbook of Adult Education in the United States.* Chicago, Adult Education Association of the U.S.A., 1960. Pp. 41-53.

President's Committee on Education Beyond the High School. *Second Report to the President.* Washington, U.S. Government Printing Office, 1957.

PRICE, RICHARD R. *The Center for Continuation Study of the University of Minnesota.* National University Extension Association Studies in University Extension Education, No. 1. Bloomington, Ind., The Association, 1943.

"Programing for World Affairs." *Adult Leadership,* Vol. 2, No. 3, July-August, 1953.

PUGH, DAVID D. *The Role of Extension Centers in a State-Wide Program.* National University Extension Association Studies in

University Extension Education, No. 10. Bloomington, Ind., The Association, 1953.

RAYBOULD, S. G. *The English Universities and Adult Education.* London, Workers' Educational Association, 1951.

REALS, WILLIS H. "The Evening College as I See It." *Proceedings of the Association of University Evening Colleges, Sixteenth Annual Meeting,* 1954, pp. 48-55.

REID, J. T. *It Happened in Taos.* Albuquerque, University of New Mexico Press, 1946.

REID, ROBERT H. "The Teacher and World Affairs." Middle States Council for the Social Studies. *Annual Proceedings,* 48 (1950-51), pp. 1-6.

REISS, ALBERT J., JR.—see OTIS DUDLEY DUNCAN.

"The Responsibility of Higher Education for Helping To Develop International Understanding: A Symposium." *Educational Record,* 37:2 (April, 1956), pp. 106-125.

REITLINGER, GERALD. *The Final Solution: The Attempt to Exterminate the Jews of Europe, 1939-1945.* New York, Beechhurst Press, 1953.

RIESMAN, DAVID. *Individualism Reconsidered and Other Essays.* Glencoe, Ill., Free Press, 1954.

——, and NATHAN GLAZER. "Criteria for Political Apathy." ALVIN W. GOULDNER (ed.). *Studies in Leadership: Leadership and Democratic Action.* New York, Harper & Brothers, 1950. Pp. 505-559.

——, ——, and REUEL DENNEY. *The Lonely Crowd: A Study of the Changing American Character.* Abridged ed. New York, Doubleday-Anchor, 1953.

Rockefeller Brothers Fund. *The Pursuit of Excellence: Education and the Future of America.* Special Studies Project Report V. New York, Doubleday & Company, Inc., 1958.

ROGERS, MARIA. Review of Ogden and Ogden, *Small Communities in Action. Adult Educational Journal,* 6:2 (April, 1947), pp. 95-96.

"The Role of Adult Education in Community Development: A Symposium." *Adult Education,* VI:1 (Autumn, 1955), pp. 3-25.

ROPER, ELMO, and Associates. *An Opinion Survey among Community Leaders about the United Nations and a Test Information Program.* New York, Carnegie Endowment for International Peace, 1956. Offset.

ROSENTRETER, FREDERICK M. *The Boundaries of the Campus: A History of the University of Wisconsin Extension Division, 1885-1945.* Madison, University of Wisconsin Press, 1957.

ROSS, EARLE D. *Democracy's College: The Land-Grant Movement in the Formative Stage.* Ames, Iowa State College Press, 1942.

ROWBOTHAM, ALICE. *Correspondence Instruction at the University of California, the University of Chicago, the Pennsylvania State College.* National University Extension Association Studies in University Extension Education, No. 8. Bloomington, Ind., The Association, 1953.

RUSSELL, FRANCIS H. "International Relations and World Understanding." *Proceedings of the Thirty-third Annual Meeting of the National University Extension Association,* 31 (1948), pp. 49-54.

SALISBURY, HARRRISON. "What Americans Don't Know About Russia." *McCall's,* June, 1957.

SANDERS, IRWIN T.—see EDMUND DES. BRUNNER.

SARCHET, BETTIE B.—see HERBERT A. THELEN.

SAWIN, LEWIS—see ARTHUR NORMAN.

SCHACHT, ROBERT H. "Annual Report 1956-1957, Bureau of Information and Program Services, University of Wisconsin Extension Division."

SCHMIDT, WARREN H., and ELWIN V. SVENSON. "Methods in Adult Education." MALCOLM S. KNOWLES (ed.). *Handbook of Adult Education in the United States.* Chicago, Adult Education Association of the U.S.A., 1960. Pp. 83-95.

SCHUELER, HERBERT. "The Method of Adult Education." *Adult Leadership,* 5:10 (April, 1957), pp. 306-310.

SCHULTZ, HAROLD A. "World-Mindedness through Teacher Education in the Arts." American Association of Colleges for Teacher Education. *Tenth Yearbook.* Chicago, The Association, 1957. Pp. 175-177.

SCHULTZ, THEODORE W. "The Emerging Economic Scene and Its Relation to High-School Education." FRANCIS S. CHASE and HAROLD A. ANDERSON (eds.). *The High School in a New Era.* Chicago, University of Chicago Press, 1958. Pp. 97-109.

SCHWERTMAN, JOHN B. "Analysis and Interpretation of Recommendations for NUEA/AUEC Action by Special Interest Groups." PETER E. SIEGLE (ed.). *The University's Responsibility for the General Education of Adults.* Chicago, Center for the Study of Liberal Education for Adults, 1955. Pp. 49-67.

——. "General Education and Specialized Education: A New Notion about their Relationship." *Journal of General Education,* IX:1 (October, 1955), pp. 54-59.

SELMAN, GORDON. "A Survey of Adult Education about International Affairs Carried on by Canadian Universities: April, 1956 to March,

1957." Canadian Association for Adult Education, 1957. Mimeographed.

SHANNON, THEODORE J. "A Study of Objectives for Selected Areas of University Extension." Unpublished Ph.D. dissertation, Yale University, June, 1958.

SHEATS, PAUL H. "The Contribution of University Extension to Learning." *Journal of Higher Education,* XX:2 (February, 1949), pp. 77-82, 113-114.

——. "Establishing Priorities in Adult Education." *Proceedings of the Thirty-ninth Annual Meeting of the National University Extension Association,* 37 (1954), pp. 38-42.

——. "A Middle Way in Adult Education." *Adult Education,* VII:4 (Summer, 1957), pp. 231-233.

——. "Present Trends and Future Strategies in Adult Education." MALCOLM S. KNOWLES (ed.). *Handbook of Adult Education in the United States.* Chicago, Adult Education Association of the U.S.A., 1960. Pp. 553-561.

——. "The Responsibility of the Evening College to the Community." *Proceedings of the Association of University Evening Colleges, Sixteenth Annual Meeting,* 1954, pp. 76-83.

——, CLARENCE D. JAYNE, and RALPH B. SPENCE. *Adult Education: The Community Approach.* New York, Dryden, 1953.

SIEGLE, PETER E. "The Adult Learner." *Adult Leadership,* 3:9 (March, 1955), pp. 16-18.

——. "Liberal Education for Adults." *Association of American Colleges Bulletin,* XLIII:3 (October, 1957), pp. 485-490.

——. *New Directions in Liberal Education for Executives.* Chicago, Center for the Study of Liberal Education for Adults, 1958.

—— (ed.). *The University's Responsibility for the General Education of Adults.* Chicago, Center for the Study of Liberal Education for Adults, 1955.

——, and JAMES B. WHIPPLE. *New Directions in Programming for University Adult Education.* Chicago, Center for the Study of Liberal Education for Adults, 1957.

SILLARS, ROBERTSON. "An Approach to Adult Education." *Adult Education,* VII:4 (Summer, 1957), pp. 240-244.

——. "Education for Internationall Understanding: A Report of a Survey." *Adult Education Journal,* 8:2 (April, 1949), pp. 91-98.

——. "An Interpretation of the Round Table Discussions." *Adult Education Journal,* 8:3 (July, 1949), pp. 156-157.

SIM, R. ALEX. (ed.). *Canada's Farm Radio Forum.* Paris, UNESCO, 1954.

SMITH, BERTRAND L. "Coordinated Community Group Action Is Functional Adult Education." *Adult Education Bulletin,* VII:4 (April, 1943), pp. 113-116.

SMITH, GEORGE H. "The Relation of 'Enlightenment' to Liberal-Conservative Opinions." *Journal of Social Psychology,* 28 (August, 1948), pp. 3-17.

SMITH, RUSSELL F. W. "Improvement of Instruction." *Proceedings of the Association of University Evening Colleges, Fourteenth Annual Meeting,* 1952, pp. 11-13.

——. *The Pooling of Ignorance? Discussion in the College Classroom.* Notes and Essays on Education for Adults, No. 1. Chicago, Center for the Study of Liberal Education for Adults, 1952. Mimeographed.

SNOW, ROBERT H. *Community Adult Education: Methods of Organizing and Maintaining Learning Opportunities for Men and Women.* New York, G. P. Putnam's Sons, 1955.

SORENSON, HERBERT. *Adult Abilities: A Study of University Extension Students.* Minneapolis, University of Minnesota Press, 1938.

SPEIER, HANS. *Social Order and the Risks of War: Papers in Political Sociology.* New York, George W. Stewart Publishers, Inc., 1952.

SPENCE, RALPH B., and ANGELICA W. CASS (eds.). *Guide for Program Service: Some Suggestions to Workers in Adult Education in Helping Communities Meet the Educational Needs of Adults.* New York, Teachers College, Columbia University, 1950. Mimeographed.

STAR, SHIRLEY A., and HELEN MACGILL HUGHES. "Report on an Educational Campaign: The Cincinnati Plan for the United Nations." *American Journal of Sociology,* LV:4 (January, 1950), pp. 389-400.

STARR, MARK. "Labor's Concern with Adult Education." NORMAN BURNS and CYRIL O. HOULE (eds.). *The Community Responsibilities of Institutions of Higher Learning.* Proceedings of the Institute for Administrative Officers of Higher Institutions, Vol. XX. Chicago, University of Chicago Press, 1948. Pp. 33-42.

"State Universities Have State-Wide Campuses." *Recreation,* 40:3 (June, 1946), pp. 126-131.

STEIBEL, GERALD L. "International Understanding and Understanding the International." *Social Education,* XXIII:1 (January, 1959), pp. 12-13 and 16.

STEIN, LEONARD S. "The Citizen's Certificate in World Affairs: A Progress Report." *Adult Education,* IX:2 (Winter, 1959), pp. 115-120.

STENSLAND, PER G. "What Is Adult Education?" *Adult Education,* V:3 (Spring, 1955), pp. 136-138.

STERN, BERNARD H. *Adults Grow in Brooklyn: The Brooklyn College Experimental Degree Project for Adults.* Report No. 2. Chicago, Center for the Study of Liberal Education for Adults, 1955.

———. "Evaluation of Student Achievement." *Proceedings of the Association of University Evening Colleges, Twentieth Annual Meeting, 1958,* pp. 172-176.

———. *How Much Does Adult Experience Count? A Report of the Brooklyn College Experimental Degree Project.* Chicago, Center for the Study of Liberal Education for Adults, 1955.

STILLWELL, HAMILTON. "Detroit's Merger in Adult Education." *Adult Leadership,* 9:2 (June, 1959), pp. 34-36.

STOUFFER, SAMUEL A. *Communism, Conformity, and Civil Liberties: A Cross-Section of the Nation Speaks Its Mind.* New York, Doubleday & Company, Inc., 1955.

STRATTON, BURTON E., and LAURENCE LIPSETT. "An Extension Division Evaluates its Program." *Adult Educational Bulletin,* XIII:2 (December, 1948), pp. 240-244.

STRAUSZ-HUPÉ, ROBERT, et al. *Protracted Conflict.* New York, Harper & Brothers, 1959.

STRICKLER, WOODROW M. "Financing Evening, Extension, and Summer-Session Programs." *Current Issues in Higher Education,* 1952, pp. 109-111.

STROMBERG, ELEROY L. "College Credit for Television Home Study." *American Psychologist,* 7:9 (September, 1952), pp. 507-598.

SVENSON, ELWIN V.—see WARREN H. SCHMIDT.

SWIFT, RICHARD N. *World Affairs and the College Curriculum.* Washington, American Council on Education, 1959.

TAEUBER, CONRAD, and IRENE B. TAEUBER. *The Changing Population of the United States.* New York, John Wiley & Sons, 1958.

TANDLER, FREDRIKA M. *Teaching about the United Nations in United States Educational Institutions, January 1, 1952, to December 31, 1955: A Report by the United States of America Under ECOSOC Resolution 446 (XIV).* Bulletin 1956, No. 8. Washington, U.S. Department of Health, Education, and Welfare, 1956.

THADEN, JOHN F. "Adult Education in the Public School and the Community." CHARLES P. LOOMIS et al. *Rural Social Systems and Adult Education.* East Lansing, Michigan State College Press, 1953. Pp. 24-51.

THELEN, HERBERT A., and BETTIE E. SARCHET. *Neighbors in Action: A Manual for Community Leaders.* Human Dynamics Laboratory,

Department of Education, University of Chicago. 1954. Offset.

THOMPSON, CLEM O. "Quality of Correspondence Instruction." *Proceedings of the Thirty-third Annual Meeting of the National University Extension Association*, 31 (1948), pp. 137-145.

——. *University Extension in Adult Education*. Bloomington, Ind., National University Extension Association, 1943.

THORNDIKE, EDWARD L., et al. *Adult Learning*. Carnegie Corporation. New York, The Macmillan Co., 1928.

TRUE, ALFRED CHARLES. *A History of Agricultural Education in the United States, 1785-1925*. U.S. Department of Agriculture Miscellaneous Publication No. 36. Washington, U.S. Government Printing Office, 1929.

——. *A History of Agricultural Experimentation and Research in the United States, 1607-1925, Including a History of the United States Department of Agriculture*. U.S. Department of Agriculture Miscellaneous Publication No. 251. Washington, U.S. Government Printing Office, 1937.

——. *A History of Agricultural Extension Work in the United States, 1785-1923*. U.S. Department of Agriculture Miscellaneous Publication No. 15. Washington, U.S. Government Printing Office, 1928.

——. *Report on Agricultural Experiment Stations and Cooperative Agricultural Extension Work in the United States for the Year Ended June 30, 1915*. Washington, U.S. Government Printing Office, 1916. Part 2.

TUCKER, RUFUS. "The Distribution of Income Among Income Taxpayers in the United States, 1863-1935." *Quarterly Journal of Economics*, LII:4 (August, 1938), pp. 547-587.

TYLER, RALPH W. *Basic Principles of Curriculum and Instruction: Syllabus for Education 360*. Chicago, University of Chicago Press, 1950.

TYRRELL, WILLIAM G. "Developing International Understanding in the First Two Years of College." HOWARD R. ANDERSON (ed.). *Approaches to an Understanding of World Affairs*. National Council for the Social Studies, National Education Association. *Twenty-fifth Yearbook*. Washington, 1954. Pp. 383-395.

TYSON, LEVERING. *Education Tunes In: A Study of Radio Broadcasting in Adult Education*. New York, American Association for Adult Education [1931?].

United States. Bureau of the Census. *Historical Statistics of the United States 1789-1945*. Washington, U.S. Government Printing Office, 1949.

——. ——. *Continuation to 1952.* Washington, U.S. Government Printing Office, 1954.

——. ——. *Statistical Abstract of the United States: 1955.* Seventy-sixth ed. Washington, U.S. Government Printing Office, 1955.

——. Bureau of Labor Statistics. *Economic Forces in the U.S.A. in Facts and Figures.* Fourth ed. Washington, U.S. Government Printing Office, 1955.

——. Department of Agriculture. *Federal Legislation, Regulations, and Rulings Affecting Cooperative Extension Work in Agriculture and Home Economics.* Miscellaneous Publication No. 285, rev. Washington, U.S. Government Printing Office, January, 1946.

——. ——, and Association of Land-Grant Colleges and Universities. *Joint Committee Report on Extension Programs, Policies, and Goals.* Washington, U.S. Government Printing Office, 1948.

——. Department of Commerce. *Small Town Manual for Community Action!* Industrial Series No. 4. Washington, U.S. Government Printing Office, 1942.

——. Office of Education. *Fact Book on Adult Education.* Washington, U.S. Department of Health, Education, and Welfare, 1957. Offset.

——. ——. *Resident, Extension, and Other Enrollments in Institutions of Higher Education, First Term, 1957-58.* Washington, U.S. Government Printing Office, 1959.

——. ——. *Statistics of Land-Grant Colleges and Universities, Year Ended June 30, 1957.* Circular 541. Washington, U.S. Department of Health, Education, and Welfare, 1959.

Universities in Adult Education. Problems in Education, IV. Paris, UNESCO, 1952.

University of Chicago. Committee on Educational Television. *Television and the University.* Notes and Essays on Education for Adults, No. 5. Chicago, Center for the Study of Liberal Education for Adults, 1953.

University of New Mexico. Community College. *Bulletin, Spring Semester, 1957-1958.* Vol. 71, No. 3, January, 1958.

University of Washington. Bureau of Community Development. "A Program for Community Development." Mimeographed, n.d.

——. Division of Adult Education and Extension Services. *Continuation Center Survey: A Survey of Existing and Planned Continuation Centers of Member Institutions of the National University Extension Association.* December 15, 1958.

University of Wisconsin. Extension Division. "Bureau of Information and Program Services." Printed leaflet, n.d.

"The University's Rôle in Adult Education: A Journal Symposium." *Journal of Higher Education*, XXVI:1 (January, 1955), pp. 10-21.

VAN DE WATER, JOHN R. "Supplementary Summary." National University Extension Association. *Preparation of Extension Leaders.* The Association and Carnegie Corporation of New York, 1947. Pp. 4-8. Mimeographed.

VAN DEN HAAG, ERNEST. *Education as an Industry.* New York, Kelley, 1956.

VAN SANT, THOMAS A. "A Community Survey through Cooperative Action." *Evaluation of Adult Education. Baltimore Bulletin of Adult Education*, XXV:4-6 (January-March, 1948), pp. 156-168.

VAUGHAN, MARILYN. *The Vassar Institute for Women in Business: A Report of the Participant Observer.* Chicago, Center for the Study of Liberal Education for Adults, 1957.

VERNER, COOLIE—see RUSSELL P. KROPP, ROBERT E. PALMER.

WANN, MARIE D., and MARTHINE V. WOODWARD. *Participation in Adult Education: A Statistical Analysis of the Adult Education Data Obtained in the October 1957 Current Population Survey of the Bureau of the Census.* Circular No. 539. Washington, U.S. Office of Education, 1959.

WARE, EDITH E. *The Study of International Relations in the United States: Survey for 1937.* American National Committee on International Intellectual Cooperation. New York, Columbia University Press, 1938.

WARNER, ROBERT S., and JOHN Z. BOWERS. "Program of Postgraduate Medical Education." *Journal of the American Medical Association*, 160 (April 14, 1956), pp. 1306-1307.

WELLS, H. B. "The Outlook for Higher Education in America." *Current Issues in Higher Education*, 1956, pp. 1-9.

"What Is Adult Education? Nine 'Working Definitions.'" *Adult Education*, V:3 (Spring, 1955), pp. 131-145.

WHIPPLE, JAMES B.—see PETER E. SIEGLE.

WHITTLESEY, E. D. "More Effective Education for International Understanding." *Current Issues in Higher Education*, 1950, pp. 118-123.

WIGGIN, GLADYS A. "Guide Lines for the Adult Educator." *Adult Education*, IX:1 (Autumn, 1958), pp. 13-18.

WILDER, DAVID E.—see EDMUND DeS. BRUNNER.

WILLERMAN, BEN—see ELEANOR E. MACCOBY.

WILLIAMS, J. D. "Adult-Education Activities in Liberal Arts Colleges." JOHN DALE RUSSELL and DONALD M. MACKENZIE (eds.). *Emergent Responsibilities in Higher Education.* Proceedings of the

Institute for Administrative Officers of Higher Institutions, Vol. XVII. Chicago, University of Chicago Press, 1945. Pp. 68-77.

WILLIS, IVAN L. "Industry's Concern with Adult Education." NORMAN BURNS and CYRIL O. HOULE (eds.). *The Community Responsibilities of Institutions of Higher Learning.* Proceedings of the Institute for Administrative Officers of Higher Institutions, Vol. XX. Chicago, University of Chicago Press, 1948. Pp. 24-32.

WILSON, HOWARD E. *American College Life as Education in World Outlook.* Washington, American Council on Education, 1956.

———. *Universities and World Affairs.* New York, Carnegie Endowment for International Peace, 1951.

WIRTH, LOUIS. "The Problem of Minority Groups." RALPH LINTON (ed.). *The Science of Man in the World Crisis.* New York, Columbia University Press, 1945. Pp. 347-372.

WOODRING, PAUL. *A Fourth of a Nation.* New York, McGraw-Hill Book Co., 1957.

———. *Let's Talk Sense about Our Schools.* New York, McGraw-Hill Book Co., 1953.

———. *New Directions in Teacher Education.* New York, Fund for the Advancement of Education, 1957.

WOODS, BALDWIN M. "The University and its Services to the Professions." *School and Society,* 69:1797 (May 28, 1949), pp. 377-380.

———, and HELEN V. HAMMARBERG. "University Extension Education in the United States of America." *Universities in Adult Education.* Paris, UNESCO, 1952. Pp. 128-168.

WOODWARD, CARL RAYMOND. "The Evolving Mission of the State University." *Transcriptions and Proceedings of the National Association of State Universities in the U.S.A.,* LIV (1956), pp. 18-31.

WOODWARD, JULIAN L. "Is the Community Emphasis Overdone in the School Programs?" *Harvard Educational Review,* XI:4 (October, 1941), pp. 473-480.

WOODWARD, MARTHINE V.—see MARIE D. WANN.

WRIGHT, QUINCY. *The Study of International Relations.* New York, Appleton-Century-Crofts, Inc., 1955.

ZANDER, ALVIN. "Student Motives and Teaching Methods in Four Informal Adult Classes." *Adult Education,* II:1 (October, 1951), pp. 27-31.

ZEHMER, GEORGE B. "The Development of University Extension Services in the United States." JOHN DALE RUSSELL and DONALD M. MACKENZIE (eds.). *Emergent Responsibilities in Higher Education.* Proceedings of the Institute for Administrative Officers of

Higher Institutions, Vol. XVII. Chicago, University of Chicago
Press, 1945. Pp. 50-67.

———. "The Off-Campus and Evening College Responsibilities of
Institutions of Higher Education." *Current Issues in Higher Education,* 1953, pp. 129-135.

INDEX

Abercrombie, Gurth I., 94
action programs 27-28, 32, 106, 109-
    110, 112. *See also* community
    development
Adam, Thomas R., 182, 237
Adelphi College, 232
adjustment, 14-15, 31-35. *See also*
    alienation
Adler, Mortimer, J., 13, 17, 237, 253
Adolfson, L. H., 83, 237
administration, *see* university; univer-
    sity adult education
admission requirements, *see* university
    adult education
adult education:
    agencies, 24, 53-54
    consumer satisfaction in, 20-29, 40-
        41, 51, 144
    content in, 19, 30-39
    definition of, 18
    "democracy" in, 19-25, 30, 39, 45,
        50, 121, 128, 148, 220
    evaluation of, 18, 39-51
    evaluation scale in, 44
    financing of, 24
    functions of, 9-16, 29, 33
    general principles of, 18-20, 29-30
    goals of, 15, 30-39
    importance of, 16
    method in, 19, 32, 35-39, 85-91,
        102-103. *See also* group discus-
        sion; lecture method
    participants in, 22, 30, 40-41, 43-
        44, 66-70
    number of, 54-55
    programing in, 20-25, 29-30
    psychological school in, 19
    rural-urban, 213
    standards in, 19, 29, 40-51
    teaching in, 33, 38, 44, 115
    traditionalist, 19. *See also* action

adult education:—*Cont'd*
    programs; adult students; discus-
    sion leaders; education; evalua-
    tion; foreign-affairs education;
    public schools; radio; television;
    university adult education
Adult Education Association, 23, 31-
    34, 36, 44, 112-113, 237
    composition of, 55
adult students, 66-72, 76
    age of, 66-67
    attitudes of, 101, 144
    characteristics of, 144
    compared with female students, 147
    motivation of, 68-70
agricultural adjustment, 223
agricultural experiment stations, 203,
    205
Agricultural Extension Service. *See*
    Cooperative Extension Service
agriculture, 205-206, 208, 212-215,
    222-226
    changes in, 214-215
    persons occupied in, 1-2, 214-215
Akron, University of, 82, 232
Alabama, 195
    Cooperative Extension Service in,
        111, 209, 211
    University of, 83, 104, 232
Alaska, Cooperative Extension Service
    in, 210
alienation, 31, 34, 38-39, 127. *See
    also* adjustment
Almond, Gabriel A., 156, 158, 163,
    171, 192, 194, 198, 238
Alter, Henry C., 19, 238
American Association for Adult Edu-
    cation, 31, 238
American Association for the United
    Nations, 162